SECURITY
OFFICERS

TRUE FIRST RESPONDERS

To John & Kathy

With Warmest Regards

George E K

George E. Kellogg, MSSM

ISBN 978-1-63630-612-4 (Paperback)
ISBN 978-1-63630-613-1 (Digital)

Covenant Books, Inc.
11661 Hwy 707
Murrells Inlet, SC 29576
www.covenantbooks.com

To "Doc Whitey" Kellogg, RIP, who taught
me more than he should have.

And to Pica, Steege, and Zander, who put up with so much.

CONTENTS

INTRODUCTION

A middle-aged man with a spare tire and deep, sun-damaged lines etching his face, stands up in a crowded room. He is about to make a confession among others like him. He has an issue that has interfered with his living a normal life. This issue, perhaps an addiction or perhaps a behavior, or likely both, has troubled him for a very long time. It has affected his personal and professional life. It has interfered with his family, with his having a normal social life. It has been a preoccupation which has done harm to himself and those around him. But now, wants to make things right. He wants his life back. He wants to be there for his family, his friends, and others who have stayed with him through such trying times.

This is it. This is his moment. It is now or never. Hoping he has the courage to carry through with what he has promised to do, he takes a breath, and looks at the man sitting beside him, who smiles and nods at him. The man's eyes are warm and kind. There is no judgment here. No criticism. Every person in this room has been there, has passed through this nigh-ritualistic moment. From this time forward, there is *only* forward. There can be no going back.

"Hi, my name is George, and I am a security professional."

"Hi, George!" responds the whole room in unison.

Notice that the man—me actually—did not say "officer" in that statement. It is true. I am a security professional, but no longer a security officer. I have branched, with the help of some good people, into emergency management, a field which likes me better. Yes… the field of emergency management likes me better than the field of private security ever did.

Now…the reason I took this approach to open this book is *NOT* to mock Alcoholics Anonymous or any other twelve-step program.

My own father quit a twenty-four-bottle per night beer habit in AA. "Dr. Bill is good medicine." I just wanted to bring a little levity to my own experience in the security field. The field of private security did do some good things for me. But I had to accept that it was time to get out of the field. I cannot keep up with the regimen anymore. I have been educated far beyond the level of line officer, but could not get into upper management for reasons that we will address here later.

The reasons for writing this book are many. First of all, I am doing this for me. At the time of this writing, I am not sure I will ever be published. I have no idea how to go about getting published. I certainly hope I can, and hope, I have learned in life, is sometimes all that we have. In this case, it is enough. Once this work is actually finished, I will seek a publisher and will do so with the intent of making my story known to the world.

My story is no better and no more legitimate or valid than any other security professional's story. But it is unique. It is unique in that I have served and loved the security field to the point that I actually hold an advanced degree in security management from Bellevue University in Nebraska. That is where the "MSSM" comes from. I earned a master's degree in security management, and I have the papers to prove it. I attended school online and read a three-foot tall stack of books. I wrote a paper on each section of each book. I learned things about door locks that I never wanted to know. I learned things about terrorism that I needed to know. I now enjoy a distinction of holding an advanced degree that only about 9 percent of the people in the United States have. Probably less than 1 percent of security professionals hold such credentials.

I went to school and worked hard because I was inspired. I wanted to make a change to the image of security professionals in the United States. But for all the idealism, all the hope, studying and hard work I invested, that change to the image of the security professional never occurred. There are several reasons why. I will cover some of those in this work. Other reasons for the change not occurring will not be addressed, simply because I don't know them. I really don't know all the "why's" and "what fors" and "how come's" of all the reasons of why this noble and honorable profession cannot change its stripes.

But more on that later. For right now I am content to write this book and hope that something good comes of the journey. Sometimes, that is what it is all about. Sometimes, God teaches us that way. We are inspired to do something, and the reasons why we are inspired to do it are not what we thought they were. Maybe these words will never be seen by the world. Maybe I will get rich from this book's sales. Maybe I will be featured on some talk show. Or maybe not. Maybe I am writing this just to make sense of things in my own life and I am the only one who will ever know that this work has been written.

And...yes, I did say "God" teaches us. And I believe he does. As you will see in some of my stories, I would suddenly feel an urge to be in that certain place at that certain time. I would suddenly be moved to change up a patrol or to run toward that back gate. I have stopped intrusions, found illicit items or substances, and even recovered cash that way. God told me to do this or that and when I did it, good things happened. You may say whatever you like, call it "animal instinct," "psychic power," "the Universe," "spirit," or whatever. But I know it is God who tells me to do these things. And I have saved the day by listening. Enough on that for now. My belief in and love for God the Father and His Son, Jesus the Christ could fill volumes and that is another book for another day.

For right now, I write this book to inform the public about what my brothers and sisters in my professional security 'family' see and do in the security field. Many of my friends and colleagues in the field have also served in the military. Others have been in law enforcement. I was never involved in law enforcement nor in the military, but Dad was. He lied his way into boot camp and joined the Marines. When he was nearly finished, they discovered his age and called his parents. They said if he was keeping up, and he was doing very well, they should keep him. They let him become a full-fledged Marine and then sent him back to high school. He graduated and then joined the Air Force who "loaned" him to the US Army. He became a Vietnam era (God bless them all) Green Beret and a combat field medic. His buddies called him "Doc Whitey" and his training me in my youth is a large part of why I am who I am, and why I do what I do for a living. This book is dedicated to him. This is Doc Whitey's book; without him it would have never been written because there would have never been a story to tell. He is in a nursing home now, paralyzed on one side and dying a little more every day. An ignoble end for a genuine war hero whose children all thought he would die on his feet, duking it out with some punk who had just done something wrong to some helpless person. Dad was big on instant justice when the moment called for it, and he had the tools to administer it.

I decided to write this book partially because of Dad. Mostly, however, I wrote it because I want people to understand that we have a class of working men and women who are willing to risk their lives for other people, who just don't get enough credit. Dad would agree with me doing this. He saw some of the stuff I went through in my security career, though not all of it. He agreed that security people are greatly at risk because their job is to be that thin line between people and assets, preventing, or trying to prevent harm to or the theft of either one. And he understood the danger of being on the front line.

He told me one day that when he was in the military, they were trained as operatives to always take out the security people *first*. It did not even matter if they were armed. When people come onto a property to do harm or commit some kind of heist, the one thing they all have in common is that they want to never be seen. Or if they are seen, they need to silence whomever it is that saw them; take them into custody, scare them into submissive silence, or simply KILL them. This is particularly important when the people who saw them have the ability to communicate in a way that will sound an alarm. They don't want people to tell the others in the building or on the property that something is amiss. They don't want any kind of response from anyone who may interfere with their plans. That puts the security professional in a very tenuous situation, and one that can go from zero to running full bore mode in an instant.

One second you are standing quietly in the lobby chatting with a client employee. The next moment, a window shatters, a fire alarm goes off, water comes pouring down the steps, some guy off the street enters the building high on drugs and cursing. Security people never know what they are going to run into any moment of any day. Things can go south and get really rough in an awful hurry. They can offer directions to someone and suddenly have a gun to their head. And while this can happen to any person, as it does every day in this world of ours, security people are willingly giving themselves up to being put in a position where the risk of harm is so much greater than for the average person. They choose to be in this position despite poor training, poor job knowledge and almost no tools to do the job. Despite the effective and professional appearance of their uniform, security professionals are often undertrained and underequipped for their post.

These are the people I seek to honor by telling my stories and stories about other security professionals. I want the public to know that they are not a bunch of "Barney Fifes," "Wannabes," or "Paul Blarts." They are not all a bunch of bumbling and well-intentioned fools trying to assert their will on the public. They are average people trying to do the right thing with their lives and, for the moment, they are putting themselves at risk to protect the property and lives of others.

And just one more thing on a personal note…the name "Whitey" was a fairly common nickname for towheaded blonde men in the fifties and sixties. Dad's hair was so blonde that exposure to the sun would turn it white. So…let's not get all excited and speculate about the name. This is where it came from. *Now* that we have cleared that up, we can get on with our story…the story of one and all security professionals throughout the United States.

Lights! Camera! Action!

THE IMAGE OF SECURITY OFFICERS

Well, where to start?

Most people in the United States think that security officers are about the biggest joke in the world. When I started in the field, back in the early nineties, the big thing was calling security officers "Barney Fifes." For people who don't know, there was a charming TV series starring Andy Griffith. Ron Howard, who grew up in television to become "Richie Cunningham" of *Happy Days* fame was the son of the town sheriff. Andy Griffith played Sheriff Andy Taylor of Mayberry.

The show was set in Mayberry, a sleepy little fictional town with lovable characters such as Otis the town drunk who would get bombed, wander into the sheriff's office, and lock himself in his own customary cell because Mayberry was a "dry" (alcohol-free) town. There was Floyd the ditsy barber, the nice ladies who would produce home distilled "elixir" only for medicinal and celebratory purposes, and then Gomer Pyle and Goober his cousin, who were, I believe, mechanics in the town.

The plot of the show always centered around the sheriff's office and interactions between the widowed Sheriff Taylor who lived with Opie and "Ain't Bea," his aunt who took care of the sheriff and his son. The residents of Mayberry getting into mischief or hilarious misunderstandings were a big part of the show, particularly where Barney Fife was concerned. Sometimes, things would get serious with an actual criminal getting loose in the woods nearby or with someone running a real distillery that was actually making folks sick. But the centerpiece of the show was comic relief Deputy Barney Fife.

Barney was well-played by Don Knotts. He was always bumbling, goofing around, taking himself and "the badge" *way* too seriously. But Andy loved the guy, so he kept him on. After all, Barney was also beloved by the town, was actually harmless and had a very good, if misguided heart. While Sheriff Taylor did not choose to wear a sidearm on duty, Barney was allowed. Barney's antics were so notorious that the sheriff gave Barney a caveat that he was not to have his gun loaded for any reason at any time. He was allowed to carry only *one* bullet on his person and that bullet had to be kept in his shirt pocket. So now you get the picture.

Deputy Barney Fife would wander around town, creating more problems than he would solve. With his hand on his revolver, his other thumb in his belt, he would approach people with this comically cocky, "Well, all right now… And what is going on here?" He looked ridiculous with this oh-so-serious sneer on his face. He would come strutting up to some kids, or some rough-looking guy, and say, "Uh-huh and just *what* are you people *up* to?"

He was ridiculously skinny, awkward, bumbling and always over-asserting his authority. He was always making problems where they did not exist and usually demanded ridiculous solutions, which always ended in him basically picking on people. That was Barney. And for many years, security officers were referred to in this way. "Barney Fife," "Barney Cop," "Deputy Fife," "Barney," etc. were all derogatory terms used for security officers, particularly if they were armed.

In a more modern vein, Kevin James, the comedy actor in *King of Queens* and several movies alongside Adam Sandler, created the beloved classic comedy character in *Paul Blart: Mall Cop*. Paul, like Barney, was kindhearted enough but still bumbling. He took himself over-the-top seriously and generally appeared foolish. What made him different from Fife was that he was actually a *security officer*. Now, the fact that he was constantly training to become a police officer, but had a medical issue of low blood sugar, added a comical element. But in this politically correct age, did anyone talk about how hypoglycemics were being misrepresented here? No, because it made the security guy look all the funnier, and that was what this movie was all about: poking fun at all the stereotypes of security officers, particularly in the shopping mall setting.

Paul's problem was that he would fall asleep at inopportune moments, like in the middle of physical agility testing whenever his blood glucose dropped. This is not the case, generally, with hypoglycemics or people who can suffer from insulin shock. Blart would drop like a rock whenever his sugar did. Having battled hypoglycemia in my past, I can tell you that is not the case. Hypoglycemia is easily controlled in many cases, as it was in mine, by eating a decent diet. I did appear drunk while not at work a couple of times, slurred my speech, slumped and actually drooled when it really got bad, but I never lost consciousness.

Paul Blart's condition was more like sleep-shift disorder or maybe even narcolepsy incidental to working around the clock. Both are categorized as sleep disorders. Both are serious conditions and can have serious effects on life and health. These conditions are related to sleep apnea, which is a cessation of respirations during the night. I was affected this way as well, and it was incidental to my working long hours, day and night, putting on weight from a poor, road-food diet and chemical imbalances that occur from not sleeping, coupled with overwork.

These medical issues are actually not a laughing matter. Combined with sleep apnea, these issues can seriously interfere with life, physical health and mental health. Currently, I have to take a special drug to stay awake during normal sitting activities and I sleep with a CPAP machine. The doctors I went to started me on this two-pronged treatment regimen so I can get normal sleep and stay awake while reading, studying, attending a movie or anything else that involves sitting still. It has not been easy.

Hopefully, I will be able to get off the wake-up pills after I start sleeping normally, if I ever do. According to my sleep study, I was waking up over sixty times during the night. This does not mean that I would literally wake up an remember it. I would slip out of a normal soundly asleep REM state 60 times a night, far beyond the 12-15 times expected during a normal sleep cycle.

I am not looking for pity, but I am trying to show the world that shift workers; security officers, soldiers, firefighters, EMT/paramedics, nurses, or any other people who work around the clock, work different shifts all the time on a revolving schedule, and who may be frequently awakened during their sleep time, suffer physical issues. My physician's biggest fear was that my heart would just *stop* one night because it was constantly being jump started by my not sleeping well. I believe that many on-duty deaths of security officers and other first responders are related to such health issues.

However, this book is not about me. So for right now, I want to concentrate on the security officer image in our North American culture and society. The image of security officers is largely negative. And yes, it is partially earned by the security industry and the people they hire. Poor training, sloppy uniforms, bad attitudes, poor conditioning/health, and people's age all contribute to this image. When I speak of age, I consider the wild disparity between the eighteen-year-old on his first job and the seventy-five-year-old who is working his last job. I have seen plenty of both in the security field. Many of the old boys try to warn the young boys to get out while they still can and let the ol' retired guys have the field. They are probably right, too.

I just want my reader to know, dear friends, that people who serve you in these capacities, or in similar ways, are putting a lot on the line while trying to keep *you* safe. Please consider that when you are giving a security officer a hard time. And yeah, now that I am out of the field, I have a hard time too, with being told what to do by people with badges. Too many years of being the guy doing the telling makes it hard to give in. So, sorry to my brothers and sisters out there! Be patient with me as I try to switch roles and actually accept your instructions.

TRUE FIRST RESPONDERS

The average person out there should understand what the term "first responders" means. Ever since William (Capt. James T. Kirk) Shatner introduced the public to "Real Stories of 9-1-1" on the primetime airwaves of the nineties, the public has been made more aware of what cops, EMT/paramedics, and disaster teams actually do. And, God Bless their efforts. But there is at least one class of first responder which is highly neglected—the security officer.

Think that one over for a minute. Not only are security officers first on the scene in many cases, but they are the ones, usually just the "one," honestly, who is holding it all together until the real heroes arrive to get the life-saving, scene controlling measures in place. That may not sound like such a "big deal." It really doesn't seem like much. Most people probably think, "Oh, okay. So the security guard called 911. Big deal. He had to call 911 because he can't handle stuff on his own." And you know what? The average Joe in this case is absolutely right. The security "dude" calls because he can't handle it. And you know what? The security person is *not supposed to "handle it"* when it gets too hot on the scene. "Handling it" alone can get him or her killed.

Now please *do* understand that the security person or team can also make the mistake of calling police for things that are just too minor and wasting the cop's time. Or security may panic at the first whiff of smoke and call the fire department to put out that birthday BBQ the neighbor is having for his friends. This is where training and experience come in. Security has to learn how to differentiate the important calls from the nonessential calls. It takes time, training and experience like anything else in life, but good security people are invaluable.

I would like to think, though, that most security professionals in the business know early in their career when to call and when to not call. Early in my career, I made a lot of mistakes. Since competent security professional training was hard to find and education was nonexistent, I had to learn on my own how to react to situations appropriately. It took time, but eventually I could handle difficult scenarios on my own, without wasting police officers' time. Sometimes... I would *delay* calling until it was almost too late. Those occasions were few and far between though, and they usually came about because a noise complaint suddenly escalated into a domestic violence event. Or maybe I made the mistake of thinking some situation was not that bad until I was in it, waist deep. But even in those cases, I had enough sense to back out of it and make the call without getting hurt. I have been injured on the job, more than once, but in all my years of doing the job there was only *one* event where I was hurt by a person. I share that story in this collection. "Hurt," by the way, is relative term. I had to be examined, but no injury actually occurred.

When on patrol, even armed patrol, it is not easy to be the guy who's Johnny-on-Spot.,. There are times when people will feel insulted that they sent "Paul and Barney" instead of city police. When that happens, you get to deal with the person who called you, compounded with the actual event. Other times, people are so happy to see you, until they discover that you are not going to "arrest" the neighbor whose dog keeps pooping in their yard. Or they become incensed that you, the security officer, don't care that some neighbor is smoking weed on their own balcony at 2:00 AM on a Saturday. You may care as a person, and not like it because it happens to be illegal in your particular state of residence, but to call the cops for that will destroy your security team's credibility with the local law enforcement. The police, in cases of college kids passing a joint around, will say that you know better than to call PD for such a small misdemeanor "in a college town on Friday night" when PD is up to their eyeballs in homicide, rape, armed robbery, etc.

Let me also say that being the first one on the scene is also quite dangerous. That danger is often compounded by the security officer being alone, unarmed, and poorly trained. Add to that the fact that the bad guy may not respect or fear city police, much less a Barney Fife do-gooder wannabe. The presence of a uniform will dissuade, discourage, or stop some people but will escalate others. The escalation of the situation can make a night go from ho-hum to "run/fight for your life." And those scenes, though they make good stories to later tell your friends, can very easily get a security professional hurt or killed.

You never hear about security deaths on the news. Very rarely is the death of a security officer reported in the news. In fact, *112 security officers were killed in 2017; in 2019 we lost 52 security officers* at the time of this writing. A lot of people have no idea how dangerous security work really can be. The average person just sees that clown on a golf cart or standing around near a tractor to discourage trespassers, thieves, vandals, etc. Under those circumstances, it is true that the work is not very dangerous. Not in most cases, at least, but there *are* exceptions depending upon the town and particular location in that town. But the fact is security personnel work in hotels, office buildings, courthouses, factories, abandoned properties, at-risk properties including but not limited to government buildings, hospitals and high-rise buildings.

But here is the most dangerous work: security officers often work in rough neighborhoods, where their presence may be viewed as a threat, with suspicion or complete disdain for what the uniform represents. In such places, security professionals are especially at risk because they most likely do not have backup anywhere nearby and often are unarmed. The bad guys know that, the public knows that, and even though they are not a huge threat, they are an "unwanted presence" because they have eyes to see, ears to hear and a mouth to make a call. That alone makes the criminal afraid of being caught and can cause a security professional to get hurt or killed.

The truth is, security officers patrol in dark places overnight, encounter criminals on a frequent basis, but do not command the respect from people that police officers naturally receive. This is because most people resent having someone exercise authority over them. And since security officers don't have true authority to enforce law, some people think they don't have to listen to security officers. Now while it is true that security officers have no law enforcement powers, they *do* have the authority to enforce policy and may apprehend persons under certain very strict guidelines. The security officers must learn and adhere to the policies outlined by their employer and/or policies of the contract set up between the client and the security company. To break these rules can land a security officer in jail and/or get them named in some kind of lawsuit in a real hurry.

It can become very dangerous instantly for the security officer. Likely unarmed and poorly trained, the security officer is often left to work alone. They may or may or not have a radio; however, in this highly communicative day and age with the Internet and cell phones, the missing radio is not quite the challenge that it used to be in the days before portable cell phones. It does not take long at all for somebody to jump a fence, cross a property line, break a window, throw a rock, and so on. Every one of these actions will provide a situation that the security officer is required to respond to, as part of their job. But even then, the security officer must choose wisely because responding to such things is dangerous; one never knows what these people may do next. A rock-throwing incident can turn into a mob coming at you. Simply getting off of or onto a light rail train can land you in the lap of a dangerous crazy person. Being on patrol can you land you face-to-face with a really dangerous person, a wild animal or a bad situation at literally any corner you turn. That is why I learned to give corners a wide berth; this is a safety measure that I take even to this day. I try to teach it to other people too.

Something else about the security profession that many people don't realize is that there are some very long hours kept by these people, even working around the clock in many cases. There are a lot of security personnel who work seventy or more hours a week, varying shifts. This is very hard on the body, the heart and even the brain. Overwork and odd hours can keep the security professional in poor health, physically and mentally. Some of them are armed *and* exhausted. That is a bad combination. When it comes down to it, security companies will work their people into the ground, burn them out and then just hire a whole new batch. It is a thankless and difficult job that is both undervalued by the employer and underestimated by the public. The low wages and potential risks do not make the field very attractive.

I thought my education would push me up the ranks in the company where I worked when I earned the degree, but I was wrong. I was actually informed by a manager that the CEO of the company asked why, if I had such great credentials, did I not have a better job? Well, I took that to heart, and found a better job. Then I ended up getting out of the field of security and pursued emergency management, now seeking to build my career in hospital or clinic administration. This is how it works though, because there just is not much opportunity in the security field. I think the people who founded many of the large companies do not have a college education and with the good living they make, many of them see no point in getting one. Back in the '60s, when many of the big names were established, there was no such thing as a bachelor's or master's degree in security management. When one gets a nice, fat shiny degree, they can either move up the ladder like they should, or they can hit a glass ceiling like I did and end up someplace they never intended.

I believe the attitude of the big companies is that they just need bodies to fill their posts. They just need to fulfill their contracts. They don't really care about the individual, about ambition or about career-minded people. Every career-minded person I know of in the field ended up either quitting or being forced out the door after they got their degree. This probably is due to the fact that people with too much education and too many critical thinking skills ask too many critical questions. This makes the bosses feel threatened. In the companies I worked for there was always this "us and them" culture. The big bosses never really mingled with "the little people." And yes, one CEO actually called his line officers "the little people" at a Christmas party where he got really loaded. He was throwing $100 bills in the air and telling people to come and get it, because it all came from the work of "the little people".

My goal in telling this story is not to discourage anyone, but it is to warn aspiring professionals that they might be in for a rough ride. I hope that any educated security professional out there lands better jobs, and has better luck than I did. I sacrificed so much in that field and got so little in return. I hope that people like me who want to excel in the field find a way to do so and carve out for themselves a wonderful career!

FIELD STORIES AND THE LESSONS THEY TEACH

MY FIRST FIND

The very first thing I found as a security officer was perhaps, upon reflection, an *omen* of sorts. I was working for a retired cop, who was a police lieutenant, and I was on about my third hour of training. I was being walked around by one of the senior security officers on that post. We were an in-house security team at a mall in Anytown, USA. He was gray-haired guy, sort of geekish. Smart but awkward at the same time. He had been on that team for a while. He had some good pointers for me, but he did not last long at that job after I was hired. He told me that high turnover was one of the first lessons I would learn about in the security field, and he set that example. Anyway, we were walking outside of the mall, around the west side of the structure. We were patrolling the utility entrances. They were big gray, metal doors of a standard type and size. All of them were locked. We were just walking along, doing our training, chatting, laughing it up a bit (sense of humor is a MUST in the security field… even if it's a little depraved), and suddenly I stopped.

"I smell something. Smells bad."

"Like what?" asked the trainer.

"Something maybe died. Behind this door."

"Well, go check it out."

He used his keys and let me into the back halls of the mall. There was a stairwell, and it was well lit. I looked around from top to bottom. Then I saw it.

"Aaaawww, maan! Gross," I said.

"Whatcha got?"

"A TURD! Someone crapped under the stairwell!"

"Ohhh, nice."

"What do we do with it?"

"Not with it…about it. We will call housekeeping."

So that was my first legitimate find as a security officer. That should have told me something about what the field would hold for me in the future.

MY WORST FIND

I was in management with a private security company in Anytown, USA. It was a normal night shift, twelve hours long. My job was to check accounts, inspect officers and make sure that things were all going well for our clients and so on. I have a certain knack for being where I need to be, when I need to be there. While this was a "needed to be there" moment, I would never want to be there on such an occasion, ever again.

It was the quintessential dark and stormy night in Anytown. I had done security work in this town for a while and I was still working on my master's. My job was pretty tough, but it paid by the hour and the overtime was pretty amazing. I had never made such money before and I had never worked as many hours, either. This job was nineteen calendar days in a row, with two days off. Three of us covered the shifts. One guy always had the weekend off. Those days were a holy grail to us. So on top of all that was about to happen, I was already exhausted.

A call came out as a "missing man." One of our officers on this post was not calling in and could not be reached. Normally, on night shift, that meant some young guy with a family was burning the candle at both ends. Up all day with the family, or what have you, and trying to work nights with minimal rest. Almost always, we would find the officer asleep somewhere, normally not on purpose. Fatigued, the officer sat down for a moment and *wham!* Nighty-night. Such events were met one of three ways: (1) immediate termination, (2) tongue lashing, (3) overlooking it just this once. The severity of discipline always was adjusted to the situation and the person involved. If it was a critical post, termination was required no matter what. But in many cases, the officer would be sufficiently embarrassed and would just get option 2 or 3. So I was ready to find this guy and probably just tell him off. He had a good reputation, even for not being on the post very long. I had met him at his hiring interview, and he seemed like a happy and fine young man.

But this case of the missing man was different through and through. Really different. Creepy different. I felt it, and I did not like it. I arrived at the office building and checked on his last location with the front desk. Our team had the building all to themselves. The only people present were security officers. I checked in with the front lobby officer and went looking for the missing man. I could not find him in the normal patrol areas. I even looked under a few desks to see if the nap was intentional and he was hiding. When I came back to the desk, my lobby officer said that he was concerned about something he saw in the patrol log, which read:

2300–FOREVER: Officer J. Doe on patrol.

"FOREVER?" said I. "That does not look good. Show me the cameras."

As my heart sped and my stomach churned, we went back on the camera footage and saw Doe's last place on camera to be the UP elevator. The officer looked normal, almost bored. He had his coat draped over his arm, something to be expected on a night like this, all cold and rainy. I called the operations manager and told him my findings. Then I called the post commander, and she came in a couple of hours early. We went up the same elevator the security patrolman took and made our way upstairs as far as we could go. We searched and searched. There was nothing to indicate where he was. I suggested that we check the roof because if FOREVER meant what I thought it did, well…

So we went to the roof access. We arrived at the doorway. What we found made us stop in our tracks. Our communal blood, mine and the blood of a former coworker—she having once supervised me—froze in our veins. At the doorway leading out to the roof, we found this young man's driver's license, company ID, and flashlight, all intentionally placed and neatly arranged on the stoop of the entry door. That did not look good. Not at all. So we took a deep breath and went out into the wet. I knew what she only suspected. We were looking at a suicide case. I hoped that I knew wrongly.

The roof was slick with rain, and water was flowing. It was darkly cloudy, and of course, there was no moonlight. We stuck together because it would not be safe to wander about on a slick downtown high-rise rooftop alone. Besides, with what we suspected, neither of us was really keen on being without company. We checked the places where someone could have fallen or jumped. But we thought it would not be onto the sidewalk below. If a jumper had hit the walk, it would have already been on the news. We were looking on the lower eaves of the roof, where a body could have gotten caught. Finding nothing, feeling relieved and yet anxious, we continued the search. We approached some of the ventilation structures on the roof, walked around them, splashing in the rainwater, when...

No! Not him! Not the new guy! No, no, no, no, no, no!

But it was. Lying there in the rain, the look of shock still on his pale face, mouth agape, eyes wide and staring blankly askew in disbelief and horror, a gaping hole in his temple with swirls of his young blood polluting the rain's best efforts to cleanse the scene of the natural aversion one feels at self-inflicted death...there lay the body of Officer Doe. He was on his side, legs curled up in what appeared to be a kneeling position. He had taken off his company blazer and laid it a distance away. After all, someone might need that jacket one day. A small shotgun or rifle, I never cared to find out which, with the barrel sawed off lay a couple of feet away. The size of the weapon allowed for easy concealment under a jacket draped across one's arm.

I stopped. The post commander stopped. Immediately, my mind slipped into command mode. I was the guy in charge. Pushing my revulsion aside and forcing my most compassionate human feelings, along with a generous portion of bile back down into my gut, it was time to act. You may think that I was being coldhearted, but the fact is that this was not a time to weep. Already my mind was racing through the possibilities. Obviously, it was a suicide, but I have over many years learned to take the obvious as nothing more than a strong suggestion of probability. We did not know, however unlikely it was, if someone else was involved and was still on the roof. Was this a murder? A suicide pact? Or was it simply what it appeared to be? What we now knew was that we had a dead man here for sure and we would treat it like a homicide until we learned otherwise.

"Okay," I said matter-of-factly. "This is now a crime scene. Post Commander Doe, you make the call to 911! I will call the office personnel."

I was in a state of being called "hyper-clinical." Medical professionals develop it too, in times of horror. Your mind knows you have to function, so you refuse to fall into the terror of it all, and you just pick out the hard facts you can deal with and not feel anything that will shut you down. That way, you can deal with the facts of the matter, settle business and do your weeping later. Now was the time for phone calls and getting help.

I could not raise my field supervisor. No surprise. Cell phone did not always reach his place. Just the way it was, not his fault. Next call was to operations.

"John, it's me. We just found Officer Doe. He's dead. Looks like a gun suicide."

"Shut up! Shut up!"

"Don't tell ME to *shut up*!"

Now, I did not understand the younger manager's slang expression of shock on his end of the conversation. He was not telling me to shut up as in "close your mouth and stop talking because you sound stupid." He was just shocked and used the words "shut up" like my generation used, "you gotta be kiddin' me." I was not angry at him, but I had a serious thing going on here and I needed to know what next steps to take.

"I am looking at a dead body, and it's not very pleasant, 911 has been called," I said. My voice tight, but not quivering at this point.

"Okay, okay. Yeah, George, I got it. Listen, I will call John 2 and John 3. You keep the scene under control. I am so sorry, man. So sorry. I'll make calls now."

I got off the phone and called human resources. I left a message. Turned out I was leaving a play by play message that took me a full minute or more to tell the HR rep that our man was dead. That was from nerves. I apologized later, and explained that I had never called in a *suicide* before. My next act after the phone calls was automatic and mechanical. I began to patrol the area, looking for other unusual things. I was also trying to keep people away, which was really weird because I was on a roof in the middle of the night. Not exactly a place folks would choose for a leisurely walk downtown. I was getting wet, but the shock prevented me from feeling it. Finally, the post commander broke the spell.

"Get in here… You can't do any *good* out there!" and she was right. So I went back in.

Cops showed up and paramedics made courtesy call, as it turned out to be. Naturally, there was nothing to be done. They were pretty sad looking when they came back down with their boxes of stuff. The sun was coming up, but it was still appropriately gray in the sky. Nature was sadly saluting Security Officer Doe's passing. As cops came, building management also arrived. Our branch's general manager and my supervisor were now on scene. The cop asked if we moved Doe around at all. I simply said, "No. It was not necessary." He had already guessed as much, but he had to ask for the homicide report. These things are always homicides until the events are properly recorded and all the requirements are fulfilled for them to legally state that the cause of death was suicide.

By this time, the post commander and I were already cracking dry jokes about the whole matter. She was chuckling and asking if it was too soon. I did not think so, as long as we weren't public about it. Not if it was making her feel better. We were alone, nobody could overhear us. So what was the harm? Then the medical examiner arrived. I knew who he was without even asking. He was about the most haunted individual I had ever met, devoid of emotion and cold. Not cold in a bad way, but cold like he did not dare feel things anymore. He was completely expressionless and just went about his business matter-of-factly. Only God knows what that poor man sees every day.

One of the building managers, a very nice lady who was clearly upset, distressed and concerned about my well being asked me, "Are you okay?"

"No," I said truthfully. "But I will be. It will just take some time."

My bosses were particularly roughed up about this whole thing. Especially my immediate supervisor. He felt ashamed that I could not get through to him. They offered me some time off with pay starting immediately, but I declined. They seemed concerned about that and rightfully so. But I explained to them that I needed to get right back into the field that very night. I told them that I had to prove to myself immediately that *this* kind of thing was not going to happen to me every night. I had to know that this traumatic situation was isolated. One of the officers on the post put my feelings together nicely during a sidebar discussion we had, worded in a way that I will always remember:

"Yeah. You can't get off the horse because you are afraid you won't know how to get back on again."

I could not have said it any better myself. I have used that metaphorical statement many times in my life since that night. Sometimes it is better to push through so that you know you will be safe from such and such happening to you again. Granted, it could have happened again that night when I returned to work. But it did not. And I have not been on a suicide call where I recovered the body ever since. Staying on the horse was the correct choice for me. As a side note, it would not be a sign of weakness to take time off, or even to quit one's job over such a thing. Individuals must do what is best for them. The *worst* thing one can do is to try to prove something; to prove you have strength where you do not. Such an attitude is based in the weakness of pride and it can have devastating consequences.

I did elect to talk with a counselor, just to be sure that I was riding the horse in the right direction. All was well, because although I was sad, the counselor determined that I was feeling normal emotions. I did not blame myself, and that was a good sign. Counseling stopped after three sessions. I had a clean bill of mental health. (Ha! If only she knew…)

One useful thing I did learn in the sessions with the counselor is that had I been there, had been on that roof with John Doe, it may have gone terribly wrong. For one thing, I may have been forced to witness something terrible that I was powerless to stop. Two, I would have, out of instinct, likely tried to talk him out of it, and that could have gone very badly. This brings me to the third point I learned: when an individual is bent on suicide, they are going to do it. There is often no talking them out of it by the time they have the place picked out, the loaded gun in hand and their jacket off. They probably see this as the only solution to their problems. If you try to talk them out of the solution, then in their warped state of mind you become the enemy. And, they may even kill you along with themselves, or maybe even instead of themselves. This is just something to keep in mind if you have seen a similar situation: *it is not your fault; it was their hand on the gun, the pills, the rope. They did it, not you.*

Later, I met on the post with the officer who was present the night of the suicide, the lobby officer who helped track Doe's last movements through the building. I was concerned because he did not talk to anyone after the event. He did not see the body, no, but he was the last one to see Officer Doe *alive*. And that has an effect on people. I visited with the lobby officer for some time. And I expressed that I was very *angry* at Doe for doing that to us, for making us deal with the aftermath of his suicide at work. We took turns expressing that anger by calling Doe a —— for a few minutes, each in turn. We both seemed to be relieved at having reached an understanding of how angry both of us were, and how that anger was perfectly okay. Crying or throwing up would have been fine too. I know that the lobby officer felt a lot better after our "therapy" session and that was the real goal, despite the rough language.

That was likely the most harrowing and terrible night I have ever seen in the security field, the worst part of it being that this was one of our own. I had met the guy at his hiring. The post commander knew him, and he was a great worker. She was glad that she did not know him better because that would have been all the harder to bear. His fellow security officers were also affected but thank Heaven none of them saw that body. It was horrible. Guys on another post in a higher floor saw the scene from a distance, out their window. It affected us all. Suicides do that.

I believe that most suicides would not happen if the victim only realized how loved and needed they actually are. And if they would stop for that one critical moment and realize how many people this one act would affect for the worst, they probably would rethink their situation. There are no perfect answers. I just know what that one fateful decision did to my guys and our bosses. I hope to never see such a scene ever again.

THE WIZARD OF OZ

I was on patrol in this apartment complex, which serviced college students. They were not on the Anystate U campus, but the apartments were close by. Car burglaries were very common. The place was too big for just one patrol officer, but that was all they were willing to pay to have on their site. This is yet another example of the universal problem with security practices; clients don't want to pay for sufficient personnel to get the job done properly.

My job was fairly simple though. and I had a pretty strong rapport with the college residents. They respected me too. I would chat with them, maybe even eat a quick burger with them at a BBQ, if time permitted. But when the time came and business had to be handled, well, business was business, and everyone understood that. All in all, it was a pretty fair and decent relationship between the residents and security.

On this particular night, it was around 0400 hours. I was off at 0500. Or so I thought. I was out of my car, which serviced as my base of operations on this post, because they would not give us an office. I was out walking around when I heard glass break. Uh-oh… another car window got smashed in. That was my second erroneous presumption within minutes.

You see, the normal procedure that we were all used to was simple: the burglars would break a window, I would move toward the sound, holler at them to stop and they would run away. Nice, neat and clean. Nobody got hurt. Nobody got busted. One night some guys broke a window out of a car and then *tried to pull a TV out through the broken window.* It was funny watching them freak out while I approached. They kept yanking on the TV, trying to get it through the opening.

I wanted so badly to yell, "Open the door, ya big dummies! You got the window out! Reach in and open the door!" But that would have made me an accessory to stupidity after the fact. But... I digress.

I carefully but quickly moved to the area from where I heard the sound. The noise led me out of the parking lot. That was quite a surprise, really, because it was very unusual. It also elevated the potential hazards and danger of the situation to a far more serious level. The hazards increased because I was now walking into the apartment buildings. There was a better chance of my being jumped and beaten, or worse, because I was walking into a situation of narrow walkways, lots of bushes and it was still dark. I was armed with pepper spray and a baton. No gun.

Not only was I underdressed for the occasion, not having the proper 9 mm accessory, but broken glass inside the complex led me to believe that I was alone and taking on one of the most dreaded and dangerous calls known to law enforcement. I believed that this was very likely a domestic disturbance, and a violent one at that. I did not believe it was a break-in because of the repeated breaking glass. A burglar would not normally break out more than one window...and would at least try to be quiet. Quiet, that is, unless he was drunk or high, and that added another whole dimension to this call. All this occurred to me while I was on my way to the noise. Adrenalin was certainly pumping by this time. I was alert and processing information very quickly.

Now that I was in between buildings, the noise was growing louder with other violent sounds. I could not understand why all the noise. This was growing more serious by the second. Soon, I realized that the noise was coming from *overhead.* That is never good. That meant that I could take a shower in broken glass. So I skirted as far away from the falling glass as I could. I slowed my approach for safety reasons. Then I saw it.

There was a lone figure in an apartment with the lights off, but I could see in the glow of the TV, I suppose, a man with a broom. This thin younger man had a broom and was breaking out the window of the apartment, metal framework and all. Then he started hitting something, or someone, that was on the floor. The whole thing was eerie because of the silence. There was not any yelling or screaming, no begging for mercy. Was someone unconscious or dead? Over and over he was swinging and hitting, swinging and hitting. He appeared to be shirtless. I called 911 and told them what I saw. They sent a unit out to meet me.

A sleepy, not-so-excited-to-see-me cop pulled up. In this particular Anytown, the cops generally did not like security officers. So he came with the "Yeah, yeah, whaddya want, Paul Blart" attitude. I looked at him and simply pointed to the window.

He looked up, made a funny oops kind of sound, and said, "Make sure he does not jump! I'm calling for backup!"

I guess he left his radio in the car because he left me standing there wondering how I was going to prevent a nut ball from jumping out of his third story window when I was on the ground. The police officer left the scene, and I had no way of contacting him.

Then I noticed that someone was standing on the balcony over my head, taking video with his camera. This was in the days before cell phones had much video capacity. I told him to get back out of sight because we did not know if that man had a gun or what was happening. Naturally, the dude just brushed me off. I warned him, and so my job was done. I was not going to add to the chaos by pushing him to get back inside. That would have just made things worse and distracted me from a dangerous scene.

Then, true to form, things changed for the worse. I saw an orange glow in the apartment and sparks flying everywhere. *A fire!* An apartment fire in the middle of the night with everyone at home is about as bad as it gets! Active shooting is the only thing that could be worse…but this was bad enough. I could not see the police anymore and did not know how far away he was, so I called 911 back and told them we needed the firefighters out to this call, immediately. I described the scene, and they completely agreed with me. Then I started pounding on doors, trying to get the drunken kids out of their beds. I was yelling, "Fire! Fire! Get up! Get out!"

Drunken and stoned people started slowly easing their way out of their apartments, slogging their ways to the pool area where they congregated. The group was fascinated with the lights and all the racket. I was fascinated too. Who could have guessed that my night would had ended this insanely? This was supposed to be a quiet shift because it was in the middle of the week, and I had to get home to drive my kids to school.

So between the police backup that had been called and fire department, we now had half of the Anytown emergency services converging on this one apartment complex. Since it was apartments, they rolled a couple of engines with pumpers and the battalion chief himself. It was about the most active scene I had ever been party to. My supervisor showed up to see what was going on. He came up, and it was kind of funny because I started talking to him like he was PD, until I recognized him.

We started speculating on what was going on. Since the real heroes were on scene, it was time for me to just back out. I would have only been in the way. Knowing when to back out is as important as knowing when to be involved. We watched the PD go up the stairs and knock on the door. The orange glow persisted. Then we saw the cops break in the door, we heard this big commotion, and suddenly...silence. Then the radio chatter started after a few seconds. The battalion chief was listening, then he started cursing up a blue streak. He ordered his men to roll up the hoses and to start packing.

The paramedics went up the stairs with their heart monitor, medicine box, and other gear. A few minutes later, the police helped the medics carry down the steps this guy who was wrapped in a blanket and handcuffed to the gurney, four-pointedly. They took him away in an ambulance. As soon as a couple of cops broke loose and came over to me, I told them about the amateur videographer on the second floor. They grabbed their lieutenant and told him that this was not anything he wanted to hear, but someone was filming the scene.

The lieutenant asked where the guy was. In a couple of minutes, the policeman came back with the tape in his hand. I don't know what he told the kid to get the videotape, but it worked. The police were satisfied, and I was satisfied. And the scene was now closed. The cops chatted with us security goofs for a few minutes. I could tell they were pleased. They even shared with us what had happened. The guy with the broom was running around naked in his apartment, going berserk. He had turned on all the stove burners, making the orange glow. Then he lit the broom afire. But no one quite understood why.

I got home late, and the kids were late to school, but it was one heck of a story to tell. I had to say that it was worth being late and all the paperwork it cost me. I was commended by the company owner over that call. He said that I responded perfectly and probably saved some lives. What if that broom had lit a curtain?

Over time, I did find out what happened. I came across the roommate of the guy whose friends now called him the Wizard of Oz. It came out finally that the guy with the broom had a problem with gremlins. Pesky, pesky gremlins. You see, the gremlins had to leave because the guy did not like them. But they would not go. Yelling at them did not help. So he grabbed a broom. Hitting them with the broom did not help. So he made an exit for them by breaking out the windows. That was what brought me to the scene. Then when the gremlins persisted, he turned on the stove burners and introduced fire to the situation, to chase out the nasty creatures. I saw him using his flaming broom to beat up the gremlins. That was what caused me to think the whole place was afire.

I asked one of the apartment dwellers what brought all of this on, and he told me that his now-evicted roommate was drinking a lot of beer by the pool. In the heat of the day, drinking in the sun can increase the beer buzz by dehydrating the brain. Then he came back to the apartment, completely sauced, and he thought it would be a good idea to try experimenting with some liquid LSD he had somehow procured. His roommate left him, not wanting to see what happened next. And the rest is history! Thank goodness no one was hurt. Not even any gremlins.

SPORT SOCKS

This was a loss prevention call in the Anytown mall. A manager of a new retail store called security. He thought some kids had stolen expensive sport socks from his store's rack. The manager told us that the kids came in, "accidentally" knocked over the rack and seemed very, very eager to clean up their own mess. The manager did not see the socks get stolen, but he was pretty sure they had them. All we could do as security was to take a description, and if we located them, we could point them out and he would have to talk to them on his own. Police would not be involved at this point. All we could do was to stand by and keep the peace for all parties concerned, including the group of young people.

You see, to have a successful loss prevention case, you must complete certain steps. Unless the standards have changed, and this is *not* a statement to suggest policy to anyone, but the basic needs are that first, you must clearly see the person select the item and then conceal it or pass it to someone else to conceal it. Then you have your eyes or better yet, video cameras on the person who concealed the item at all times. You cannot lose sight of them at any time because even a couple of seconds is enough time to dump the merchandise. Then with eyes on them at all times, you must be sure that they have passed the *last* point of payment with the merchandise still in their possession. Otherwise, you could have a false arrest/apprehension case on your hands.

So as it turned out, the kids did not have the socks in their duffel bag. The manager had seen that bag on the floor, unzipped and was pretty sure that they had had slipped the socks into the bag while they were cleaning up the mess. But when he stopped them and talked to the kids while we watched, he found that they had nothing on them. I called the supervisor over to tell him it was a bad stop made by the store manager. The father of these kids was understandably irate, but his behavior was truly out of line. He was screaming all kinds of profanities at us, calling me a "Paul Blart ——" and so on. It was quite a scene right there in the mall.

The security director of our team asked the family to come into his office. He was interviewing the family, trying to get to the bottom of what happened, and how it all went so wrong. He excused my supervisor from that closed-door meeting. While they were in their meeting, I once again showed my knack for being in the right place at the right time. A young Hispanic lady approached and asked in her best broken English if I was looking for socks. I said yes, I certainly was, and she told me to look behind the gumball machine. She saw one young man put the socks there when the manager started catching up to him. This just proved why you can't let a suspected shoplifter out of your sight, even for an instant.

Sure enough, there were the expensive sport socks. As big as life and twice as beautiful! Well, I got the supervisor on the radio and said that I needed to see him right away. I showed him right where the socks were stowed. He picked them and hustled to the director's office.

Slick as a whistle, he covered the socks with a file and laid it on the desk, dropping the socks in the director's lap, saying, "Here's that file you were asking for."

The director did not even blink. He examined the file, then said very calmly, "Well, folks, I guess we are all about done here. But just really quick, young man, have you ever seen these socks before?" He then held the socks up and the kid's eyes bulged in stark terror and looked at his dad—WHACK! Dad smacked him across the head. And then Dad started yelling about how he was working hard to provide the boy with a living and how he didn't have to steal because his dad was a provider, and so on.

The family left the director's office and came back past the sports shop where I was standing. The dad walked right past me strangely silent and clearly embarrassed. I was quite satisfied at the turn of events, but I did not gloat. I really felt bad for that father. I guess that father's big gripe was that his family could not go to a shopping mall without his kids being harassed by security officers. He could not understand why his kids were always targeted. Well... I guess that now he knows there is more to the story than what his kids were telling him. I would not have wanted to be that boy when

GEORGE E. KELLOGG, MSSM

he got home. I think a traditional homemade butt-whooping was coming to that young man and his siblings.

VALENTINE'S DAY EXPRESSIONS

On Valentine's Day at the Anytown mall, a young shoplifter was caught in one of the anchor stores (a large retail chain store). He was trying to steal a heart-shaped basket of bric-a-brac. The store was concerned and involved us because they had only one loss prevention officer and this guy was getting jumpy. I handcuffed him so as to discourage any foolish or desperate acts. The top priority is always that nobody gets hurt.

So I was there with this young man, who was obviously stressed. He was upset because he got caught shoplifting. He started asking me questions about the case. I told him I could not help him with the legal questions he was posing, but I could tell him the procedure. Now that he was caught, the store was filing a report. My only report would be a statement to say that I was there. In this particular case because the matter did not turn into a pursuit outside of the store, the Anytown mall would choose not to be involved. The police would come, take a statement and run a check on his ID. If he had no other warrants, the police would most likely turn him loose with a shoplifting charge and a citation.

He had other questions I could not answer. The most striking of those questions was, "Do you think this will affect my job interview?"

I stopped and looked at him like, *really?* Then I told him that I had no way of knowing if this would affect his interview. It would depend on criminal background checks, how long it would take for this arrest to appear, and a number of factors. I had no way of knowing if this would affect his chances of getting the job. But I did suggest that if it were *me*, I would not bring up the arrest unless they specifically asked the question.

This dumb move really complicated his situation. He had a girl; it was Valentine's Day. He had no money. He stole something. He got caught. He had a job interview. All this stress and bother, his actions quite possibly endangering his job opportunities, both today and in the future. All because he wanted to take something that was not his to give to his girl. Then he arrived at a conclusion. After carefully thinking things over, he said, "I guess I should have just gone to the interview, huh?"

Well, duh! I chose to hide my derision and agreed that, yes, it would have been a better present for his girl, to have gotten a job. She would have liked that over a court date. At least, I think she would have. But not knowing his girl, who's to say? Maybe she thought it a Romantic gesture to risk breaking the law to please her. I hope not… but who knows?

This is a case where a young man made a true error in judgment. He did not act like a rebellious thug. He did not have gang colors. He just wanted to please his girl and he chose the wrong way to go about it. He was nervous, naturally, but he was cooperative and rather humble the whole time.

Cases like this, people risking their entire futures over a very inexpensive item, never cease to amaze me. Full grown people, some over thirty years old, lose their integrity and affect their employment possibilities over $3 and $4 items. That is just crazy to me. I don't understand it. And most retail chains have *zero* tolerance for shoplifters, prosecuting every single case. Fifty cents or $500, it does not matter to them. They prosecute them all. Imagine being a full-grown adult facing a judge for fifty cents worth of stolen merchandise…

BUSTED…AND STUPID (A QUICK SERIAL)

Episode 1

One night at Anytown mall, we got an assistance call from an anchor store. They had confirmed shoplifters heading toward the mall entrance from their store. These two young men were carrying backpacks full of store merchandise and were headed into the mall. This loss prevention guy was alone that night and he was one we trusted

GEORGE E. KELLOGG, MSSM

to make good calls, so two of us went to the entrance and waited behind the pillars. When we saw them coming out of the store, we stepped out.

I shouted, "You two! Stop right there!"

When I saw them stop, both looking awfully guilty, I knew we had control of them. So I said, "Sit down! Keep your hands where I can see them!" Having them sit down is the best way to make the scene safer. It makes it hard for them to run away or to fight. They sat down quickly, like two kids who had gotten caught and had a guilty conscience.

The loss prevention guy came out and told them both, "Now listen, you guys, all I want is our stuff back. I don't wanna bust you. I really don't. So just give me the stuff in your backpacks."

They both looked at each other and completely denied they had anything. The LP guy was really in a genial mood, or more likely, it was late, and he did not want to mess with the report. He gave them a last chance to fess up and return the stuff. They did not. They got busted.

All they had to do was give it all back. Cops would have never known. Their parents would have never known. The judge would have never known. There would have been no entries on a criminal record in their name. I am sure that these young men both regret their actions to this day. They were not a day over eleven-years-old, and they decided just like that, making such a far-reaching decision. For the rest of their lives they would have a juvenile record. I guess they were thinking not to admit it, no matter what. They did not want to get caught. But they probably did not understand, in that kid-way we all have lived through, that they were caught already and the LP guy, for whatever reason—late night, compassion, what have you—wanted to give them a break.

Episode 2

Another sad case of ignorance was unnecessarily long, drawn out, and actually took me into court, needlessly, as it turned out. This drawn out event was over a balloon animal that some little kid, about ten-years-old, grabbed out of a box of balloon animals. No one was there, there was no sign or price on the box, and he innocently thought it was free. It was an innocent mistake anyone could have made. But what happened next drove the situation out of control.

I had just come on duty and was called to a disturbance in the Anytown mall center court. When I arrived, there was this family of born-again Christians simply losing their *minds!* I was hearing them yell and using some very filthy language, yet calling down legions of angels in the name of Jesus, in their very next breath. There was probably ten people just making a crazy ruckus. The police arrived moments after I did. The cops helped us restore order. And because of the ruckus, they ended up charging the kid. I could not believe it.

This whole thing could have been settled very calmly and equitably as a misunderstanding. The balloon would have been returned, an explanation calmly rendered, and everyone would have gone about their business. But instead, this kid got a ticket and a court summons, and so did I. I was supposed to be getting ready to go camping that day, but I ended up prepared to testify against this kid.

So here I was, in Anytown court, wishing instead to be packing my car. I had some trout to catch, roast and eat. But here I was in the courthouse. As it turned out, they never even called me as witness. I don't know why they summonsed me, of all people, because I never saw the theft. All I saw was them raising heck with the security team and creating a disturbance. The disturbance was not even the issue. This was all over an unmarked, unattended $5 balloon animal.

I sat there and waited, watching the case get called to the bench. The prosecutor actually told the judge that in the interest of justice the case should be dismissed. Mom was there with the accused, her eleven-year-old boy. I was relieved to hear the prosecutor say that. The judge was in an agreement with the prosecutor. I don't think, though, that Mom understood fully that the boy was being sent free, no harm, no foul. She said that she did not accept the terms of the court, that she wanted the boy to be tried.

I think that she had probably been coached by some legal mind from her peer group. Some guy who once had a "cousin that knew this one guy who worked in a law office" kind of thing. And she was probably advised to not take any "deal" because the boy was (truly) innocent. So not knowing any better, Mom thought that the prosecutor was trying to pull a fast one and cause the boy to cop to a plea. There was no plea. There was no crime. They just wanted to dismiss the case. But Mom did not understand, she was just not going to let her boy be tricked.

Like I said, as it turned out, I was not even called to testify. My time there was completely wasted, and I was late for my weekend in the mountains. That was pretty aggravating, but it is one of the hazards of being a mall cop. You actually do get tied up in some legal situations and may be subpoenaed to court at any time. Believe it not, the company can opt to not pay you for that time, arguing that you are performing a civic duty, not a work task. Kind of cruddy, right? Personally, I would have given up the overtime just to get out being at court on that day. But they did not even offer the OT.

Episode 3

This old man in Anytown, USA, made the papers when a bundle of white grapes turned to manslaughter. There was this produce market and a well-known customer tried to get out of the store with a bag of white grapes. Not having a trained loss prevention or security professional on the scene, the best thing that store manager could have done would have been to let the man go with the grapes and just called him on it the next time he came in. Have him either pay for the grapes or simply don't come back to the store ever again. That would have been the smart thing.

But instead, the manager completely lost his head. He not only chased the old man out the door, but when the customer jumped into his car to speed away, the manager jumped on the hood of the car, Mel Gibson-style. All he had to do was get the license plate number and call the police if he was that anxious to prosecute the old man for the grapes. Instead, he had to go completely nuts all over this guy. Tried to be a super cop.

The old man panicked, gunned his car out of the parking lot, the centrifugal force dumping the manager.

Now, we see this stunt all of the time in the movies! We've all seen the trained stunt person working at controlled speeds in coordination with a trained stunt driver. They simply roll with the fall and always somehow tumble onto their feet with a perfect Mary Lou Retton-style landing. No breaks, no sprains, no injuries, and on to the next scene.

It would be nice if things really were always as neat and cool as the movies. The world just does not work that way. In reality, without the equipment and professional drivers and stuntmen used to keep actors safe, the man clinging to the does not tumble well at all. There is no tight roll or tumble and no picture-perfect landing. Instead, his body flails all over the place. He flops around for a moment and goes into a blind panic. He slides off the hood like a rag doll. He hits the pavement, slides, rolls, whiplashes his spine, and finally, he cracks his head on the parking lot pavement. His employees run to him.

And he dies.

Then, in reality, the old man does not go home and have a couple of movie-clever laughs by the pool over a cognac. The old man is now distraught. He is driving in traffic, completely stunned. Not knowing what else to do, and probably crying wildly and going into emotional shock, he somehow manages the drive home. Carrying his grapes—those precious, precious grapes—he goes into the kitchen and drops them on the table. He is not even interested in eating them anymore. He wanders the house, and everything is in order. He sits down to watch TV. He tries to relax. He is SURE that the manager is just fine. After a few seconds, he breaks down again. He becomes horribly upset this time. He stands up without even knowing why. He sits down again. He thinks of the store manager. The crowd he saw gathering around him. He's sorry. So very sorry. Why did he steal in the first place? He shakes, trembles, cries again, and has a heart attack.

And he dies.

Two men, now dead. Two parties have lost their lives over a pittance. It was all so unnecessary and all so regrettable. This is what happens when someone lets his emotions get the best of him. This is the very thing that people are warned against by their local police department. Stop and *think*, people…stop and think. What is the item, and is it really worth risking your safety over? It is almost never worth all that.

In this case, all that had to happen was for the manager to stay calm. Be reasonable. Or all the old man had to do was not steal the grapes. But instead, a bad choice on the old man's part led to a shoplift. Then the manager, who was in this case the guy in charge or "mission control" went hysterical and everyone went crazy. When the leader on the scene blows his cool and becomes irrational and behaves foolishly, it causes a ripple effect. Such ripples wash over people and in this case, so many lives were completely changed that day. It was all so very tragic, so very unnecessary. People went home with the most unexpected answer to the question, *how was your day?*

Let's think for a moment of all the people who were affected and their involvement in this tragedy, and those who tried to help on the scene. The person dialing 911 and trying to get help *now* instead of answering "dumb" questions from the operator. The panic. The fear. The terror. The employees of the store who lost their boss, liking him or not, and who had to endure being questioned about an event that killed their boss before their eyes. The owners of the place who had to deal with the natural heartbreak that always occurs when someone dies. And on top of all this, they had to suddenly find a new manager. Their small business was now in the papers. Customers knew the manager and maybe even the old man. The community was changed. Funerals and other final arrangements had to now be attended to. The impact was incredible. It all was so avoidable.

These are the two main questions that all security professionals should consider:

1. Are my next actions for the *best*?
2. Am I prepared for *all* consequences?

If the answer to either question seems to be shaded or in the least degree questionable, it is probably time for a "checkup from the neck up." Pause before making any move that may create regrets. Think for a moment beyond the passion, whatever that passion may be. Consider for a moment if you are acting in anger. Are you over-reacting? Is this situation really worth endangering myself and/or others over? Is this really worth taking a chance that I might not go home? These are not easy to answer when your judgment is clouded.

A helpful piece of advice might be for every security professional or every person who is involved in the retail sector to think ahead. Create a scenario and work through it. If a man steals something, how will you respond? Will you try to tackle him? Will you pursue? What are the chances that he will be armed? Will you just let it go? Will you call the police? What information will you need for the police? How will you gather the information? How will you control the responses of people around you? Do you even have the ability or authority to control them? And so on. The questions are unlimited. The biggest consideration should be the health and safety of all people around you, including the perpetrator.

CASPER THE FRIENDLY MALL COP

One morning, early in the week when security teams run classically short in shopping malls, I was on patrol at Anytown mall. I was on the upper level of the mall when my boss called out that we had a group that looked like trouble. She wanted me to get rid of them without looking like I was *trying* to get rid of them. Well…wasn't *that* going to be tricky?

So sure enough, here they come. Kind of rowdy, they were a group of young men who wanted to be tough. They were not wearing any classic gang apparel or colors. So I had them pegged as some local neighborhood boys who wanted to pretend they were real tough guys. I quickly referred to my days back in the log woods when my boss would play "cowboys and Indians" with me. The trick to that game was to disappear by using the environment and then pop up somewhere unexpectedly in an "ambush." Not with real weapons, mind you, but the principle idea was to get the drop on the other guy and scare him.

So… I came up with a plan. I let them walk past me on the upper level without saying a word. Then I fell in behind them at some distance. Far enough away to be noticed, but not close enough to make trouble was the general idea. And I achieved that goal. I put on my best poker face, which I am told is pretty creepy, and followed them. They approached the escalator and one of the "homies" turned around and stood up straight, "staring me down" as he disappeared from sight down the escalator. I have to admit, he was pretty dramatic and had a good tough guy stare. I stopped and did my best to look scared.

Then I hustled quietly over to the bridge and let then cross under it. I timed it for just under a minute. Let them have "clean air" for that long, with nobody in sight, thinking they are home free. Then I ran down the escalator and came about fifty feet short of them, again hustling along quietly so they would not hear. I put on that same indifferent facial expression, easy paced walk, as if going nowhere in particular. After a moment or two, one the home-boys looked back at me, did a double take, and said something to his crew. Then they all looked back with the most darling startled expressions and hauled for the next mall exit. I started laughing. I could not help it.

Next thing I know, the boss was on the radio: "Hey, [call sign], I don't know what you did, ha-ha, but it sure worked."

I met up with boss lady and told her what I did. I told her I was "Casper." Then I explained how I disappeared, and apparently frightened them off by reappearing suddenly, like I had fallen out of the sky. Nobody could move that fast, right? Not in their minds. It always appeals to someone's superstitious side when you appear suddenly. And I guess these guys believed in ghosts.

I had a pretty good reputation after that, for a while, anyway. That was a stellar morning. It was the perfect solution. I got the drop on the bad guys, no words were exchanged, no confrontation was made, and no report was necessary. Funny thing is, I don't recall ever seeing those young men at the mall for the rest of my tenure there.

THE BAD SHOOT

Here is a story about a security professional gone wrong. In this book, it is only fair to present the bad with the good. The right with the wrong, the fair with the unfair. And this is a situation that went all wrong. I did not have anything to do with this particular story, but it was in the papers. The funny thing about this is that I am pretty sure I met this particular security officer on his post before the papers met him.

When I saw this guy, I pegged him for trouble. You could tell that he really liked looking powerful. He relished wearing that uniform. He really liked carrying that gun. And perhaps the most telling thing about him…he wore leather fingerless gloves with holes in the knuckles. He just loved looking tough. You could tell he was really into the tough guy role. This was not someone you wanted even wearing a uniform. And you *really* did not want him wearing a gun, especially not in your name. He did not appear to be overly smart, and this is not good either. In fact, he is what everyone expects, culturally, of security professionals, but he is the last guy that should be in that role.

Everything that I just relayed here, I reasoned out in about ten seconds of seeing this guy, basically in passing. I never met him, and I wanted him to stay as far from me as possible. A man like this, a real tough guy, not too smart, belonged in a backstreet bar or a truck stop. This is *not* to take anything away from a bouncer's job. I would be a lousy bouncer. I really would. What I am getting at is there are different kinds of personalities for different security functions. This man was severely miscast for the role. He was at one of those corner stores. Apparently, the owner of this particular place wanted armed security. I certainly understand why. But what he needed was someone who was subtle, with less ego. He needed someone who would make the right decision with a cool head.

This security officer, who probably worked for a local company, ended up making the papers. His was the story of someone who had not only the wrong attitude, but was also poorly trained. If he was trained, well, it only means he should have never passed the training course. There was a case of snatch and grab. A young man ran into the store and grabbed a six pack of beer then ran out the door.

So let us review the shoplift rules: The subject has to be seen selecting the item. Check. The subject has to conceal the item or at least keep it in their possession. Check. The subject has to pass the last point of payment with the item in their possession. Check. The subject must be kept in sight by either a person or a camera for the entire time they are in possession of the item and they pass the last point of payment. Check.

So...here we have a potentially good loss prevention stop. Fully justified. But in this case, the security professional did not *arrest* the thief. He *shot* the thief. In the back. Now did the thief live? Yes, and he was caught. But he also, probably, sued the place. Now was he in the wrong? Clearly. But the law does not allow for *anyone,* as far as I know, to shoot an unarmed suspect of a misdemeanor, who is fleeing (or standing still for that matter). Not even law enforcement officers can legally do that. The law treats felons who are fleeing and known to be dangerous quite differently. A law enforcement officer may fire on such people under very limited circumstances. Again, unless there are laws, rules, or circumstances I am unaware of, a security officer who is NOT a sworn peace officer may not shoot at fleeing dangerous felons. The only time security may shoot someone is in the defense of self and others. It needs to be a very clear case of life or lives being endangered by a person who has obvious means and has expressed the intent to kill or seriously injure someone. There are NO circumstances I know of under which a security professional may shoot someone in defense of property only.

In fact, the only reason a security officer can shoot someone is for the same reasons that any other private citizen can shoot someone, and that reason is to save someone's life from the criminal. If the beer thief pulled a gun or a knife and openly threatened a life or lives, the security officer would have been justified. But only for as long as the thief would have been actively pointing his weapon at someone. If the thief came in with a weapon, grabbed the beer and then fled, the security officer could *not* shoot him in the back as he was running away. A security officer cannot fire at someone once the threat to lives has ended. There is no such thing as shooting someone to protect property. Security officers, as private citizens, can only fire a weapon in defense of themselves or another person. And that officer had better prove that there was no other option than to fire.

But in this case, there was no weapon, there was no dangerous threat, there was only some guy grabbing a six pack and running out of the store. The security officer could have easily grabbed him, and held him for the police, with reasonable force. *Reasonable* force. Handcuffs, yes. Reasonable hand to hand force, yes. These would have been proper, acceptable and reasonable measures. These measures would have not gotten him into the papers and certainly would not have gotten him put into jail. And his employer could have avoided being sued.

Thank Heaven that this suspect survived. Because if not, that security officer would have ended up in prison for a very long time. The original charge would have probably been second degree murder, a homicidal act not premeditated, but intentional. They may have pleaded it down to manslaughter. But I don't know. There are aggravating circumstances we may not know about. The bottom line is this guy was not the right man for the job. He was hired poorly, and he was likely trained poorly. Instead, it landed him in jail, the client got sued and the security company was also, I am certain, held responsible. Another case of completely avoidable difficulties and anguish.

LACK OF SELF-AWARENESS

I once worked with a company which serviced armed accounts. I was in charge of a couple of those accounts. We were fully uniformed, armed, and very professional. Or at least many of us were. There was this one guy who thought himself to be a real hotshot. Another guy with leather gloves. What is it with these guys and their leather gloves?

Anyway, this fellah was very popular with the company. He was trusted and was granted special favors. He had an ego that would not quit. Supposedly a Marine, but I doubted it. The Marines I knew were very stand up guys. Tough, but humble, and they never felt the need to prove it. This guy was always out to prove something, always talking tough. No one liked him; no one trusted him.

The company had this inane policy. They demanded that while we carried guns for them, they needed to be company issued weapons. That was fine. But they also wanted us to carry company approved ammunition. These bullets were full metal steel jacketed rounds. Such bullets pass through bodies, instead of stopping inside the intended target. Very dangerous. These bullets are a hazard to everyone around the shooting site.

When a client hires a security company to provide armed protection, they often don't know the proper questions to ask. The client should discover how well the officers are trained, who trained them, the proficiency level of the officers in the use of their firearms, what kind of firearms they are bringing to the post, how much ammunition they carry, what caliber are the weapons, the type of ammunition, the level of experience in using the weapons and if they have experience in "shoot / don't shoot" and other safety scenarios. The client should also discover how well the company is insured for liability and insist upon at least $1 million in liability insurance in the event of a shooting. They should also know the potential firing condition of the weapons of the officers on scene. In other words, are they carrying revolvers or semiautomatics and are these weapons ready to fire or will the officer need to "chamber" a round?

Unfortunately, this particular company required the officers to carry a semiautomatic 9 mm with only ten rounds in one magazine and that magazine was to be in the pistol which was not chambered with a round. Anyone who knows anything about shooting scenes understands that you probably will not have time to draw your weapon, say, "Excuse me, Mr. Bad Guy, while I chamber a round," and then bring your sights to target. No security officer in his or her right mind ever *wants* to be in an active shooter scenario. But on the same token, any officer in his or her right mind knows that when you are carrying a weapon, every bad guy in world assumes that you have that thing "cocked, locked, and ready to rock." No one expects a security officer to have to pull the weapon, chamber a round and then put the sights on target. Only the unknowing and naive would carry a weapon in that state.

The reasons for such thorough critiquing of your potential security company are reflected in the story of this security officer who came to the post. He showed up, his usual cocky self, and he was going to *show everybody* that he was going to be against company policy, even though he was from the office. His leather gloves fastened, and sunglasses polished to a high sheen, he pulls out his gun in front of everyone and chambers a round. Then the bullet that was already in the chamber pops out of the ejection port and this guy has to chase the bullet down the inclined sidewalk. He then had to drop the magazine, holster his gun, put the bullet back into the magazine and reload his weapon, resulting in the need to chamber it all over again. All this time, my guys are trying to not crack up while hoping no one was watching that whole embarrassing scene.

The worst of all this was that this security officer was not aware enough of his weapon to realize that he already had a round in the chamber. And he should have never pulled out his weapon in front of the other officers. The safest possible thing to do was to have the round chambered while he was alone, at home or maybe in his car. Your weapon should never be clear of the holster anyplace on the post unless there is an occasion that calls for it. You may need to enter a building to clear it, or you may have an actual armed encounter which are the only occasions for an officer to pull his weapon out of the holster. Security personnel should never have their weapons out for display or to "check" them. Those occasions need to take place off post, in a place of privacy/concealment. You don't want the public or client to see this happening. This is also how accidents happen.

THIS GUY SHOULD HAVE NEVER BEEN ARMED

In Anytown, USA, there was once a guy who loved to brag about stuff he used to do. He would brag about an Ecstasy binge he once went upon, stoned for a week and apparently became essentially endowed with superhuman strength. He used to tell the most outlandish tales about things that would happen to him on the job. He was a shooter, but not a very smart individual. He claimed that he was some kind of specialized military man. One look at him would tell you he is not, if you have any discernment at all.

One day this security officer, John Doe, reached into his trunk and pulled out a long gun case, which he opened while it was in his trunk. I had no problem with that, looking at the AR-15 he had in his trunk. I did have a problem, however, with him pulling it out, putting it to his shoulder, and sighting it in like he was going to fire. And this in broad daylight, in full view of the public, where anyone walking by could see what he was doing! Then he told me that he had permission to keep this rifle in his trunk, on patrol and that the manager really liked having it available. I was not sure, and for good reason.

I found out later that he actually was told that if had been at the shooting range and did not trust his AR-15 to be in the trunk of his car, that he was to put the rifle in the office, discreetly, under lock and key. He was *not* under *any* circumstances to take his AR-15 with him in his patrol car. In fact, they would prefer that he not bring it on the property at all, even in his private vehicle. But…if it was with him, then these were the only circumstances under which he was to have the AR-15. He certainly was not allowed to have out, in firing position, checking his scope anywhere on company property or in a patrol car.

These are the types of people who cause big liability issues for their employers. These are the types of people that you never want to arm. They are reckless and irresponsible. And they love playing military/cop. These guys get into security because they want to have some kind of event happen where they may have "adventures" and get into shooting scenarios. Any responsible person knows that they never want to get into a shooting scene, but they are nevertheless prepared to do so if called upon to protect themselves or other people.

So anyway, Officer Doe got called onto the carpet one day. The company had received a disturbing report. There was a post that had some exposure to a field, a bit of undeveloped land. This post was a patrolled post where security would drop by and hit checkpoints on various landmarks around the post. On this post, it was said that there was a rattlesnake somewhere. So just to get ahead of the curve, we put together a procedure for the snake. If one of our officers (fat chance) saw the snake, the general order was that we could shoot it if it posed a threat to someone (fat chance again), but then we had to call it in to the supervisor and to the local police.

Well, Officer Doe was on that particular route one night. He met up with some of client's employees. Doe found a trash bag of leaves and weeds. He had apparently been bragging it up to the client about how our security personnel were allowed to carry AR-15s in our patrol cars. He basically made all of us sound like *him*. None of us wanted to be like him. Not remotely. The smartest of us wanted to see this clownish parody of a security officer get fired.

In the midst of his bragging to these guys, he felt that he had somehow impressed them. The fact was, they were keeping an eye on him because they were afraid to turn their backs. They thought, correctly in my opinion, that this guy was half nuts. When he saw the bag of leaves and stuff, he told them to stand back because the rattlesnake might be under the bag. The problem was that it was about forty degrees out on a fall night. Anyone who knows anything at all about a snake is going to realize that it is too cold out at forty degrees for a snake to be wandering about for any reason. And at best, the snake, if it was stupid enough to be out in the open in this season, is going to be too sluggish to hunt, slither or bite anyone. It likely won't even be able to move.

But here was Officer Doe. Representing our entire company, and hunting rattlesnake rumors in forty degrees. He approaches the bag ever so carefully, *pulls his weapon*, and lifts the bag with his free hand, turning it over, his gun at ready to shoot the rumor. Nothing! Phew! Officer Doe saved the day!

Good thing that snake wasn't there. At that close of range, shooting at a suddenly unveiled target on the ground with people around was a recipe for tragedy. You never want to have one hand busy while the other holds a loaded, cocked gun. Particularly not when you are leaning over at a bad angle, off balance and in a poorly lit area. Had Doe actually fired that weapon, even accidentally, there was a fair chance of a ricochet off the ground or wild round zinging around the post. That could have badly hurt or killed somebody.

Well…needless to say, when the managers got the call that next day, they were not pleased. They called him in and asked him with some clearly spoken terms just what he thought he was doing. Bragging about carrying AR-15s in our cars. Drawing a weapon in front of the client. Unsafe firearm practices. Aiming at a target that did not exist…etc.

And what did they do? Instead of pulling him off armed duty like any responsible person would do, they left him on patrol. But they would not let him carry his gun for thirty days. They left him in a contracted *armed* slot, but *unarmed*. The supervisors were furious because first of all, everybody figured this guy for the clown that he was, and nobody with brains thought he should be armed in the first place. Secondly, what liability would they be under if he arrived at an armed confrontation, but did not have a gun to defend himself or the client? That could apply to both the company and the supervisors who were personally responsible but had no control over the management's decisions. They should have just pulled him off armed patrol all together. That would have been the best thing to do.

This example shows how people who manage security teams don't always think their way through a situation. I understand that managers want to be "nice" to their employees. And they should be. But in this case, that was the last thing that should have been on their minds. This guy had shown himself to be incredibly irresponsible on more than one occasion. He was sliding further and further downhill, and this time, he did it in front of the client! Not to mention, he openly endangered people by unnecessarily drawing his firearm in a situation that by no stretch of sane boundaries was warranted. And, not only that, but he showed how ignorant he truly was. I mean a rattlesnake at forty degrees? Get real. That was not a proud moment and one which negatively reflected on the entire company. Anyone wearing his uniform was now lumped in with him. Thanks very much!

360-DEGREE FLIP-OFF

In Anytown, USA, there is a place where people who cannot stop their drinking may be sent by a judge who wants them to come out of the twelve-step program a sober and responsible citizen. The security officer, and there was only one on site, had the duty of keeping people from selling beer in the parking lot to the residents of the dry out facility. I never personally encountered anyone there, but I did find a resident who was giving me a rough time.

This young man seemed nice enough at first. But then came his problem with authority. No one was going to tell *him* what to do! He was out to show the world that the rules did not apply to him. Well, fancy that! Apparently, some judge *did* think that some of the rules applied to him and so, this young man ended up in a place where he could be taught that rules *do* apply to him.

Naturally, there were rules to staying in the facility. Most of the people there were in for crimes such as DUI, public intoxication, maybe assault/battery, creating a disturbance, disorderly conduct, etc. They had sinned against society to the point that it was time to either put them in "big-boy jail" or send them to the detox center. So here, almost everybody I was watching had a criminal history directly linked to an alcohol issue. My job was to keep them in their rooms and not let booze get into the facility. Now, I was not searching people, but if any alcoholic beverages were discovered or if there was someone on the post who was misbehaving, then I would be pressed into service.

Well, true to form, one guy decides to break the rules. I had to keep sending him to his room and he would get tough and verbally abusive with me. I have found in my long career that whenever you have a habitual rule breaker, a rebel, a criminal or any of the like, they always know just where the line is drawn. They know what security or law enforcement can and cannot do. They know the rules and they know just how far they can go. That gets old after a while and it wears on the patience because they keep poking that same old bruise over and over. Many a security officer has quit his job, been fired and maybe even jailed, I am pretty sure, over somebody pushing the wrong button on the wrong day. No matter what the excuse or how bad one's day has been, there are just some things security professionals are not allowed to do. When I was reaching that point, I knew I had to get some help.

Finally, sick of him, and having worn out my arsenal of "stay in your room" lines, I began involving the nursing staff. I went in to speak with them, telling them that I had several encounters with him, and he was starting to get abusive. They told me to keep an eye out for him and whenever he came outside, to call them because if he wouldn't listen to me, he *would* listen to staff. In this particular facility, because the residents were there under a judge's orders, they would have the authority to boot him from the program. If they had to do that, he could end up in jail.

I thought that was fine, because it took me out of the classic "middleman" position of enforcing *their* policies. Now, that would normally be my primary function, yes, but in this case, I was dealing with subjective and legal rules. Whenever rules are subjective and legal, it can get very sticky, particularly within a behavioral health setting. I could make an innocent mistake with even the wrong remark, that would normally be acceptable, and I could end up getting my company sued. So as of now, the staff was just using me as their spy and snitch (security professionals call it "observe and report"), and I could live with that.

The rules were now changed, and I loved it. His "spoiled bratness" would no longer have me to abuse. From then on, if I caught him outside, doing stupid stuff like throwing rocks at the patio plant life, climbing around where he had no business being, or tossing pebbles at the window of other residents trying to wake them up to come out, I would just call it in. The staff would call him and talk to him. No more name-calling or defiant remarks from him.

As a side note, I am a pretty big guy, and these old bones have been through a scuffle or two. That, coupled with martial arts training here and there, plus the tactical training from my paternal Green Beret makes me rather formidable. Now here comes this young punk, obviously coddled and spoiled his whole life, and he is giving *me* a hard time? Really? That was not such a smart thing. Not if you consider the odds which were against him if it got physical. But he, again, knew exactly what he could get away with. And he knew I had to play by the rules. So…in this case, I decided that if I simply *outsmarted him*, it would pain his pride in a really bad way. Not only that but I would have done my job without any violent expressions, the way I truly prefer it.

My strategy was a simple one I picked up from both my old man and our endless kids' games of neighborhood hide-and-seek in the country. I learned how to hide in the shadows. And wearing a pair of forest green BDUs and a black polo shirt with minimal patches, etc. on it was perfect for that scenario. I was well hidden in the patio scenery. I chose a perfect spot where I had minimal exposure to light, could tuck myself back into the scenery, but I could see the whole patio. I could see where he came out, to where he was going and so on. But he could not see me.

Well, he came out the nurse's office for about the third time. This time he was *mad*, boy, I'll tell you. I think they must have told him that he was going to go back to the judge if he goofed up one more time. This young man was very defiant. Very accustomed to pretty much doing whatever he liked. Now his game was ruined. He was not getting away with whatever he wanted to do anymore, and he was really gonna get me. He knew I was somewhere watching him, but it drove him completely *crazy* to not know how and where.

But you see, the "last word" is very important to a little brat-man like that. So he was going to get the last word. And he did.

He marched out onto the concrete portion of the patio, held up his hand, and with great intent *lifted his middle finger, and then spun around in a circle.* He was going to flip me off, no matter where I was! And so, he did. His intention was not to provoke a fight, but only to flip me off and give himself the satisfaction of having the last word! I knew he did not want to fight because he did not challenge or call me out. He simply flipped a 360-degree bird and went inside.

I started chuckling, and I was so pleased with myself that I rode high on getting the best of that little booger for the rest of my shift. It was a fantastic "psyche." He did not know *where* I was or *how* I was getting the word out on him, and it made him nuts. He knew it was pretty pathetic of him to do what he did, but that was the closest thing he had to telling me off. I was very happy too, though. I got my job done, nobody got hurt and I outsmarted the smartest little jerk in the whole facility. It is not often that security gets the best of someone. But that was one good night!

MANAGEMENT INCOMPETENCE IN THE DESERT SUN

I was put in charge of a post one time. This place was an exclusive jewelry store. It was very nice to work there. I liked the sales staff who were very pleasant people. The managers were wonderful people too, all except for one. He was in charge of security, and we kept running into problems with this guy. I could not keep the post staffed. He kept firing people for infractions which could have easily been corrected with a verbal counseling.

Patrolling for ten hour shifts in 110 degrees Fahrenheit is possible without anyone getting hurt. You just need to find any shade possible, drink plenty of water, and make sure you are getting at least some kind of electrolytes in you. The paramedic/fire team I consulted with said that a good ratio was one quart of good quality sports beverage to every gallon of water consumed. This was optimal.

You see, sports beverages often contain sugar in the form of corn syrup or other sweeteners which may actually hinder hydration if they are drank exclusively, absent of plain, clean water. But drinking sports beverages in conjunction with water was great advice. Or even a concoction such as an infant electrolyte formula is good too, when added to water.

This is not medical advice from me; it is just what the fire department taught me. I would encourage investigating this for yourselves to see if that remains good advice. What I just told you was from about fifteen years ago: the fire department and I had a strong connection. I had someone call them up on the telephone and they came right out there to give me that advice.

Of course I was strongly connected with them because I was having a drink with them after work... I will explain why.

I was out in the heat, fifth or sixth day in a row. I was drinking plenty of water, urinating normally and all that, so I thought all was well. I would sweat, I would drink. I would sweat, I would drink. Just like you are supposed to in the desert. I had been a desert rat for many years and was supposed to know what I was doing.

It turned out that what I was doing ended with me walking around in a circle, aimlessly, giggling to myself. I remember one of my guys calling me over. Next thing I remember, I was sitting in the shade, sucking down two full quarts of sports drink. The the manager in charge of the security team was taking my pulse for some reason, and I ended up being disarmed by the manager, who took my 9 mm and "tried to unload it." We were lucky that this alleged ex-military guy didn't shoot somebody or something.

You see, the genius took my gun from its holster. Okay, fine, that was the correct thing to do because I was delirious. But... I remember him pulling my piece, pointing in a safe direction and jacking the slide back. The round popped from the chamber and he declared that he had "unloaded" the gun. *Nope!* Even in my current state of stupid, I realized that he done nothing more than pop one of my bullets out of the gun and chambered a fresh round. I prayed he wouldn't "test" the trigger to show how unloaded the gun was. Although, in retrospect, that might have been tragically funny to watch him get fired on the spot. He was some tough guy, that one, ex-military, survived an armed robbery, etc. But *how* any military man could *not* understand a semiautomatic's basic operation was beyond me. One of my guys saw what he was doing, saw me trying to instruct him in my slurred, broken English, and took over the situation. He safely unloaded my gun.

So there I was on the floor with my legs elevated. It was awkward., but at least I was cooling off. They dimmed the lights to let me rest until the paramedics arrived. Then the medics turned on the lights without warning, making me holler. They apologized and went to work. Yep, it was time for a drink; they all agreed. And the drink was on them. Time to party!

They hooked up the IVs, jabbed a tube in each arm, pulled the needles and left the plastic catheters in my veins. Then they went full bore, wide-open, and dumped all the water, normal saline they could into my veins. I was hauled out on a gurney and zipping toward Anytown hospital at code 3 (lights and siren). I was coming around a little, and they started asking me questions. That was when I got the lecture on how to hydrate but to add electrolytes. They explained that I had sweated out my own electrolytes, and while I was drinking plenty of water, I was not replenishing them. I had effectively watered down the potassium, calcium, sodium, etc. in my blood. That knocked my chemistry out of whack, and that was why I had become so goofy.

So I was seriously ill, yes, but it was an easy fix. They got me to the ER, and by that time they had to hang more bags of saline. They just kept the fluids coming. With two quarts of sports drink already on board, two more liters of saline en route to the hospital, two more fresh liters of saline hung up at the hospital bed, that was about a gallon and a half of fluid being dumped into my system in less than an hour. Boy, did I have to take a leak! Immediately, they gave me one of those handy bedside urinals and told me to go to town. They had the curtain pulled so I did not have to worry about stage fright. I turned the faucet on and filled the urinal. They emptied it. Then I filled another. The most impressive thing for me was that the fluid leaving my body was hot.

Finally, after about the third emptying of liter-sized bed urinals, the ER doc came over and apologized for not being available. I understood, and I was feeling better. I had enough medical training as a nationally registered EMT and a CNA that I understood the danger was minimal once hydration was restored, so I was not too worried. The doctor kind of chuckled and said that I was "peeing up a storm." Well…yeah. What did they expect? And he told me what I already knew to be true, I had suffered from "heat intolerance." Yeah. No kidding. And the doctor said I had hyponatremia, which I had never heard of before that day. It turned out that hyponatremia is the $9 word for "not enough sodium in your blood."

I came around, got over the heat issue and drove myself home with a three-day pass from the doctor to rest. Now stand by, because there are two more experiences related to this event and the girl I was married to at the time.

BAD COMMUNICATION

One thing that I did not mention about the above experience was that I had asked one of the people at the jewelry store, a person I trusted, to be sure to call my wife. The paramedic said that they would take care of that at the hospital. I thought they had done that, so I did not worry about it right away. A member of the management staff from the security company I worked for came by to visit. He told me that I was fully recovered, just like he knew I would be. We chatted for a moment, and when I realized how late it was getting, I finally asked if anyone had called home for me. He kind of flinched and said, "I will be right back." Well, I figured that meant nobody had called home for me. When he came back a few minutes later, he had the funniest look on his face, like somebody had broken off a broom handle inside his rear end.

I laughed at him, my boss, because I had actually earned the right, and said, "Ohhh...nooo...you got a hold of her, didn't you? Ha-ha-ha! And just, how is she? Hmmm?"

"Oh, um, well, she's fine now," he said. But I knew better than that. She was only receding for a moment. She was going to tear into somebody else before this over. I could feel it in my bones. That being said and done, doctor's excuse in hand, I went home. When I arrived, my wife was, as expected, fuming. At least it was not at me. I was glad of that. We talked over what had happened. And she told me what the office had put her through.

You see, I have a long-standing policy, which I still live by today. I always let somebody know where I am, and I always let somebody know if I am going to be late coming home. That way, if I am late, *really* late, somebody knows that they need to start looking for me. And she had. She started looking for me at around two and a half hours past my normal arrival home by calling the office. They told her that they *did not know where I was*. And they really made a mistake by telling her that it was "not their problem" when she said I was three hours late and it was very unusual for me. She was very worried, but they did not care.

I have to say at this point that I had a very good reputation with the company, and on the day I was hired they said they loved to take care of their employees like family. Well, they had some people in the office who did not take care of us like we were family. Their response to my wife's concerns was not appropriate. I would have at least shown some concern for their employee. The office knew me well enough to realize that I had strong character and was not given to carousing or running around. They should have had some concern for my whereabouts, or least pretended. Anything was better than telling her that it was not their problem and blowing her off.

If someone had simply taken the time to look at the previous shift's notes, they would have found out I was sick in the hospital. And what about the off-going shift? They should have made it quite clear that we had a man down. But no one thought that through. No one was concerned enough about the situation, a dangerous situation, to even pass it on to the next shift. That was certainly a problem, and it caused my family undue distress. The office staffer my wife spoke to acted like I had gone out drinking or something and it was just too bad for her. That was not the way to treat anyone, particularly not a trusted employee.

The next morning, the phone rang around 5:00 AM. True to form, being the post commander, I sat straight up in the bed, ready to answer the phone. In those far-off days, most telephones were wall-mounted in the kitchen or on a bedside table, or both. Our place had the phone in the kitchen. My wife told me that, no, she was going to answer the call because we both knew it was the office. I was under a doctor's orders to rest, and *that was* entered in their notes. We knew it because the office manager, captain by rank, saw to it personally. She answered the call and said that no, they could not speak with me. The man on the phone insisted that he be allowed to speak with me because there was a problem on my post. We had an officer call in sick and they needed to get coverage. She started yelling at him because he would not let go of the idea that he was going to speak with me. She really lit into him, calling him an idiot, stupid, etc. She told him that he was not going to talk to me because I was resting after the security office allowed the manager of the jewelry store to leave me out in the sun until my brains were baked. Her parting shot was, "THEN LOOK AT YOUR NOTES NEXT TIME...IDIOT!" and slammed the phone down in his ear.

All that grief could have been avoided with a simple phone call to my wife telling her that I was in the emergency room but was recovering nicely from heat exhaustion and I would be home soon. The fact that the simple phone call was not made, and nobody bothered reviewing notes was a reflection of the competence level so common in the security field, even among management teams.

THEY THOUGHT THEY SAW A GHOST

Back in the days before GPS and cell phones were so widespread, if you were stuck in traffic, that was it. You were stuck. And you had no way to tell anyone.

On my way to work one day, I was caught in really bad traffic. The freeway was gridlocked. It turned out that there was an accident, a fatal accident. This was a horrible scene, because when passing by, you could see the charred spot on the road where the SUV had been burning. Sadly, there were Christmas gifts scattered all over the road, and all the litter from the paramedics, the bandage wrappers, and so on were blowing everywhere. That was a hard thing to bear. So sad, so sad.

When I got to work, I just knew I was going to be in all kinds of trouble. I thought it was at least a write-up or even worse. I was in a big old hurry but did not dare speed, especially not after seeing that burning car scene and those presents all over the road. I had the radio on, and they said there was a fatal car crash on the freeway (no kidding) and that traffic should resume its normal pace soon (not soon enough). I did not think much of it; I was just trying to get to work. It was a very hard thing to see, and the memory is still hard to carry with me to this day. So it was not that I did not care. There was just nothing I could do about it, and now I was an hour late for work.

I pulled into the parking garage, ready to take my lumps. I knew it was going to be tough. I worked my way to the door and badged in. Well, at least I was not fired yet. They would have left me out in the cold by canceling my badge and reassigning me to the office. Then the office would have had the option of either giving me another assignment or not. When you are not immediately reassigned, you are in essence, fired. But not technically. And on that technicality, they did not have to pay out unemployment or put up with wrongful termination suites. That was just one of the many loopholes so many security companies used when they had to get rid of somebody.

I made my way to the office, and I badged my way in. I did not expect what I saw on the other side of the door. I had often heard of the expression, "You all look like you've seen a ghost!" But this was the first time I had ever been greeted by people who looked that way. The entire control center was packed with two shifts of security officers. A sea of white, short-sleeved polyester and embroidered badges. All staring at me, eyes wide, mouths agape.

Then the security team manager said, "All right, everyone. Kellogg is okay. Dayshift, go home. Swing shift to your posts. Kellogg...you call home!" I wanted to explain, and the boss repeated the order. Well, with no points to be made by arguing with him, I called home. On the phone my wife at the time was very upset. She explained what had happened. She and my parents got word there was an accident with at least one fatality on the Anystate Freeway, northbound, and I was missing with no way of contacting me or knowing if I was safe.

She had called in to my job to see if I had arrived safely. When I had not, my boss asked her to keep them posted on what she and my parents found out. Meanwhile, word spread across the shift like wildfire. Everyone stayed after their shift to wait and see what would happen. My wife and parents in the meantime, were calling all the hospitals and such, trying to locate me. No news was good news indeed, but it was very hard not knowing anything as well. As it turned out, yes, I was fine, and everything went back to normal.

This goes to show you the camaraderie which security officers develop. It seems to almost be an unconscious sort of situation. When you put on a uniform that separates you from the general public, it does something for you. It gives you an identity. And it does not matter if you are with the FBI, police, fire, housekeeping, or security. You have an identity. Should the job be dangerous in some way or another, it is all the more so.

In this case, it was unheard of for security professionals to stay after their shift for any reason. People just never hung around to chat or anything like that. At 1430 hours, shift was done, and *zoom!* Out the door we went. It was kind of alarming for me to see everyone hanging around and to hear the "Kellogg is okay! Go home now and the rest of you to your posts please." It was very strange to not get called to task for being an hour late to a job that normally accepted no excuses. But I guess when death is on the line, and people think the call was for you, there is room for some forgiveness.

Another interesting part of this story is that many of the guys who stuck around did not even like me all that much. Certainly, none of them wanted to see me *dead*, but we were nowhere close to being friends. I guess the pressure of the moment, the peer pressure and the camaraderie all combined to keep these folks glued in their seats. I was touched and deeply appreciated their concern.

I suppose peer pressure was part of it because no one wanted to be "that guy, the one who left when we thought one of our own could be dead." They would have gotten "the look," and they would have in some subtle ways been treated differently in the following days. Their loyalty to the team and their ability to have the other guy's back would always be questioned, even if nobody would have vocalized it. That is just the way it is.

About half of these guys were in the military and that is the way it always is in your branch of service, particularly in combat. Security professionals should not enter into combative roles, but sometimes it just cannot be avoided, and we all knew that. We knew that we had to be able to count on each other. And they proved it that day. That day, I knew that I was part of a real team, conscious of it or not. I regret not having a greater appreciation of that at the time.

A COP SHOOK MY HAND

The relationship between security professionals and police is a complicated matter and will have its own chapter in this or some other book. But here, in the real-life experiences section of this work, I wish to address the personal experiences I had with police officers who shook my hand. This handshaking business may not seem like much to the outsider; I understand why. And no, this is not a situation where I had some grade-school brand of celebrity fascination with a "real live cop." No, these were both situations where cops *congratulated* me on matters that I took firmly in hand and gave them a lot less to worry about.

I have actually provided solid assistance to police several times in my career. I have put my foot in my mouth too, and made my mistakes as well. In these matters, I took my mistakes as a "lesson learned" and moved forward. My mistakes were reflections of my lack of training or my inability to cope with verbal abuse, things like that. I was embarrassed and the cops were annoyed, but in the end, well, I learned. As for the assistance, there is usually a "thanks, guys," and this is always nice. But the heartfelt congratulations I have found were usually reserved for security professionals who did the job exactly like the police themselves would have, or even perhaps excelled past what they could have done, alone.

Now the first time I experienced the heartfelt handshake was in an upper-crust section of Anytown, USA. This place was where the wealthy hung their silk scarves and sipped $40 espressos. Well, I was on the Unnamed Property in Anytown, having a mildly boring conversation about execution and police shootings. These topics often came up with former or retired cops when I was working with them. It's not morbid; it is just a natural part of conversation. Same with soldiers and particularly special forces operatives, who are commonly in the security field.

Anyway, we were watching some police officers interviewing a suspect. This little blonde girl was getting shaken down for something outside of Anytown Grocery Store. Suddenly, when the officer got off of his radio and approached her with his hand out, she ran! Holy cow! It was now a foot pursuit! We didn't commonly see those in the security field, much less in Anytown's poshest neighborhood. So the girl was not wasting any time with zigging and zagging. She was beelining away from the cop, probably hoping to outrun him in straightaway. The problem was, she was running straight for my client's property line.

"Well," said I to myself, "that just ain't gonna happen!"

I knew I could not let that foot chase, and possible breakdown-takedown thing, happen in my client's parking lot. If I did, the client would be simply livid!

I watched close, and being a rather big guy with a sidearm, I thought I could scare her into stopping before she crossed onto the property, at the edge of the curbed cedar-chipped landscaping. So timing it just right, in an effort to put myself directly in front of her as a barrier and hoping the cop could catch up and nab her, I put my hand on my holstered weapon, pointed my finger right at her so I had her attention, and yelled, "You! Stop! Stop! Stop! Stop NOW!" And she *did!*

Now in all fairness, she could have easily skirted around me and ran right across the property. A more experienced fugitive, used to running from police, would have done that very thing. But in this case, my gamble paid off. She looked angry, almost hurt, really, and gave me one of those "Where did you come from, and why are you involved? I hate you!" types of looks, and she stopped dead for the cop to grab and cuff her. He walked her back to the patrol car some hundred yards away.

I went back to my retired cop partner, a sheriff's deputy who had been in an "officer involved shooting" and was telling me about it, and I said that the police normally don't like it when we get involved in their business. Such had been my experience in different Anytowns in this particular Anystate of the United States. The whole county and surrounding areas of this particular location just had it in for security. They generally did not like us. As I was saying that, I saw the policeman approaching. I thought, *uh-oh, here it comes!*

Then I said aloud, "Uh-oh! Here it comes! I'm gonna get my tail end handed to me in a wicker basket!"

My partner told me that I really did not know that. and I should give it a chance. Well, yeah… What else was there to do? The approaching PD had a captive audience. I could not leave, and I sure was not going to back away or try to avoid him. Certainly, I did not want to have this conversation where the police would be seen chewing me out; which would be very bad for the client to see, and then the client would chew me out. With only so many inches of chewing flesh left on my butt, well, I felt obligated to leave some for the others. Gotta spread it around, you know?

And here came the copper. Okay…what is it going to be? The standard "What you did was very dangerous" or the "You don't have the authority to…blah, blah," or maybe it would be the standard "Look, buddy, we appreciate your efforts [a lie], but please don't interfere with police business from now on, okay? We don't want you to get hurt!" So I braced for it and my former deputy partner just stood there, kind of smiling. I think he got the feeling of what was coming but did not want to blow it for me. I was dreading this. Turned out to be wasted dread!

Well, this police officer—a Hispanic male with no stripes or rank on his uniform—approached me and probably saw the forlorn grimace on my face. He broke into this huge white-teethed Eric Estrada-type smile and offered me his hand! I could hardly believe it. A bit surprised, pleasantly so, and maybe even bewildered, I waited for what he had to say. He *thanked* me for helping him with that stop. He was *glad* I was there. Wow! That was unexpected. When I asked him what the girl did, he sort of paused and gauged whether telling would be some breach of professionalism, then he said that she was kiting checks, and the grocery store caught her. I was satisfied with that response, and he went back to work, glad that some Barney Fife was on the ball.

I was suddenly feeling pretty great that afternoon, and my retired deputy partner smiled and suggested that maybe I should learn to give the cops in this town the same chance I hoped they would give me. And he was right. Security and police personnel do need to trust one another, each in their respective roles. We need to trust the cops to be professional with security and give them the credit they have due. And the cops need to trust security to not cross over the boundaries. In this case, I did just that. I did not cross the boundaries. I did not scream or curse at the girl. I did not grab her or slam her to the ground. I had my weapon on my hip, and it *stayed* there. No gun drawn on this one. It was not the appropriate thing to do. I used minimum force to divert the suspect's direction of travel, and that gave the cop the only edge he needed to make the arrest. That was a good day.

DOC WHITEY VS. ANYTOWN PATROL

Since one purpose of this book is to present both positives and negatives of the security business and its personnel, I want to relate this story my old man told me. Dad was a pizza delivery guy for Anytown Pizza. He would drive around, make his stop, deliver the pie, and move on. He minded his own business and got along fine. On a side note, Dad would carry a red-colored 4 D-cell Maglite with him. Pizza in one hand, big red (the flashlight) in the other. One day, some kid, sitting in a group of miscreants that frequented the neighborhood, asked in that "hey-old man-let-me-mock-you-in-front-of-my-friends-tone":

"Hey! Why do you carry that big flashlight around?"

Dad stopped, looked square at him, and with a completely humorless, matter-of-fact tone said, "Because they won't let me carry a *gun*."

Then he stood there for a moment and just looked at them, waiting to see what was next.

"Oh," said the kid. And they never bothered him again.

Then one day, while minding his own business, he saw the red-and-blues light up his rearview mirror. This was nothing new; police often stopped Dad to talk to him. They would not really want to pass time, necessarily, but they would ask him about things he was seeing around the neighborhood.

Pizza delivery guys see things around neighborhoods because no one thinks twice about a pizza car. They are commonly seen; they are around all hours of the night, especially on weekends; no one thinks to hide anything they are doing because, after all, he's just the pizza dude.

So cops got to know Dad, and they started to realize that he was generally on their side, and he did not mind giving them tips on what was going on or not going on. He would sometimes see this or that activity, this or that car, this or that person in the area. So when Dad got pulled over, he really thought nothing of it. Just another quick chat and he would be on his way. Only this time, something was off. The guy that climbed out of what appeared to be a cop car was dressed all wrong, and he carried himself all wrong. The uniform was powder blue, the outdated color for Anytown PD. The cops had given up that color and had been for years dressed head to toe in black.

Not only that, but he was all sloppy and fat-looking, shirt was not well pressed as one would expect for PD, and this guy sort of saun- tered up all "Barney Fife-like" with his thumbs in his belt (I mean... seriously?). As soon as this security officer approached the car, Dad knew that this was no cop, not from any jurisdiction. So when the "officer" stood at driver's window, Dad, true to form, forced the guy back by pushing open the door and jumped out of his car, something he would never do to a police officer. He knew better than that. But this guy, a "pus-gut," as Dad called him, had it coming. And he was about to get him a tiger by the tail without knowing it!

"And what are you doing pulling me over on a public street?" asked my indignant father.

"Going a little fast, weren't you?" And he still had his thumbs tucked firmly in his belt with all his pus-gutted glory oozing all over the place.

"What? That's none of your business. Get back away from my car right now! You can't pull me over! Pulling me over on a public street is illegal! Who are you anyway? Oh...you're from that security company, where you guys are loser wannabe cops! You back away from my car right now! Tell me why I need to listen to anything you have to say! Why? Why should I listen to you?"

"Well...uh... I got a gun!" And he put his hand on the pistol grip.

Now, at this point, it must be understood that this Barney Fife, a true one and not a representative of any true security professional in any part of the world, was wearing a full duty belt. That means this guy had on a leather belt, a pistol, handcuffs, a Billy club, magazines of ammo, and pepper spray. These guys were decked out! Now... I have no problem with security officers being equipped. I really don't. I have worked in parts of town where I know that such gear is actually necessary for the work because the security pros are in true danger.

Now...these boys, who worked for this company were authorized to wear the gear by the company owner. But they were not trained in its proper use. I mean I saw firsthand these guys finding unlocked doors on homes in a retirement community, and bursting into the house to clear it with their guns drawn like they were going into a drug bust or something. They were training each other, and the owner of the company had little to no supervision or control over what his people were doing.

So getting back to the gun remark. Oooh, boy! That was the wrong thing to say on so many levels. I mean, seriously! That was just a...well... I don't know what that was. I would definitely say it was a threat of some kind. I mean, think about it, an attorney could have gotten some serious mileage on that in court. An apparent authority figure, in a uniform that was designed, rightfully so, to evoke a response of authority to give an edge over the people they approached and to win the trust of the people they were there to serve, to protect. And this man performed an illegal action in a car designed to make people think they were seeing a real cop car in their rearview mirror.

In fact, these are actually decommissioned cop cars, which is fine for security people or taxi companies to use. Even laypeople who don't run a business in security or transportation can simply just buy the cars and use them. But the thing they must do to buy them is to take all the police markings off and they should not have used the red and blue light bars. The Anytown patrol company did not have police markings, but they did have the light bars. I don't know if that was illegal in those days, and I don't want to do the research to find out. But I know that legal or not, those light bars were to be used only in emergencies such as blocking intersections against people breaching fire zones, medical emergencies, etc.

The light bars should have *never* been used to pull someone over on a public street. Retirement community or not, that was a bad thing to do because this community was not a gated community with private roadways or walkways. This was simply a housing development built along city streets that was designated for retirees. The streets were public property, and the security officers had no authority to pull people over for the commission of infractions on those streets. Besides, how did he know that Dad was speeding? All he had was his own judgment to tell him that the car was going a little fast. There was no radar gun, and if he thought he "paced" the car like police officers do, fine, but did he have the certificate to prove that he finished that training? And even if he did have the certificate, he was not a police officer and that makes the whole issue a moot point.

Getting back to the conversation, Dad said that if pus-gut pulled that gun he would take it from him, use it on him as suppository, and pull the trigger. I don't know for sure how it all ended, but the police never were involved. I think that Dad pretty much just ended the conversation by getting back in his car and driving off. Personally though, I think that he should have called the police. I really do. I never like to see security people get into trouble with the local police, but in this case, it was really needed. That guy needed to be taught a lesson and have his security license pulled.

As it turned out, with little surprise, the Anytown patrol company ended up in official trouble. I guess someone finally reported that their officers were now dressing in black just like the police. To the untrained eye, you could not tell cops from the security people, and this is completely unacceptable. The public should always be able to easily differentiate security uniforms from police uniforms. That way, there is never room for security people to pass themselves off as police, and there is no way for police to be mistaken for security personnel. Security has its role, police has theirs, and there is a terrible legal mess here just waiting to happen in the event of a multi-agency incident. We cannot have any mix-ups in those circumstances.

Eventually it became the law throughout the great state of Anystate that no security officer could wear *any* colors of *any* police agency on *any* part of their uniform. So let's say that I went on duty, in uniform. I have gone through all of my training and all my weapons are secure on my person. But under my security uniform shirt is my T-shirt. And it happens to be charcoal black. The authorities could take legal actions against me and my company. Why? Because that shade of black is now used on the T-shirts of the Anytown swat team. And as a security officer, I cannot wear *any* part of my uniform the same as theirs.

That all started statewide because the Anytown patrol company had their Barney Fifes go off half-cocked and they started picking their own uniform colors. They were dressed like the PD from head to toe, and that was okay with their boss. You see, the company owner set out the idea of running the company just as close to Anytown PD as possible. Noble gesture, yes, but the plans that he had cooked up were not wise. He had a hiring process that consisted of an interview:

"Jim says you're looking for a job."

"Yes."

"Okay. You got a gun?"

"Yes."

"You know how to use it?"

"Yes."

"Okay. You got these hours open?"

"Yes."

"Okay. Here's your uniforms and gun belt."

The idea behind this company, when it started, was that the owner wanted to run his company to be as close to Anytown PD operations as possible. Now think for a moment of how incredibly bad of an idea this was. Not only did his company attract guys who liked to pretend to be cops, but he had them looking like cops as well. Obviously, this was a bad idea. He had guys looking like cops, he had some actual police academy washout running things, unofficially of course, and so he had them acting like cops. It was hurtling out of control at breakneck speed. These security officers really were getting off on this whole routine.

And that was why that Officer Doe approached Dad the way he did. He was pretty bold until somebody assertively objected to his behavior, and obviously, he had no de-escalation training. He did not have proper backup. He did not even know the laws, which he was trying to "enforce" without authority. And they carried guns. Real guns with *plenty* of bullets. It is a wonder that no one was actually shot, intentionally or by accident.

I once had the opportunity to sit with a cop who had some dealings with this company. I just asked him a direct question about how much trouble, if any, that they had with Anytown patrol. He did not mind telling me this story about how one of Anytown patrol's guys wanted him to talk to a man who was jogging through the retirement community, on a city street. That jogger was wearing a sidearm, in an open-carry-firearm state. He was on public property, in the street. There was no law or even any rules being broken. The Anytown patrol guy demanded that the police officer go speak to the jogger.

"Why would I do that?" asked the cop.

"He's carrying a gun," said the Anytown patrol.

"Yeah, so? I have a gun, you have a gun, and he has a gun in an open-carry state."

"Well… I want you talk to him and find out what he is doing."

"It seems to me that he's jogging on a public street with a legally carried firearm. What else would you like to know about him? He is not breaking any laws or rules of carry."

"I don't like your attitude. I want to see your supervisor."

"Oh…you do. Are sure you want to see my supervisor?"

"Yeah! I don't like your attitude, and I want to see your supervisor!"

"You are *sure*, then, that you want to see my supervisor?"

"Yeah! I am sure I want to see your supervisor!"

"All right then. Remember…you demanded this."

"Hey! Sarge!" The jogger then changed directions, arching back to the Anytown police and the Anytown patrol. He met the two guys.

"Hey, what's up? What can I do for you?"

"Well, this guy here, Patrolman Doe, wanted to talk to you."

"Okay. What's up, man?"

"Um…"

"Well, what is it, Patrolman Doe? You called me over here," said Sergeant Jogger.

"Uhh…"

"Sarge…this guy says he wanted to talk to you about me."

"Okay…what about you?"

"He doesn't like my attitude."

"Really? What is it about your attitude that he doesn't like?"

"Well, he wanted me to talk to you about your gun. And I told him that it was not necessary because you have a gun, I have a gun, and he has a gun, in an open-carry state."

"Oh? What about my gun?"

"Well, Sarge…you're carrying it."

"Oh…and…well, I have a gun, and you got a gun. He has a gun. We are allowed to have guns and to carry them openly by Anystate's laws. What about it?"

And they both just sort of stared at the Anytown patrolman until he felt stupid enough to finally start his outdated, unmarked patrol car and just drive away, light bar and all. This is a pretty sad commentary on the state of affairs that exists in some security companies. This is why state laws have cracked down on private security operations in the legal sense. But this still does not address the core problem of poor or nonexistent training and zero standardization of what training does exist. There are very few states who require any serious licensure, and they don't have any core skill set for what security professionals are supposed to know and be able to perform.

And the types of people who work for Anytown patrol are the results. Such security officers are commonplace enough that this creates the stereotype of security people. This is why security professionals are not respected, nor are they liked in general by the public. It is easy to imagine what changes could occur in public perception if there was a skill set required by the states in which security companies operate. We could very quickly and easily eliminate from the ranks these "Barney Fife"–type companies; they would simply not be able to operate. The existing security companies would have to comply with the training requirements and so forth. We will talk in another section of the book about training and so on.

NOISE COMPLAINT: ELDERLY LADY VS. THE EXERCISE MACHINE

One night on patrol in Anystate, for Anysecurity Company, I got a noise complaint at an apartment complex. This nice elderly lady was complaining about the neighbors making a racket. "A treadmill or something," she said. It was a typically busy Friday night, nothing really special happening, it was just hectic trying to get all the patrols completed before the shift was over and these complaints were the biggest waste of time for the most part. I mean, really, there was just not much we could do about it.

Think about this for a moment:

Someone is playing their stereo too loudly. I get called. I answer the dispatch. I go to the apartment. I knock in the door. I see someone use their peephole for its intended purpose. They see who it is. They know their rights. They know that I am private citizen working for a private company. I cannot demand entry. I cannot issue them a ticket for the noise complaint. If they open the door or ask me through the door what I want, I can only politely ask them to turn down the music. And they may either turn it down or not. Or maybe they just turn it down long enough for me to go away, then they just turn it back up again. It would be inaccurate to say that everyone always did that, because most people understand that, yeah, it's getting late.

But if the person chooses to not answer the door and just keeps the music up without responding to me, there is nothing I could do but call the police. Which is all the residents of the apartments can do too.

I was just sort of a middleman in the case, who served best by saving time for the police who did not have to deal with the call.

Friday in every police jurisdiction where I worked security was by its nature very busy for the cops and they were working on real crimes. Muggings, stabbings, shootings, rapes, robberies and homicides. This was their night for getting out there and gathering material for the next episode of "Cops." So no, they were not interested in hearing about me or any other citizen with a noise complaint, unless that noise complaint was caused by something really serious.

In the interest of providing proper customer service for the client, and in the interest of keeping the actual crime fighters on the streets where they belong, I went ahead and answered the complaint. I knocked on the lady's door when I did not hear anything on the floor. This was to make sure I had entered the correct building and that I was contacting the proper complainant. She assured me that, yes, I was in the correct place, and yes, she was the one who called. So I stood by with her there, her hair in curlers as she was obviously ready for bed. After all…it was seven thirty, and the sun was down! (Just kidding.) It was actually past ten o'clock and yes, she was well within her rights to demand a little quiet.

So I stood by with her and listened…and listened and listened. There was no more noise. She asked me to knock on their door. She wanted me to speak to them. That, I ended up explaining to her, was a bad idea because if I knock on a door when all is quiet then that can become a serious matter very quickly. The person who is now quiet can become understandably upset. And we don't want that. Because we don't want to stir up a mess where none needs be stirred, we did not knock on the door after all was quiet.

The elderly lady, who was nice enough, insisted that the people next door kept using exercise equipment. She was annoyed and had to get some rest. I understood, but I could not do anything about it. She understood my position, as well, and was not getting aggravated with me as people often did in these cases. But she did have me back two or three times. And it did start to get old. I mean, it's not such a hard thing that she was asking of me, but it was time-consuming, and I had other accounts to check up on.

So finally, on about the third or fourth time I went out there, I heard the noise. The old lady said, "So now you know I am not crazy!" Well, it was not that I ever thought she was crazy or lying. And she was not attention-seeking because she did not have that way about her; you can always tell when somebody just wants the attention. She was genuinely upset and just trying to get some sleep. And now, *I* heard the noise, and it sounded like, yeah, a treadmill...

Okay...but at *this* hour...aw...heck no!

Squeak...squeak... Well, yes, I could see why this lady was annoyed...and it was just ridiculous. Well...maybe I would go speak with him...*squeak-a-squeak-asqueakasqueaka!* Uhhh...hmm... well...no. I was NOT going there—*squeakasqueakasqueaka*—to speak with the neighbor because...yep! There it is!

"OHHH...OHHH...YEESSSS!" PANT! PANT! "OOOH! OHHH! AWWWWYEEEAAAAH! YEEEEEEEEEEEESSSSSSS! YES, YES, YES, YES! Ahhhhhh... hhhhhohhh ahhh! (Silence.)

And...that just kind of ended the whole misadventure/mystery of the treadmill. I just kind of looked at this innocent, sweet little old lady in her curlers and night robe and just said, "Ummm, well... I think that the treadmill issue is resolved. I doubt you are going to need me anymore tonight. Rest well and stay safe."

Then I got the heck out of dodge before she actually figured out what I was talking about. I mean, yeah...it was time to go before she started asking me questions about the treadmill that I just did *not* want to answer. And who knows when some innocent old lady might get some ideas...

THE CRAZIEST PATROL NIGHT... EVER!

On this particular patrol night, I received preauthorization from the branch manager to take my two boys with me on patrol. Because they are my boys, they are not going to be John Doe 1 and John Doe 2. They are going to be "Bravo" and "Alpha" for the purposes of this experience.

They were both minors at the time of this adventure. I was going to just take Alpha because he was old enough to drive and could get himself out of harm's way in my vehicle if something went terribly wrong. My ex-wife, married to me at the time, told me that Bravo was feeling pretty bad about being left behind, I called my manager back and got permission to take him too. That made me pretty happy, because, yeah, it really was not fair to take one without the other. And it was a good thing this worked that way because it was quite a night.

On this job, I held the rank of captain, which never means anything outside of the company where you work when you are on a security team. Rank is just arbitrarily assigned at the whim of the manager. No special requirements, your rank is just whatever the branch leadership says it to be. That being said, we arrived at the site and I found that my "co-captain," a man whom I greatly admired, named Captain Doe, was talking to Officer Doe. You should understand that Captain Doe was well educated and well-spoken, and a retired cop on top of it all. Officer Doe was a doofus who did minimal time in the armed services but made it out to be that he was the baddest of the bad. You can see about where this is going to end up.

I brought my sons into the office and I introduced them around, when all of a sudden, something started between the officer and the captain. It started out as a discussion, then Major Doe, in charge of the standing post accounts and not at all affiliated with the patrol team, came into our office. Officer Doe had gone to the major with some kind of issue. The captain was not pleased.

He started off with, "But, Major, with all due respect, we have our own major to whom we report. Now if you will excuse me...YOU, OFFICER DOE! What the —— are you doing going behind my back to a boss we don't work for? You better —— never ——..."

At this point, when he started yelling at Officer Doe, I saw the look on my boys' faces, and I shooed them out of the office. I told the boys to wait outside and just be patient while we worked this all out. I rushed back into the office, not because I was concerned, but because I was curious about what had just happened. I had never seen the captain go off like that. As it turned out, Officer Doe had an issue with some policy or ruling on a policy Captain Doe had made. He took issue with it, so he went to Major Doe because she was major, and Officer Doe thought she outranked the captain. Apparently, the good major thought so too, because she was there to "take charge," and this was where I wandered back in.

"—— and again…don't you ever go behind my back again! You have an issue with something I have said or done, you bring it to me! Then, once it's all said and done, if *we* can't work it out…we go together to the major OVER OUR —— DEPARTMENT and we work it all out together! If I'm wrong, then so be it. If you are wrong, then so be it! But we work it out in our department! We are SEPARATE FROM THE STANDARD POSTED OFFICERS! She runs *them*, the other Major Doe 2 runs our department! You never —— ever go over my head especially to the wrong major! If you do go to the correct major, then you are still going to get it from me and *him* for going —— over my head. Around here, as you —— know, we don't go around behind each other's back! We —— deal with our problems like *men*…like adult, grown mature men!"

I believed then, and I still believe now that this was one of the greatest lessons a young person could have gotten in leadership and office politics. The lesson being that you need to have integrity in communications, and you need to follow proper procedures. Plus, there was a chain of command issue at play here. You *never* in any job go to a boss who is *not* over your department. Now, we saw here a situation where a young officer, who truly knew better, went over the head of a captain, to a major not over his head. Not wise, not smart, and very manipulative!

The underlying issue here was that the officer was friends with the major he went to and thought that he could use her to bully my co-captain. Not only that, but the major apparently thought she could also bully my co-captain. And that was the real problem. When a leader allows a subordinate to try to use the leader's authority inappropriately, then that leader has just become the problem. Not only is the leader being manipulated, but that leader is failing to teach the subordinate a valuable leadership and organizational lesson. They are delivering the message to the subordinate that they can play one end against the other like a child of divorce plays the ex's against each other to get that one-upmanship thing rolling. This is not only counterproductive, but it is also destructive.

So the message my co-captain delivered to both the officer and the major was that there was a way to do things. That way is written in the post orders and office procedures. Everyone knows the rules and the major especially should have known better than to engage in this foolishness. Now, the co-captain in this case was quite shrewd. He was chewing out the subordinate and the major at the same time. But the major could not say anything or prove that he was chewing her out because none of his remarks were leveled at her and at no time was the major told that she needed to stay for the meeting. So everything the co-captain said was pointed at the officer, but splashed all over the major, making her look like a fool. And I don't think she even noticed. But…that was kind of what she was known for, too, so no great surprise there.

Getting back to my boys, they were outside in the foyer. It was late enough in the evening that the building was emptied of employees for the other business, so nothing was overheard by anyone but my sons. I went out and retrieved my sons; they were laughing quietly between themselves. I knew what was on their minds before they even told me.

"Dad, I don't know why you sent us out here. We could still overhear everything, including the bad language," said Alpha.

"Well, son, I was not worried about you hearing that. You were raised around your grandfather. I was, however, worried about you laughing out loud while Officer Doe got his butt chewed off."

"Well, yes, we did do that out here."

"And you understand why I did not want you to do that in the office."

My co-captain later apologized and said he did not mean to frighten my boys.

"Ha!" I said. "They were not frightened by you. They have a former Marine / Airman / Special Forces grandpa and they know what being yelled at is. They are tough enough to sit through your training tutorial, and they were starting to become highly amused because Officer Doe is a doofus. That is why I took them outside. They were out there laughing, and I did not want them to laugh out loud in the office and spoil the 7th *Heaven*-style father-and-son chat you were having with Officer Doe. If they could have sat quietly, I would have probably let them stay to learn the lesson you were teaching, but they simply were not going to make it."

"Oh," said the Co-Captain Doe. "Your daddy was all that, huh?"

"Yep."

So after the butt-chewing, I needed to get out on the street with my boys. I was supervising, but I also knew the co-captain was my leader behind the scenes. He was the one who led the team, even though I was "in charge." If I got into some kind of a pickle with the guys, which was frequent, the co-captain would give me sidebar advice. You see, I was still the new guy and I was still in the habit of giving some guys on the team more credit than they deserved for the brains in their heads. So he would tell me what he thought would happen next if I did this or that and how to best control the team. After a while, I caught onto to how things ran, and I was okay. No matter how much education one has, it is good to defer to experience and wisdom. My co-captain had both, and I respected that.

Now on this night, it was my boys' first ride along. They were ready to go out and they knew what to do. They had their standing orders. The boys knew that if I got into some kind of trouble, Alpha was to drive off with his brother in the truck and call 911 once they were safely out of the way, even if they saw me get *shot*. Was that going to happen? Naw. But it could happen. And we all knew it. But really, if this job was all that dangerous, I would not have ever brought my boys into it. The branch managers would have never allowed it either. I mean, in this particular Anytown, it was not all that dangerous. Not really. But we carried guns for a reason, too.

So that being said, we were going out on patrol and it was getting late. With the extra time allotted me with the supervisor's route being intentionally set up to service fewer clients, keeping time open for supervision duties, we went to dinner. We went to the local Maxburger place, and the night got really interesting. The boys needed to use the john, so I sent them to the counter to get a restroom token. Bravo went in there first and then came out with the oddest expression on his face.

"Dad...there's some weird guy singing in the restroom. He won't come out. Can you do something about that?"

"Well, son, you will need to talk to the store management. I don't have any authority here, and the restaurant will have to tell you what to do."

Now, we had seen this guy sitting in the dining room, just kind of talking to someone. They were not eating. Odd, but not unheard of. When the restaurant manager heard Bravo's complaint, he called to the man sitting there to check the situation. Hmmm... I guess he was the in-house security guy. Plain clothes. Essentially, he was a bouncer. And he was about to go to work. The bouncer got up, went to the restroom, and with Bravo and Alpha standing there, the bouncer asked the guy what was going on. It turned out that the potty singer was a little whacky, no big surprise there.

The bouncer then called the guy out; he had to abandon his bathroom vocalist routine, and leave the restaurant. So Elvis Toiletry went over to the table where he had his customary backpack full of stuff spread out all over the place. He was told that he needed to gather his things up and go. The caca crooner proceeded to do so, but he picked his things up one at a time veeeeeery, veeeeeeryyyy slooooowwwwwwly. He looked the man right in the eye while he was doing it...just daring him...and I knew that this was going get interesting very, very quickly.

The bouncer finally got sick of the nonsense, so he grabbed the guy, who in my opinion had it coming, and physically forced him out the door by shoving him unceremoniously into a belly flop on the sidewalk. Then all the stuff, hastily gathered, was thrown out too, all over him. Now, a uniformed security officer working for a private company would have been fired for that stunt. It could be argued, potentially, all day long whether or not the bouncer was completely justified. Justified or not, it was rather amusing. And from a certain perspective, the trespasser did have it coming, after being warned several times and then behaving defiantly in a generally rude manner as he was supposed to leave the premises.

That was how the evening began. And with us having eaten our dinner during all of this, we had to get on the road. We got in the truck and headed off to my first call. We had a medical center for the indigent on our roster. We were assigned to check this property three times during the course of the night. One point of special concern was this park bench that sat beside the public sidewalk. We were to prevent homeless people and trespassers in general from using the bench. The trouble with the bench was that it appeared to be a city-owned bench. It looked like the bench was just there for anyone to use. Naturally, it was understandable for people to use it. On the other hand, the people who would use the bench were not very nice about it.

The whole reason people were forbidden to use the bench was not some kind insane turf war with a bunch of sore-footed people. The users of the bench would leave litter and old food, liquor bottles and nasty garbage in general behind. The place was becoming smelly, disgusting, urine-soaked and there would even be feces. Our job was to check the doors because the medical clinic obviously needed to keep their place secure. And since they did not want their staff to have to run off unconscious drunks, or clean the filth and stench every morning, the clear alternative was to hire someone to watch the bench and keep the people from using that bench.

Speaking of drunks, we pulled up to the medical clinic and first I checked the doors, then I went to the bench. I had the boys wait in the truck, with Alpha sitting in the drivers' seat, keys in the ignition, ready to take off if something went wrong.

There were two guys on the bench and you never know how it will go when you approach a stranger and try to tell them what to do. People on the street are at times high, drunk, mentally compromised, handicapped and in extreme pain. Or maybe they are not even "street people," but just had a fight with their family or significant other and they are really in an aggressive mood. Any one of these people will, if treated badly, react aggressively, and they may even use physical violence.

That is why I had Alpha behind the wheel. There were two men, and I was convinced they were alone. But there was two of them after all, and I didn't know anything about them or their state of mind. I didn't know if they were strong, or armed. I didn't know if I was safe approaching them. If I really sensed there was serious danger, if they were, say, gang members out in force or something like that, I would have stood down and retreated. I would have gone to a safe area and called for backup from either more armed security officers or the police, whichever would have seemed reasonable.

But in this case, it would have been very poorly received, in security and police circles both, to not approach a couple of apparently harmless, homeless guys on a bench. Pulling back, staging, and calling out for police or other security personnel would not have been appropriate. Even so, there was risk anytime you approached a stranger, particularly if you were about to run that stranger off the property where they were standing. I found that generally, unless they were really looking for trouble, homeless folks would respond favorably to your kindness.

These two guys were just a couple of homeless, harmless drunks. One of them was quite a bit more sauced than his buddy. In fact, his friend kept falling asleep…passing out. And he smelled like urine and hand sanitizer. Since he did not seem to be exceptionally concerned about his general hygiene, and with his apparent serious state of inebriation, I could only assume and believe that he was sucking down bottles of $1 hand sanitizer for the alcohol content. As most people know, rubbing alcohol or isopropyl alcohol is very dangerous to drink or ingest. It is very hard on the body and the brain especially.

I also noticed at this point how wet his pants were. He was soaked in his own urine, and he was shivering. It was quite cold that night. The wet man's friend realized that it was very important for them to leave. I had approached them nicely and asked them kindly to leave the properly, explaining why and telling them that I could not leave until they left. But the friend could not wake up his buddy to get him to go. The guy would wake up, talk to us, and then pass out again. He would holler a bit about what a nice man I was, then he'd pass out. At some point, I realized he was not shivering anymore, and I know this to be a classic sign of hypothermia.

I was becoming afraid for this drunk's life at this point, and I knew that I was now responsible for a medical scene, so I called 911, and I called in to our team by a general radio transmission. I did not require backup, but I would be busy for a while. By this time, my boys were in the truck, wondering what I was doing. They could only see one guy talking to me and the other one with his eyes closed and not moving. They thought that the drunk was dead. He was not, not yet, but he was likely not going to last the night out in the cold. And again... I was now responsible because I was on the client's property, and I was in contact with a trespasser.

The police car arrived, so Anytown PD was now in charge of the scene. They called an ambulance. The paramedics came, took a look, and would not take him. Personally, I thought that they should have taken him, but they believed he was just drunk and did not want to deal with it. Now I was here with a cop, and my sons were almost sure that the drunk was dead because the ambulance did not want him, and the cop appeared to be investigating the scene.

The police started making calls to get this guy into a drunk tank. I had pointed out to the cop that the old drunk was not shivering anymore, and I told him that I could not leave until this guy was gone. The police officer asked me if I wanted to trespass the old boy, and I said that, yes, I did. The police officer looked at me sort of shocked and mentioned that this guy couldn't pay the ticket. I told him I did not want the man to be cited, but I did want him to be removed from the site. That was a relief to the police. We agreed at that point that we needed some help.

The Anytown cop called more police cars to the scene, and after one of the officers discovered that the drunken man had already been thrown out of one drunk tank tonight, we realized this would be more of a challenge than we at first thought. Meanwhile, the old drunk's friend was concerned and standing by. We had four police cruisers by this time, and at least one policeman was calling the different places, trying to find somewhere that would take him. He finally did.

Now, the question was, how to get the unconscious, urine-soaked drunk to the people who will take him in to sober him up for at least a few hours. At least he would be warm for a while, until he was put back on the street. We finally determined that one of the police officers would take the old boy to the drunk tank, wherever that was. The cop got into his trunk and found some plastic bags so the urine would not stink up the back of the patrol car. The policeman had to drive that car, no matter how it smelled. Once the seat was covered with plastic, we had to glove up for self-protection and four or five of us grabbed hold of this guy and tried to move him.

In the 1970s, I remembered watching hippie protestors just go "limp" as a method of passively resisting police. They would invade a piece of property, public or private, and when told they were trespassing, they would fall on the ground. Then they would just lay there and relax completely.

A completely limp, relaxed body is incredibly heavy. And you have to be careful not to injure the person, particularly if their limpness is chemically induced in some way. Dead people are similar, but worse. I had handled dead bodies as a certified nurse's aide, under controlled circumstances, from a bed of a specific height. The dead person was definitely sloppy and hard to handle, yes, but on a flat hospital bed, you have some control over the limbs, using the bed as a sort of work bench.

But this…on a cold night, outside, a man who was chemically compromised, smelly, and wet, far too cold for his own good, completely flaccid and slipping in and out of consciousness—it was a completely different deal. We had to get him off the park bench, this soggy, floppy being with a soul and a truly human identity. And we could not injure him during the transfer. We had to move him off of the park bench, over to the police car, through the open back door, and we had to securely buckle him in so he would not roll around during the vehicle transport.

It was like lifting a four-appendage meat sack full of wet, sloppy, gelatin. He was dead weight, which made him deceptively heavy for a lean man. The five of us fought and wrestled him over to the cop car. We struggled, dragging and pushing him across the seat without sliding the plastic off. Finally, we got the old drunk positioned and buckled in, and the police took him away. Off to…well, who knows? The point was that I was finally able to call in an all clear and get back to the truck. We were locked onto that scene for almost an hour.

I sat there for a few minutes, explaining to the kids just what we did with that guy. The boys thought the old drunk was dead. They asked me what was going on and why it took so long. What about the ambulance? I explained to them all that happened. They were pretty impressed with the impact that one security patrolman had. I staved off death for one guy, even if it was only for a little while.

After that call, I decided I needed a little break. Even though that took so long, I had time for the boys and I to grab a quick snack at the convenience store just around the corner. We drove over there and picked up some snacks and drinks. Then we sat in the parking lot, just watching the people go by.

Then I said, "Boys, watch this guy in the hoodie."

"Why do we want to watch him?"

"He's about to provide some entertainment."

"What's he going to do?"

"I don't know, but he will do something."

"How do you know?"

"I have been around this kind of person for a long time, and I can just tell he's going to do something."

You see, when you hang out on the street long enough, you get good at reading body language. This guy just had the right posture, bearing, and mannerisms. I could see those freaky wheels turning inside that dude's head. The look in his eye told me he was thinking about something. When a dude is stoned, you see, he often loses all impulse control. Whatever occurs to him, he will do. Good ideas, bad ideas, whatever. They have no judgment and no discernment. They can't think ahead to the consequences of what their actions will cause. A dude on dope will just walk into a place and start doing the most random things. And I knew this guy was about to get fully random.

We have all eyes on him, watching him. He walked onto the sidewalk and suddenly stopped and just got sort of twitchy. Then he reached around and started scratching his butt, just on the outside of his clothing. Then he walked a few steps, and he reached down and scratched his crotch. He took a few more steps, stopped, and reached down the back of his pants on the inside and scratched. Then moving onto the front, he reached all the way under his boxers and really started scratching.

Meanwhile, we were starting to laugh. We were sitting in the patrol truck. I was in uniform laughing my head off, and I've got these two boys just rolling in laughter as well. People were starting to look at us because I didn't think they knew what we are laughing at.

Then the guy *really* got going and jammed his hand down the back of his pants again, and I'm telling you…he was mining for gold! I mean, he was getting in there, and it really was gross. And to top it all off, after he was done digging for the tingly methamphetamine-induced, hallucinatory worms inside his pooper, he just went into the store and starts randomly fingering the merchandise—chips, candy, whatever—that people were expected to BUY to EAT! *Eccch*!

After we left the convenience mart, I finished my patrols without even one incident, and the boys slept in the back seat. That was just one crazy night. I had seen busier nights at that job, but none crazier, especially all at once like that. That night had more nutty stuff happen all at once than I would probably see in a normal month on the job. If there ever was a solid night to take the kids on patrol to see the madness of the world around them, that was it.

I think back on this, and the boys actually did learn a lot. They saw how quickly things can get out of control in an office when someone breaks the chain of command. They saw Officer Doe take his chewing out from my co-captain. From that, they learned an important principle of effective leadership.

Then they saw the homeless guy acting up in the burger joint. They saw random and very odd behavior out of that guy, and by letting them contact management by themselves while I kept a close eye, they learned how to get out of a pickle like that. Plus, I taught them by example the boundaries of a security professional's so-called "authority." I intentionally did not act because I wanted them to understand my limits on the job. My security uniform did not mean that I could just do whatever I wanted, even if I was wearing a gun.

They also learned that defying authority, like the homeless man tried to do with the bouncer, can get you a butt-whooping. And they learned that there is more than one way to skin a cat. That bouncer did something that I was not allowed to do. He got physical in a situation that was not directly related to self-defense. They also learned that a uniformed professional, no matter what business they are in, represents their company everywhere they go. When you are wearing somebody else's name on your clothing, you need to be careful how you represent them out in public.

At the medical clinic, they learned just because a bench sits near a sidewalk does not make it public property and security will likely tell you to move along. They saw the pathetic condition of someone who has used entirely too much alcohol in his lifetime and learned that the homeless all have a story. This man, his story was of a bad habit that became a vice that ruined his life. He could have lost his life that night, had I not been doing my job. This event, then, taught them the importance of having a set of eyes watching things. Compassion also was shown by the cops, if not the paramedics. When you get all torn up like that, people just won't deal with you. Nobody wants to be around the end result of an alcohol-soaked lifestyle, that's for certain.

They learned about the vice of street drugs from that fellah outside of the convenience market. Drugs rob you of your money, your reason, and your ability to cope. They saw firsthand, the "funny stuff" aside, how big a wreck drugs make of your life. In fact, you have *no* life. No life at all. Whatever time you have on earth, you don't want to squander it away using drugs. You can't see clearly, and obviously you don't act right because you lose your inhibitions. The boys saw witnessed gross and disgusting and how shameless people become when they are all doped up.

The boys saw that in this man's life, all that mattered was how he was going to satisfy his latest urges. Whether it was hunger or thirst or a need to relieve himself, he just did not care how awful and disgusting he appeared to the people around him. He truly had no idea what he was doing. He was just acting out on his immediate, most-bothersome needs with no consideration for the people around or for his personal appearance.

Just these simple lessons alone put my kids far ahead of many people who will have to make these mistakes themselves to learn how bad it can get. If my boys were at all paying attention, then they have quite a head start in what *not* to do in life, which is almost as important as knowing what *to* do in life.

THE TRACTOR

I was working in this one Anytown mall, and I just could not get my feet under me in this place. For whatever reason, I just could not grab hold of the job and run with it. I was great as a security officer, but I got promoted too fast into a position that I was not actually prepared to do. They made me a lieutenant, another one of those arbitrary ranks, and I fell for it. I was not prepared to deal with the incompetence of the security team. I was not ready to deal with getting blamed for not being able to do a job I was not trained for. I still needed to learn my way around that business; retail security involving an entire mall and all its clients with their particular whims and wants. I was not ready to lead a team at that mall and I was set up for *failure*...

The guy who promoted me, the director of our security team, had all the faith in the world that I was capable of doing the job. He believed I had the personality and the leadership qualities, so I took the promotion. I tried, I really tried, to get the job done; but at that time I had my associate's degree only, and I did not have the necessary background in leadership to handle what was coming, and what came was a terrible wave of doo-doo that got stuck all over me. And once you get the doo-doo on you, you might as well leave the post because they will never let you live it down. Your subordinates will do all they can to bury you while your supervisory peers will distance themselves from you so that they don't get any stink on them. That is just the way it is, and I hope the reader learns this valuable lesson from my hard experience.

One of the first and biggest mess-ups ever was represented by a picture posted in our office as a reminder. I was reminded about that farce every day I walked by it. And it hammered at me. I suppose I should have exercised stronger will and put it behind me, but

I just could not. This was a *huge* embarrassment and a completely ridiculous situation, which just did not have to happen. That stain remained with me in the mind of the mall manager for rest of my tenure at that mall. It was not fair for that manager to see me that way, but that was how he rolled, and nobody could talk him out of it.

You see, I was put in charge of the day shift. Fine. But there was a trick to being in charge. I had to enter what I called "forced marches" in the computer system. The team I worked for carried these little boxes around, and the security officers had to scan bar codes to prove they were here or there. I was okay with that to a point, but the security manager really went off the deep end. There were two settings on the machine. One setting allowed you to just hit any point at any time, and you were good. As long as you hit all the points within the assigned patrol hour, it was considered "done." That was fine by me. I could work with that.

It was the other setting that was my Achilles' heel. The other setting was a completely predestined route. The box said that you had to be at this point by this time, or you were considered deficient in your patrol. If you did not hit that certain point within a five-minute window, you would not be able to have a complete route and that was almost certainly going to be a disciplinary action on your employee record. It was a ridiculous way to do things. The reason the security director did it this way was because he did not have control of his staff. He did have a background in social work, and he thought that he could help everyone become something they did not want to become. He thought that he could discipline them into having character. But he could not, and I ended paying the price for this social experiment.

To sum up, I was tasked with supervising a bunch of unwilling, not-so-competent people who basically did not want to work. And every one of them thought that they should be the one running things. They had *so* much more experience at the place than I did. They had *so* much more of an idea of how things should be than I did. And yes, there was some validity to that argument. There really was. But they did not have the smarts to understand the picture beyond what they wanted for themselves. I did have the smarts. But

I did not have the know-how to realize my vision. Had I been on the mall team for another six months or so, I would have been ready for that supervisor position. I needed to be trained and groomed more than I was if I were to succeed.

Part of the supervisor's job I was promoted into was to set up these predestined routes. And they had to be set up in this not-user-friendly software, which I could barely operate. It was very time-consuming because I was not adept at it. On top of it all, I had security officers in the mall who were so very experienced, much more than I, so I trusted them to do the right thing. THAT WAS A MISTAKE! I did not read the situation for what it was; I had people there who wanted to see me fail. Dealing with their stupid ways was one thing, but having them secretly rejoice at my being held fully responsible for their incompetence was another. I could successfully manage one or the other. I could handle stupid ways, or I could handle people not caring for me to be their leader. But I did not know how to handle *both* at the same time. It was like trying to catch a greased pig while roller-skating through a stampeding buffalo herd on a field of ball bearings!

One fine morning, I came into the mall to do my job. I was monitoring the radio traffic while setting up the routes. And these routes, to the discerning eye, could be predicted if one watched the activities of the security for long enough. That is why I don't like using routes that demand you be at this place at this time. Bad guys don't take long to figure out that security has a routine, and when they are over here, they are not over there. They simply go and do their bad things where security is *not*. So while dealing with my professional differences and trying to set up routes that would maybe make sense, and trying to generally fight with the software, I let the team do their job unsupervised. I trusted them like a naive schoolboy would trust his peers who were actually out to take his lunch money.

One fine morning, just as the mall was getting really to open, and I was just about ready to make the magic happen with the routes, I get this call from the mall manager over the radio to meet him at the center court. Okay...so I finished off the routes, all set and ready to go, and I walked down to meet the mall manager. From a long way off, I saw him, and I froze. There he was, his facial expressions never changing, but readable at the same time. I was caught with my pants down, and I knew it! Here was the mall manager, understandably upset, but never showing emotion, no matter what, and he was standing in front of this giant cherry picker. The machine was very large and very obvious. It was used to put Christmas (yes... I said the C-word) decorations along the mall, suspended from the ceiling. That is how tall this machine was. And the manager found it.

Normally, this would not be a big deal. Because *normally*, with a team including a man who boasted thirty-plus years as a mall cop at this very same mall, someone would have found the tractor and called it in. Then they would have either by their own initiative or under supervisor's instructions, left an officer there to keep an eye on the machine. The rest of the team would have then retrieved the velveteen barriers from the basement and had the whole thing ornately cordoned off. They would have posted, "DANGER: DO NOT CROSS," or other such signs all over the barriers.

I told the manager that I was busy setting up routes, and I had three patrols out here, and none of them reported anything to me about a machine in the middle of the mall. Well, that was just fine and dandy, but I was still responsible, and he held me responsible for that until the day I left that poorly run team. The mall manager would bring it up from time to time, even months later, and it made me sick every time I heard about it or saw that *full-color posting of the giant machine that patrolmen never reported!*

Even that man with thirty-something-years on-the-job experience did not get the fact that when something is that *glaringly unusual, you report it, even if you* THINK *that there is nothing wrong!* The biggest problem with all this was that the mall was about to open its doors to the public for the day. Moms, dads, and kids were going to be in the place soon and we had this big, yellow, shiny tractor there with no warning signs or safety cones or anything around it! Anyone worth their salt, to any degree, would have at least called it in. But the excuse, the prevailing attitude was that this tractor was engineering's problem. After all, they had it brought into the mall, and why would security deal with it?

Well, security had to deal with it because it was now a safety issue. And I should have never had to remind my people to do their job to that level. That was just inexcusable, what they did. In that mall manager's eyes, I was solely responsible. Can I argue that? No. I cannot. I was responsible, even if I was truly not "at fault." Fault does not actually matter when it comes to accountability. Responsibility trumps fault every time. My issue with that mall manager was his inability to, with some degree of understanding, realize that bygones were bygones, and he needed to drop the matter. He chose not to, and I had that albatross around my neck until I left that job for some greener pastures. In the new job, I completed two college degrees and was promoted into upper-level management.

SILVER PANTS, HAIRY BUTTOCKS, AND THE UNACCEPTABLE PUBLIC DISPLAY

These are actually three separate events that are related by the same topic, not by them being in the same case. These are cases of apparently deviant people who were spotted in public doing off-the-mark things and being called on it. These cases are from different Anytowns in different Anystates. These situations were reported for their singularity, and because these people disturbed the public with their behavior, they were either arrested or asked to immediately leave the property where they were caught hanging out.

One person, he would have been left alone if he was just moving around, shopping like everyone else. We would have never approached him, but a call came into dispatch in a form of a suspicious person that was hanging out in the store. Loss prevention was calling for a uniformed presence to an anchor retail store to help with an odd-looking person. This man was reportedly wearing "Elton John-style sunglasses," a "colorful top," and "silver spaceman pants." That was worth going to see, even if just for the entertainment value.

I reported to the anchor store, and the suspect may have heard the call go out because by the time I got to the retailer's toy department, there was no one there. We got a second call of the same description a few minutes later. I arrived in time to see that our people were already talking to this guy. I did not get in on the conversation because it was not necessary. The security personnel present were sufficient to handle the matter. One more would have been too many and could have provoked a reaction. So in this case, I just sort of held back and watched.

The store manager was talking to the oddly dressed man and eventually told him that he had to leave. Again, it was not that the man appeared to be a threat. A person can dress as strangely as they like. The problem was that this man was not actually shopping, but loitering. And the fact that he was loitering in the toy section made it a bit more concerning. He left when he heard that security was coming, but then came back again. And he was just standing there, looking odd.

He was not buying anything, he was just standing there, in the toy section. And that was what had people worried. It was his behavior more than his appearance, but his appearance just enhanced the worry. *No* fully grown man in his right mind is going to continually hang about in the toy section of a major retailer, unless he is actually there to buy toys. No man, or woman, for that matter, should just stand in a toy section, for extended periods at a time, for no apparent reason. That is equally bad for male and female, and it will get a person ejected, as it should in this day and age.

This shows the public perceptions of adults where they relate to children. The media is full of stories about people seen hanging around, and then suddenly, someone's child disappears while waiting for an ice cream truck or on their way to school. The point here is that if you are an adult and seen lingering for no particular reason in a place where children are going to congregate, you can expect the other adults to question it. This is a very important principle of good security. Seek out and question the unusual. If something does not "seem right," it is worth at least asking questions about it.

This next tale of odd appearance is of a man in an anchor retail store who was shopping, but his attire was unacceptable. A man wearing women's attire is not a crime, not in our day. It was reportedly one of the crimes for which Butch Cassidy was wanted. How times have changed.

But this modern-day guy, in a dress, wig, and all the accessories, had a short skirt on and his hairy rear end was sticking out. His buttocks were exposed, and it was offending shoppers. They reported, rightfully, and the man had to leave the mall. This was a case of just simply being gross. No one was mocking him or giving him a hard time. There was not a scuffle because someone tried to point him out the door. And I can honestly say that if a woman came in dressed that way with the same type of exposure, she would have also been asked to leave. This was enforcement of a public decency policy, and it was rightfully enforced. This is just one of the many things that security officers will see and deal with.

This next incident is a bit graphic, but I will attempt to handle it tastefully. This was not a situation where security actually responded. This started out as a completely innocent and random camera check and became a courtesy call to the Anytown PD.

Let me explain.

We had just gotten on the post a brand-new camera system. It was not the standard black-and-white screens either. This was full-color, and we had PTZ, or "pan the zone," features on more cameras than we ever had before. This post had always boasted the top of the line in its camera features, and now they had surpassed themselves.

Since this was a new system, the console operator decided to put it through the paces and test the capabilities. After all, what's the point of having new toys if you don't *play* with them? The console operator started working with the zoom feature. He was very happy to see that we had greater distance than ever before. In fact, he believed that he could zoom in on objects and people from far across the campus. He confirmed it. And with such detail! Well, since we can go all the way across the campus, can we go *off* campus? Like to the park across the street? Why *sure* we can! Why not?

The more the console operator fiddled with the controls, the more he could see. And the more he could see, the more he wanted to push the capabilities. Pretty soon, he was looking all the way across the street and deep into the park. He zoomed in on birds, trees, playground toys, and so forth. And oh…there's a nice lady in a black dress, just enjoying the park. Could he see the color of her eyes like the satellites in space spying on earth? Well, let's check. And…oh, well, that lady has brown eyes and *way* too much make up. Is that a wig? Yep. Oh, heck no! Hairy legs? That's a *guy!*!

Again, that is just something you see in public. No law against it. This guy, cross-dressed in fine women's attire, was just minding his own business. He was not bothering anyone. He was not hanging out with kids. He was not soliciting for money or doing anyth—oh no. Is he…? Is he reaching up inside his skirt? *Oh no…he is!* And is his hand gyrating? Ohhh…it is. Yep. Pretty obvious what's going on there…in a public park. Gotta call that in before some kids see what is going on.

So the console operator called this in as a courtesy to the Anytown PD. They were anxious to make this man's acquaintance. The console operator still did his job on the post, but he kept one camera trained on the guy. The police never did call us back, because the console operator was able to pinpoint the place in the park well enough for the cops to know exactly where to pick the dude up. And they did.

RABID, OBNOXIOUS LOSS PREVENTION

When you are setting up a uniformed security team to stand a post, it is important to have people in uniform who can hold their tempers. They need to be diplomatic and be able to do their job without taking it personally. This is a given. The same principle applies to loss prevention (LP) teams. And it can be even more important because LP team members often carry handcuffs and must be very familiar with the rules and laws of arresting somebody. It is vital to learn how to handle different types of people in different situations. Adults are handled differently than kids. Tough, aggressive types are handled differently than calm and compliant people. This is just how it is. I am not suggesting that some people are "better" than others, but let's face it; a repeat-offender of violent felonies is not going to be handled the same way as a ten-year-old committing his first misdemeanor. This is what makes loss prevention a different type of security work.

That being said, on one of my first security jobs, I was a mall cop at Anytown mall. We had this particular anchor store with a loss prevention team that was completely berserk. I am not exaggerating either. These guys were nasty, aggressive, and literally screamed in the faces of their suspected shoplifters. They were not there very long, thanks for that, but while they were there, it was certainly colorful.

They had this one agent that was a very big guy. Obviously working out all the time and probably on steroids, from his aggressive demeanor. He had long, well-kept hair, a moustache and did that `80s thing where guys let their facial whiskers grow out only so long and kept them there, in a constant state of four-day's growth. I mean the guy did take care of his appearance, but he was always yelling at the top of his voice.

One day, while on patrol, I just happened to be in the right place at the right time to see this. Some little kid, maybe nine or ten years old saw some shirt and tie combos sitting at the entryway from the anchor retailer in the mall. I saw him select and grab one of the shirts and ties. He started walking for the exit. As soon as he crossed the property line into the mall, this big ape was on top of the kid and yelling at him loudly enough to be heard across the mall. There is a command voice you can use to get control of somebody, but then there is just yelling and screaming for its own sake. This guy was yelling and screaming for its own sake.

To make this arrest, which, yes, was necessary in this case, all the LP guy had to do was quietly slip up on the kid and say, "I'm Agent Doe from Anystore Loss Preventions. Please come with me, we need to talk to you about some items we believe are in your possession," or whatever it is they say when they are taking someone off the floor to have them charged.

Instead, the big ape came roaring out of the store, yelling, "Hey you, Kid! You stop right there!" Understandably, when the boy saw this guy thundering up behind him, not even knowing who he was, he bolted. Heck, I would have run too. That muscle-bound dude was scary-looking, and he never identified himself.

The kid tried to run off, and the ape chased him around the pillars of the mall, inside the mall itself. He should have never done that either. The moment a private officer of any kind crosses the boundary line of their own property, they lose all their "authority" to do anything. It is like being in one's own yard, and then chasing some trespasser off the property and pursuing him down the street. That property owner has no more rights to apprehend the trespasser after he leaves his yard. It becomes a police matter after the property line is crossed. In this shoplift case, their loss prevention should have asked mall security for help, as we have seen in other examples here.

That whole scene was just pretty ugly. This massive, loud, obnoxious, screaming idiot chasing some little, terrified kid through the mall. After he caught the kid, he was huffing and puffing way too loud and yelling at the boy about how he "was going to jail." It was ridiculous of him to treat the boy that way. Not only was the loss prevention guy being abusive, but he had no business threatening the boy with jail. Yes, the kid did something wrong, but to repeatedly abuse him was just pointless.

We once had some people who were suspected of shoplifting, and they got outside when they knew LP was onto them. They made it to a car that had California tags on it. I called out the plate as they pulled away, but it did not help. They got away...except for one. He was left behind, but he had no evidence on him. As mall security just arriving on the scene, we had nothing to hold him for. But the LP guy from the same store where Big Ape worked came unglued. This skinny little blond guy from their department came running out the door, screaming at the top of his lungs.

I could not believe what I was seeing. They also had nothing on this guy. All we could do was to let him go. Now I agree that he was probably up to his eyeballs in the mess. I am pretty certain that the group found out they were caught and bolted for the rear doors of the mall. They all got away except for this lone man, and he knew we had no evidence for which to arrest him. All he had to do was to keep his wits about him, and he would be left alone. That was exactly what he did.

We could not arrest him, but we thought that we might need to arrest the LP guy who came outside with us. The guy that the LP personnel started going after was the subject of interest, a man not quite a suspect but more interesting to us than the average shopper. And this one LP guy in particular came completely unglued, yelling and screaming. The person of interest gently touched him on the shoulder and said, "I respect what you all are trying to do." Now, understand that the casual observer, or even the witnesses who were on the scene watching intently, as our security officers were, did not or should not have seen any true threat. Granted, the man should not have touched the LP guy, but his response, "You don't be touching me, Man! You don't be touching me because I'll deck you! I will knock you out right here in front of all these people!" was not very appropriate.

In fact, my partner on the scene said, "No...you won't." And yeah, both me and my partner were ready to jump on the LP guy and stop him if we had to. That would have been some irony, wouldn't it? Two security officers pulling a loss prevention agent off of a suspected shoplifter! Imagine that...this would have been a very crazy situation to explain to the police, but they have seen crazy before.

There is an appropriate way to perform security, loss prevention, and private officer duties, and that is not the way. Yelling like that is not acceptable. Especially when you go all red in the face and make vicious threats. I am happy to report that this guy and his buddy, Big Ape, were not around for a whole lot longer. They were likely dismissed by their own people. I am sure that the mall had a thing or two to say about the way they mishandled things and were yelling and making a whole bunch of noise outside of their own stores. The shopping malls don't like public scenes of the loud variety.

DRESS CODE VIOLATIONS

In some Anytowns, it becomes necessary to have dress codes for the shopping malls. These codes are usually put into place to discourage violent behavior. The behavior can be triggered by certain colors being worn in certain parts of town. The news is full of gang crimes, and it is well-known that the gangs all have their ways of dressing. When I was in the business, the Crips were dressing in blue and the Bloods were dressing in red. We had other gangs who dressed in different types of clothing, some of it sports related. There was a gang from Pittsburgh, Pennsylvania, who dressed in Pirates baseball gear, for example. We had to be kept up on all the latest, and we had to know whom we were dealing with.

Some of these confrontations could get dangerous. Some of them were humorous, particularly with some of our local "wannabes." Now, don't get me wrong, the wannabes can be more dangerous than some of the OG (original gangsters) or leaders, because they think they have something to prove and they don't have orders from above to sanction or prevent their actions. But normally, in the particular Anytown of which I am speaking, the local wannabes were pretty funny. Particularly to me, because I lived for a number of years in an Anytown where the "real" gangs had a pretty strong hold on the town. So I knew the real thing from the wannabe.

In this one case, I risked my safety to approach a Blood. I had spoken to him twice earlier that week. I think that he may have been sent out on a scouting mission of some kind because he kept hanging out in the part of the mall where I was posted and he knew that I would approach him. Twice in two meetings I approached this well-built, apparently well-conditioned and trained Blood. He had some muscles, and he was real.

I was taught by police officers that these gangs will send out scouts to get a feel for the town; to figure out weaknesses and strengths. They would just send them out and have them check around for potential markets for drugs and/or crime. These guys would stay at their own safe houses or with people friendly to their cause. They would then move about town and visit different neighborhoods and landmarks, such as shopping malls to see what places had loose policies or poor enforcement of existing policies. I think the Blood was testing me to see what "Paul Blart" would or would not do.

This Blood would dress in normal young man's clothes such as jeans, shirt, and ball cap without "representing" the Bloods, but would fly his "flag." His flag was a red bandanna that he would hang out of his back pocket. His general demeanor. gave him away and that flag was the clincher. I knew he was a Blood, and I knew that I could not give him an inch if I was to have his respect. In this case, I had to make a difficult choice.

The choice was difficult because I understood that if the young man was of the mind, he could probably whip me pretty good or even kill me so approaching him had its risks. But I also understood that I was hired to do a job. If the job was beyond my personal risk tolerance, then it was time to move on and take up a safer profession or a safer post. I also fully realized that if I let this guy get the upper hand, he would put the word out and the place would be crawling with Bloods in a very short time. I knew the neighborhood was rough enough without encouraging the "real" gangsters to start.

Every time I saw him with his flag hanging out, I warned him per our policy to put it away. We also had a "three strikes" thing in place. If I caught him three times, I could bar him from the mall. The first warning came and went. No problem. The second warning, a couple of days later, came and went. But the third approach, now that got interesting. It was interesting because of a few aggravating factors that were present, not the least of which being I had to throw him out.

It was an early Sunday morning when I presented him with his third violation of the dress code policy and ejection from the mall. We were just starting to open for the day. He came walking in with his red bandanna clearly hanging out of his back pocket. He stopped in the food court at the gold exchange booth they had set up there. He had a couple of screwdrivers and some other tool in his other back pocket. These were clearly the type of tools that one could potentially use in a burglary.

He walked up to the gold booth and I held back and watched, not wishing to cause any problems for the merchant. No point in making a fuss; I just let the transaction happen because I understood that I could endanger the merchant if the Blood decided to get a little crazy. He got the money and put it in his sock. Then he tried to walk into the mall. I sized the situation up: I had one other guy with me, and he was out on mobile patrol. I had no police. I had no other security officers, short of the dispatcher who was clear down in the control center. So on this approach, I was on my own. Already having a sort of loose rapport with this guy might give me an edge, if I was bold and respectful enough at the same time.

Displaying a lot more courage than I actually felt, but turning the fear into strength…which is perhaps what courage is… I approached my li'l buddy, who towered over me by a couple of inches. He was lean and athletic. I was broad at the shoulders, rounder at the middle than I should have been, but bold.

"Hey, what's up?"

"Nuthin'. What up wit' you?"

"I thought I told you about that flag you been flyin' in the mall"

"Yeah. You did."

"I told you that you would need to leave if you showed it again. That's the third time."

"Uh…it's put away."

"If it was put away, how'd I know you have it?"

Silence.

"You need to go, now."

"Well, I'm gonna buy a shirt…then I'll leave."

"No…no shirt today, man. Look, I saw you turn in that gold. I saw the money in your sock. I saw your people out in that car. You did your business, and now you gotta go."

Silence, but some wide eyes.

"Now," I said gently, "you need to go out to that car where your guys are. You get in that car. You drive off the property. I will have a car out there too, with a yellow light on it. You don't worry about him. He won't approach you. He's only there to make sure you leave safely. Okay?"

"Okay, we're outta here."

"Have a good day."

He walked away, and I gave my mobile patrol precise instructions on what to do. "Give these guys plenty of room; don't wave, don't nod. *Do not approach them or make them feel shadowed.* Hang back, and let them leave. If they stop or turn back toward you, immediately retreat, and I will call the police. Stay *out of harm' way!*"

With that instruction, I watched my mobile patrol do exactly as I said, and they left the mall. I did not see that guy again for the rest of my tenure at that mall.

I found out later that he likely did not shoot or stab me because he did not have authorization to bring down that kind of heat. The Bloods were not ready to fight the cops. I think he did not want trouble with me because if I was watching him closely enough to know his routine that day and where his boys were, then I likely saw the burglary tools. And he could not afford to get caught with them. So not being able to kill me, and not wanting me to call the cops on him, he just left, and I am sure he reported on this old, fat man that was not stupid and showed some guts. Not the kind of security that they wanted to deal with in the Anytown mall. I cannot vouch for what may have happened recently, but in the time that I was there, the Bloods never came back, at least not that we knew of.

GETTING IN TROUBLE FOR DOING YOUR JOB

There once was this Anytown mall, which tried its hardest to keep their image as a safe, clean, and family-oriented shopping mall. There was the trend of gang members who would show their gang colors by "sagging" their pants. When the pants are sagged, or when they are partially down, but somehow cinched up so they don't fall completely down, the boxers or the gym shorts or whatever they happen to be wearing underneath stick out. The color of the underlying garment becomes their identifier.

I don't know how many young men know this, but the whole sagging tradition started in prison. In prison, they let their underwear hang out as a signal to other inmates. That signal alerted those so inclined that the "sagging" inmate was willing to have sexual relations with other inmates. That, in effect, was a clarion call for homosexual relations. And here we had kids thinking that it looked "cool."

The bottom line of all this is that the mall I was working in had a "no-sag" policy because they were a family mall. At least, they wanted to appear to be a family mall, despite someone having been killed there not long ago during a gang-related gunfight. This policy was all part of a new image they were trying to create. They saw it as cleaning up the mall. I saw it as an opportunity for people to heap more abuse on the security team. Guess who was right? We both were, actually.

The "no sag" policy, put in writing, and conspicuously posted was appreciated by some elements of the community. But it was not appreciated by other elements of the community. And if I am not mistaken that mall got rid of that policy for "cultural" reasons. I never bothered to check into it; it just does not matter to me because I do not shop there. I believe it to be fairly safe; I just don't make it to that part of Anytown very often.

At the time I was working there as a security officer, the ban was in place, and security was to enforce that policy. We were to approach the young men sagging their pants, and ask them to pull their pants up. We were specific, telling them over the hips, because they would ask, "Well, what do you consider to be not sagged pants?" As if their mothers never told them to not let their undies hang out over their waistband. They knew what we meant; they very well knew. They just wanted to argue the point.

Well, when you are attempting to write such policies, enforcement needs to know—whether they are cops or security—how they are to go about enforcing the new rules. This one was going to be a tough one due to the nature of the clientele. This mall was putting forth a rule that was blatantly anti-gang, and they were catering to the kinds of stores which stocked the kinds of clothing and accessories which gang members and even prostitutes would want to buy. We were told to restrict the activities of gang-type people and other lawbreakers. I guess they did not think of the repercussions of this kind of policy enforcement. There was bound to be blowback. We were bound to have problems.

One day, there was this particularly obnoxious young man with "MOB" tattooed on his shoulder. One interpretation is profane, the other is "Member of Bloods." Well, that tattoo coupled with these two guys who did not want to pull their pants up led to their ejection from the mall. I was the lucky boy who found the men sagging their pants. That made me the one in charge of the scene. It was time for me to get them to leave the mall. We put them out and had the police nearby. One of the PD from the Anytown police substation at this mall was a SWAT officer.

These kids were giving us a really tough time. They were leaving the site and cussing all about the mall, yelling and calling us names, calling the mall names…it was just crazy. Then they stopped moving off the property, and that was when then cops decided enough was enough, they were trespassing. One was probably a Blood; the other guy was acting like he might have a gun under his shirt by using some street/gang sign indicating he was armed. In concert with police efforts, per our policies, we assisted the PD in putting them on the ground. They were then handcuffed for safety purposes, but they did not end up in jail. The cop questioned the kid with the tattoo, and he gave the police an alibi as to what MOB means, which was not a direct admission to being Bloods affiliated. Nothing came back during the ID check the police dispatcher ran on the boys.

So they were cited for trespassing and released. The cop could have given them disorderly conduct too but decided to go easy after everyone calmed down. The kid with the MOB started looking a little sad and my boss softly asked if he really wanted to fight us. The young man just looked up at him with apparent regrets and just said, "No." One of the police got a little chatty while we waited for the ID check and asked the kids if they had any hobbies besides making problems at the mall. The MOB said that he was a martial artist from Anytown Aikido Academy. The cop said that he found that hard to believe because he knew the *sensei* of that school personally. And he knew that school to be very disciplined and no-nonsense. The cop could not believe that one of the students of that academy would even act this way. MOB just sort of hung his head and got really quiet. I hope that he actually learned something that day. I know I did.

You see, something about this action just set these guys off. Boy, were they mad. I guess they maybe just fed off each other, almost like a hysteria of some kind. One said one thing which gave an idea to the other, these inspirations just ping-ponging off each other like a brain storming session with only two guys involved. The longer it went, the bolder they became, and the anger fed off the boldness. But that is not the lesson I learned. No, the lesson I referred to came from the mall management team. We got in trouble that day for doing our job the way we were told by the management team to do it. They told us *zero tolerance* for sagging the pants. Anyone caught sagging their pants was to be ejected from the mall, and if they refused, they were to be criminally charged with trespassing. *No exceptions.*

On Monday morning, the security director was called into the mall management office for the morning briefing. This time though, they had the item to bring up. Normally security would basically run the meeting and give the mall managers a rundown of the weekend activity. But this time, the managers ran down security because of the activities of the weekend. Apparently, word got back to the management team that there was a couple of young men on the ground kicking and screaming and making a really loud fuss, cussing out the mall and everyone within earshot. This customer who complained said that this was not a very good image for our community.

So…mall management became concerned. And they asked about the event. The director described the whole scenario to them, and they confirmed it was also what they had heard.

Then they asked, "So what did these guys do?"

The security director said that they were sagging their pants. The general manager at this point came sort of unglued. He told the director of security that this scene was unacceptable and that he could not believe this was all over a sagging issue. What he did not know was that we had probably two or three of scenarios a week; it just happened to be that someone complained this time. So the managers still wanted the zero tolerance, but without the "dramatic scene."

When one considers what the GM was asking, it was completely unreasonable. When you are dealing with kids so tough and rebellious that they don't fear the police and even signal that they may have a gun on them right in front of a police officer, you are going to get a "scene" if you tell them anything at all that they don't want to hear. It is just the nature of the beast. We have here a shopping mall that wants to have zero tolerance of an unpopular policy enforced on wannabe gang members (and OG alike), but they want nothing to get *loud?* It is not going to happen, because these rebellious types love making a fuss. And they love making a fuss when they don't get their way.

I believe that such people do this because they know that if someone complains, then a place like a shopping mall, which wants good relations with the community, will start to change things so that the rebels and wannabe gangsters start to get their way. I think that this behavior is intentional because they know that somebody, somewhere is going to get security to back off and let them do their "own thing." The GM should have realized what the complainant was actually saying. She was telling the mall managers that our guys on the security team were working very well with the Anytown Police Department in stopping potential gang activity in our Anytown mall. *That* is what the GM should have taken away from this, if he had any courage at all. But no, he did not see the whole picture. He did not see that we were doing exactly what we were governed to do by policy. *His* policy. We enforced it the way we were supposed to, we did it by the numbers. Only in this case, instead of being contrite after security and then police showed up, they rebelled and were criminally charged—*precisely* by the book.

I understand what the GM was saying, I really do. I agree that is not desirable to see that kind of behavior in the public eye, but half the clientele in the place were gang affiliates, gang members, OG, and wannabes. The retailers would stock the kind of merchandise that would sell in such an atmosphere. This was just the kind of neighborhood it was. There was no way to have a winning position in such a place because it was a self-perpetuating problem. The customers came from the community and would only buy stuff that appealed to them. Many of the younger set wanted to have that "gangsta" look, and they knew that the Anytown mall would have it, so they went there to buy their clothes and then hang out. It is a hard thing to tell somebody that they cannot wear *in* the mall clothes they bought *at* the mall. You have to try to explain such a goofy rule to people who hate all rules in general. It's a huge challenge, trying to explain to them that retailers have the right to sell whatever they like, but that the mall will not tolerate that merchandise being worn as intended in the halls of the mall itself. The merchants' rights of sale end at that entry to the mall. But people don't understand that. And I understand why that is. The public sees the mall as one entity. They don't understand the rules under which malls operate.

Each different store is allowed to carry different merchandise. For instance, a gift shop may sell T-shirts with profane slogans and nudity on them. The customer can purchase that shirt and parade all around the store where they bought it as much as they like. They can do that because that store is allowed to set the rules, within reason and within the rules of the lease, inside their own store. But when that customer steps across that magic line where the merchant's leased footage ends, the customer is now under the mall rules. And the mall rules will say that the customer cannot wear profanity or nudity on their T-shirt while in the mall. Such policies are necessary to prevent small children or persons offended by such material from seeing it while at the mall so that all people feel welcome in the mall. If people who appreciate such things are so inclined to read or view T-shirts of these types, then they may step into the store and read/view them. People who prefer to avoid such things may do so by staying out of the store that sells them.

If you sit back for a moment and consider it, this is a very reasonable way to run things, and it is no different than rules against public intoxication or consumption of alcohol. It is the same as rules against someone bringing a "dirty magazine" onto the street and showing it to passersby. If you want to see or display certain things, you have a place in which to do it, but you cannot do in the common areas of the mall where such things may cause offense or create a disturbance. As for the law, well, you can have a private place and allow or disallow just about whatever you like, as long as you are compliant with the laws. If a mall has a policy or rule against wearing orange socks for whatever reason, then if you wish to be in the mall, you will have to comply with the "no orange socks" rule. Otherwise, you will have to leave the mall.

This Anytown mall had a rule against gang attire, subject to the mall's discretion and definition of "gang attire." It did not matter if you bought at OG Outlet or Ganstas B Us right there in the mall; you could not wear it in the mall's common areas. It was tough to enforce such rules because the people inclined to break them were not going to like *anyone* approaching them about *anything* that might be contra gang attire or gangster appearance. And they certainly were not going to take the time to listen to a Paul Blart or Barney Fife explain to them why they could not wear it. Such conditions make it nearly impossible for security teams to enforce dress codes or other rules and to do so without somebody yelling, cussing and making a fuss in public that will embarrass the mall.

This is a very common dilemma for security professionals. Often, the security team is under the direction or command of someone who does not understand the role of security, how a security team functions or how the public responds to security officers who are trying to keep order. For a manager in an environment where the security team is in direct contact with the public to be effective, I would highly recommend that they adopt and follow a routine I saw on so-called "reality TV." The premise of this show was that the CEO of a company would go into his own establishment under conditions where the front-line workers would not know who the CEO even is. They would get "hired," become the "new guy" and "train" on the job that were "hired" to do.

That way, the CEO would see just what their employees were putting up with every day. The CEO would know and understand firsthand just how the company policies were affecting the staff at the level where all the work gets done. The upper management of a company that expects people to behave or execute policy in a certain way need to understand how their policies affect the people who work on the security team and how the public perception of the security team is affected by the enforcement of certain policies. I think that after about a month of enforcing the "no sagging" rule with zero tolerance

GEORGE E. KELLOGG, MSSM

and dealing with the problems that rule was causing, they would think of something different.

The problem with security people is that the good ones are a special breed who have compassion for people, a desire to perform a service and to protect the property of their client as well as the population occupying or using that property. The good security people actually develop a "feel" for what will work and what will not. This was a case of what was not working. I am not complaining here about the policy. I am complaining about the management who wanted perfection in two different arenas. The manager wanted to have perfect enforcement of his no sagging policy, and he wanted perfect public response to it, and if they did not get said response, security was being held responsible. It was a no-win situation as it often is for security officers. Either security would get in trouble for not enforcing the rule or they would get in trouble and take the blame for people becoming upset about the rule being enforced. This is a case of actually getting into trouble for doing your job. And nobody ever wants to be in that position. That's all I have to say about that.

PEOPLE GETTING BUSTED FOR DRUG ABUSE

I was once in a medical setting as a security officer. This particular facility, call it "Anytown Clinic," had a lot of homeless clients wandering in. Part of the job of the security team was to clear the backpacks of all patients who came into the facility. We would turn all of the paraphernalia items over to the police officer stationed there. The police officer would take the items and our report on how the items were confiscated. The handwritten report would never contain any name or room number by which the police could trace the owner of the stuff. Basically, the clinic did not feel like they were in the business to "bust" people for drugs. If word got out that the clinic had become a "narc," many people would remain sick rather than seek treatment, and that can cause some serious problems among the vulnerable populations, particularly with wound infections and contagious diseases.

114

We found some of the most ingenious appliances for smoking various substances:

A plastic ink pen heated and bent into a crooked shape with a "bowl" made by flaring out the pen barrel was one of the items. I once saw some pot in a baggie with the barrel of a thick magic marker the owner cut and fashioned in a clever way. The tip of the marker where the nib pokes out was cut off, allowing an appropriate-sized piece of the barrel to form a nice pipe bowl. Of course, the felt core was removed and discarded. The hollow barrel had a hole drilled in it. Now the tip of the marker barrel where it tapers down to hold the nib in place was stuck tip first into the hole. The butt end of the marker was also cut off, making a hollow tube through which the smoker took his hit. It was both cheap and clever. It actually looked like a pipe. Naturally, the owner of the pot and pipe claimed it wasn't his. It was confiscated and promptly turned over to the police.

Something very common was for homeless people to keeps pieces of tinfoil in their backpacks. If the foil appeared to be heated or had black stains on it, we would confiscate it for destruction by the police. The heroin user would put the dope on top of the foil and then heat it up, melting it. They would then inhale the vapor of the melting heroin.

One of my more humorous catches occurred as a homeless man was leaving the hospital. When someone is prescribed medication, they are to have the right medicine, have the prescription in their name, have the right amount, it cannot be expired, and it must be taken by the correct route. Well, as this man was checking out to get back out on the mean streets of Anytown once again; he was given his meds to take before he left. I noticed on a camera that he had pulled a silver tray table over to him. He was bent over it and was crushing his medication. I called out the nurse on duty.

"Room XYZ is getting ready to snort his meds!"

The nurse rushed in there with a couple of medics and caught him with a straw, halfway through his first line. He claimed it was the same as taking the pills by mouth. Medical staff begged to differ and made sure he was off the property posthaste.

We found crystal methamphetamine, usually in tiny little Ziplock baggies. Little tiny things. These must have been some kind of portioning tool as well as a container. Nasty, nasty, nasty. We would see so many lives ruined by that stuff, otherwise-decent people who pick it up and cannot put it back down.

A really bad case was a man who came in unconscious. They were establishing an airway and found a piece of aluminum foil. He kept coming around with every dose of Narcan but crashing within moments. They took an image of his stomach and found that he had several foil balls in his belly, most likely full of heroin. The conclusion was the foil was compromised, and the heroin was leaking into his stomach. That is why he kept crashing after medication was administered. I don't know if made it or not, and honestly, after all I have seen in the business and how dope destroys lives and even whole cities, I did not and do not care if he lived. The guy was some dealer's "mule." It was his third time in for the same thing.

COYOTE UGLY LIVE

I was at an apartment complex and working the night shift. I overheard and then confirmed a rumor there was going to be a wild party at one of the apartments. As people came into the party, I heard one of them remark that he was "still paying off fines from the last one of these" he went to. I just shook my head. I guess he did not learn from the first time. So I was around the area and keeping an eye on things. Then he showed up. Oh boy!

Some kid who was two days away from turning eighteen was looking for trouble. He was still a minor and thought that he could just do what wanted while just a child in the court's eyes and not be tried as an adult. He was getting lippy with some of the residents, and he claimed that he lived somewhere in the complex. I was trying to convince him to leave, knowing there was booze running around and people would not be on their best judgment.

Well, the kid started throwing around racial epithets, and that did it for this particular group that was already half drunk. I tried to stop them from approaching the kid, by telling them that cops were going to remove him, but they would not listen. They skirted right around me, and then the fight began. I had never before seen a drunken brawl. It was very strange to watch people who were not even involved in the original argument start fighting with each other, thirty yards away from the scene.

Then I saw the girl, whom I called Coyote Ugly, who was with the seventeen-year-old troublemaker. She was in a verbal tiff with another female. The other female hit her on the head with a beer bottle, breaking the bottle. Wow! I had seen that in dozens of movies and on TV but never knew that could happen in real life. Well, it did. It happened. The bottle broke.

It was chaos; there was no reasoning with people, and I called 911. When people heard that cops were coming, they bolted like scared roaches. I had about five squad cars coming onto the scene with lights and sirens. These people were gone for the most part, and when the cops arrived, they were disappointed.

The police sergeant asked me why I did not just start pepper-spraying people. My reply was that I had to come here to work every night, and I didn't want to have a bad problem with the residents of this complex. I spray them tonight; they come looking for me tomorrow. Besides, no one attacked me, no helpless person was being attacked, and that was what the chemical agent was for. I would have used it in my own defense or that of an innocent, but why risk my safety for a bunch of drunks who were engaging in mutual combat, some of them attacking people they came with and who did not even know what the fight was about.

No one got arrested. The girl with the bottle busted over her head refused hospital transport, and her buddy who started the whole melee got his butt kicked.

Then he had the nerve to blame *me* for his beating. All he had to do was leave the area. All he had to do was be peaceful. Either one of these options would have prevented all this. He chose option D (none of the above) and got his rear end handed to him. Amazing how he started a fight with half a dozen guys and then wanted me to protect him. Not gonna happen. The cops were saying that he was seventeen, yeah, but with only two days before his eighteenth birthday, the judge could make that call that he was to be tried as an adult.

As it turned out, because nobody got arrested, I don't think that the sergeant of the PD believed things were as bad as I said. Well, here is a classic example of how a security professional was a "true first responder." I took the initiative and instead of getting involved in the fight and adding to the insanity, I called the police and told the brawlers that the cops were on the way. That broke up the fight, and by the time the cops arrived with lights and sirens, things were more or less quiet. I did my job. I did it right; I did it well.

Later on, I found out that one of the partiers was going to creep up and punch me in the back of the head. But because I had a good rapport with the fine citizens of the apartment community, they stopped him and said, "Not George. He's doing his job." And I expressed gratitude to the one who stopped that potential assault on my person because that *would* have resulted in somebody getting hurt with my pepper spray and baton, assuming I was conscious enough to finish business. That would have been a mess because at that point, all bets would have been off. No more Mr. Nice Guy, no more rules of restraint.

THE SAMURAI WARRIOR

This experience shows my ability for turning on/turning off my "anger" in a crisis situation. I guess that this shows I am not really angry, but it is more like I am "acting angry." Let me tell the story, and you can arrive at your own conclusion.

I was walking around, minding my own business on patrol—which is really a funny thing to say because while on patrol, you are minding everyone else's business and being nosy. That is what patrol is all about. Security is supposed to be an alert, uniformed, and in my case, armed presence. I did not carry a sidearm for the Anytown Security Company, but they did arm me with pepper spray and a baton. It was a nice, chrome-colored collapsible baton. Compact and easy to draw. I would practice with my baton so I could access it quickly. Laugh if you'd like, but if you are going to carry a weapon of any sort, you need to keep it in the same place on your duty belt and practice deploying it over and over until it becomes second nature.

Over the years, I had practiced with various weapons, including firearms during my security training courses, and knives and swords during martial arts coursework. I took aikido in college under Nagasawa *sensei*. Phil Nagasawa was an employee of the phone company and an aikido practitioner and instructor. He taught philosophy and life skills as well as the martial art. He saw aikido as a sort of religion or at the very least, a life-skill practice, as well as a martial practice. I learned a lot under him, and he was pleased to teach me. His only regret was that he wished I was a younger man because of the potential for injury. The relevance of this bit of personal trivia will become apparent in just a moment.

One night, minding my own business on patrol the same way I always mind my own business, I saw something that looked a little off. In fact, it was a lot off. In fact, it was way off, and someone was in real danger! *Crap!* The scene played before my eyes in this way:

A young woman was just walking down a sidewalk in a parking lot. It was well lit, not sketchy, and everything looked normal until this car started creeping up behind her. I froze, watching carefully, completely focused on that car. The car stopped, and the girl reacted by backing up a little bit, away from the car. She seemed to feel threatened.

The next thing I saw, the driver of the car was talking to the young lady. He stopped and put the car in park. Then he got out; she backed up. But her back was to a garage, and she had nowhere to escape. As soon as he encroached on her and she said, "No," there was a definite sense that she was in danger. This went to from 0 to "OH CRAP!" in about half a second.

I started toward her, and when the passenger got out of the car, I broke into a dead run. The adrenaline was pouring on. I had a daughter about her age, and that inevitable, paternal instinct kicked right in. I had that fight-or-flight thing going now, full bore, and I was fleeing...*toward* the danger.

By the time I got there, both the creepers had their hands on her. That was *not* going to happen. It looked like a rape or forced abduction more than a robbery, because they were both in close proximity to her, and they were not grabbing at a purse, wallet, or for her pockets. They were interested in her person. Whatever it was, she was not going to give it up; she was not going down without a fight. As they struggled, she bought herself a few precious extra seconds for me to arrive. I did not think she even saw me, but she did not have to. DADDY GEORGE (my daughter's pet name for me) TO THE RESCUE!

I was a few feet behind the three of them, and they were struggling, and there was some hollering. They did not see or hear me, so I said, "Guys! Hey, guys!... GUYS! SHE SAID *NO!*"

And knowing that I was now fully engaged and completely committed at this point, for right or wrong, good or evil, life or death, as I yelled "NO", I pulled out my baton without even really having a conscious thought about it. The baton was out, in my hands, *chink*, fully extended and glittering under the streetlights in its full-chrome polished steel glory. I had, again without thinking, assumed the aikido/samurai sword fighting posture.

This proved to me the idea that was presented to me long ago that "under duress you will assume the posture and methods that you use most of the time in that situation." If you drive slow and calm, under stress you will drive slow and calm. If you have trained with your fists, you will resort to your fists. If have trained with a weapon, anything that you get in your heads will be used like that weapon. It was true. Here I was with a collapsible baton, brandishing it like my *katana*.

When the men saw me, their eyes got big, and I went on the offensive before they got over their surprise. "Back! Back! Get BACK!" I yelled as I advanced on them, stepping forward with my front foot and bringing the rear up behind it. This way, I could stay balanced and not stumble. Plus, moving in and pushing forward like that, one could tell I had some training. My baton was now in my left hand, out of their reach, and over my head, ready to strike at any second. I was watching their hands and yelling at them to keep those hands where I could see them. They did. And they backed up to the wall, now afraid, as they should have been. I meant every inch of what I said, and I would have beaten both of them half silly if one of them even flinched.

With their hands up, they were now against the wall. The girl was loose of their grip and out of their reach. I looked back to see if anyone was coming from behind me, and I saw that the girl was starting to almost wander off, carelessly, like none of this mattered. I saw what she was doing, and I thought she was in traumatic shock. One of the guys made a remark about her being his girlfriend, and I told him, "SHUT UP! I DON'T CARE WHO SHE IS!" Then I moved to her and warning them to keep their hands up and not to move, I asked her if she knew these guys.

"Uh-huh," she mumbled. I asked her if she was in any danger, and she said, "Uh-uh, no," as she continued to just wander slowly.

Now, sensing that there was no immediate danger to her or to me, I lowered my baton to a less aggressive position and asked, "Then just what is going on here?"

One of the men sort of raised his hand, and I gave him a nod to please talk. "Um, she's my girlfriend, she's drunk, and we're trying to take her car keys away."

Oh jeez! Really?

"You! Stop!" I said as I stepped in front of her. "Give them your car keys right now, or I will call the cops on you and have you arrested for DUI!"

She stopped, scoffed and fretted a bit, pulled out her car keys, gave them to her boyfriend, and then we three just let her walk off.

I looked at the terrified pair and thought, "Oh man. What am I going to do now?"

To appear less imposing, I tapped my baton on the sidewalk to collapse it, and then I started to softly chuckle as I put it away. Suddenly, I was *so calm*. I was no longer a raving madman. My heart was beating at a nice pace but was already slowing down; my breathing was normal; the urge to fight or flee was fading rapidly and nearly gone as quickly as it appeared. I looked up at the guys after my baton was put away, I was still hunched over.

"Guys…," I said calmly and slowly, "I am so very sorry." I was shaking my head at my own reaction. "But you have to understand how that looked to me. I see a young lady minding her own business, a car pulls up slow, some dude jumps out, she resists, the car parks, and another guy gets out? Man, I thought it was a rape or a kidnapping something… I am so sorry, guys… I just don't know what to say…you were doing the right thing, taking her keys. You may have just saved some lives."

The young men both just sort of looked at each other, realized that they were not about to get the beating of their lives, swallowed hard, and relaxed a little. I stood back up, still nervously chuckling and coming down from the adrenaline.

Then one said, "Aww, no, dude…don't be sorry…that was awesome!"

The other one said, "Aw, yeah man! You were nuts! That was great! You looked like a samurai, man! We knew if we even moved wrong, you meant what you said. Hey, man, you are awesome! We know you're DA MAN! Ain't nobody going to mess around with you here! We are so glad, man, that you are keeping us safe."

"Well, guys, I am glad I came off that way, because yeah, I did mean every word. You were smart, you listened. Sorry to be so rude when you were trying to explain yourselves, but I had to control the scene."

"Hey, no problem, man," they said.

We exchanged first names, shook hands, laughed a little more, chatted a bit, and said good night.

And yes. I meant every threat I was making either verbally or with my body language. When you go into a situation like that, there is no room for weakness. You have to come off like a mad dog killer, because there is only one of you. And you need to convince them that they will get hurt. In this case, those boys would have gotten hurt. I would not have hit them on the head like most people think of when they see a baton. Smack on the head and put their lights out, right? No. No. No. You hit someone with a collapsible baton on the head, and you will fracture or even penetrate their skull with not much effort. Steel is very hard, that baton has some weight to it, and the bar has not much surface area. Combine all these, and you are looking at a penetration surface on the baton, not just a striking surface. Add adrenaline to that, whether from fear, anger, or excitement, and you are likely going to strike someone harder than you intend.

Plus, I have been trained in some swordsmanship. The posture I automatically assumed was aikido, based on the samurai arts. Aikido and other Japanese sword martial techniques were created over many, many years to allow your body, mind, spirit, and the sword to work together with maximum efficiency. Samurai blades have been known to cut people in half, split down the middle. That is *not* legend. Now, while I am not an expert or even a black belt, I do have more skills with edged weapons than the average college kid, and those techniques were about to applied to the baton.

Anyone who has been trained on a collapsible baton knows that it is deadly if applied to the skull. My striking points would been the shoulder joints, collarbones, the trapezius muscles, the back, the chest, the ribs, the elbows, knees, and ankles. Essentially, I would have started on the most dangerous or closest one of the two young men, and then alternated strikes between he and his friend. Each blow, particularly from over my head and coming down onto the target, would have been delivered with the intent to break bones or separate joints. Those boys would have been seriously injured before I was done.

Please understand that when you are outnumbered and without backup, you must go into such a situation with the intent to win. Or just don't go into the situation at all. And yes, for a security professional, that is actually a viable choice. Each security professional needs to know his or her capabilities and capacity for assertive, decisive action. I entered this situation because I was very confident that there were just the two young men and they posed a serious threat to the girl. I had to make a choice, and I did, because that is what my personal system of values demanded.

Remember that security officers do not have the same training, tools, backup, or legal powers that cops have. And security does not have the backing of the legal system to get them through a tough situation. We don't have the same city resources that police have. We don't have immediate, effective legal counsel unless we have arranged for that ourselves. We also need to remember the city has an ulterior motive for protecting their police officers: the city may also be sued for that officer's actions. As private citizens, security officers don't have all the advantages of such legal protections. In fact, the city will likely join the efforts against the security officer because it is their prosecutor who is trying to score another victory in court for political gain. Sad commentary for how our society treats its security officers, true first responders though they be.

This is why when a security professional makes a choice, it is important to understand that any act of violence will always have both professional and even personal consequences. There is the risk you are taking of personal injury. There is the risk of injuring someone. There is even the risk of going to jail if you cannot prove that you were absolutely correct in deploying your weapon. To be absolutely correct, you have to prove beyond reasonable doubt that someone's safety, be it yours, someone else's, or both was in jeopardy. You also have to prove that there was not a reasonable alternative, even if it was walking away, that you could have taken. Even if you convince the police that you were right and you don't get arrested or charged, you still have the civil situation you need to worry about. Even if you were legally correct or found "not guilty," you can still be sued! Sound crazy? Remember the O. J. Simpson trial? He was found "not guilty" by a jury in a court after only twenty minutes of miscarriage of justice—oops—I mean *deliberations*. But then…he was found "responsible" in a civil suit and was *sued!* The bad guys can actually sue for personal injury and may recover monetary damages even though they were behaving criminally.

So…before you become overly inspired by the thought of a heroic act, remember that I walked into the above situation as a matter of personal choice. That choice was backed by years of experience in the security field, martial arts, weapons training, some knowledge of the rules and laws of self-defense. I also had the natural mental conditioning that came from years of being taught "tactical thinking" by one of nation's finest soldiers over the course of a lifetime. I would never advise anyone to just jump into something like this. I did, yes, but I also understood the possible ramifications of what I was doing, and I weighed out carefully what I was about to do on my way to the scene. If you have not been trained and conditioned to do that, then maybe you should not try to be "heroic," if that is the proper term for such actions.

A SALUTE FOR SANTA

This is a very lighthearted moment I am about to share. The retail world is very tough. It is tough because competition is high, shrinkage from theft and shoplifting is always a concern, profit margins, despite what we may think, are not very high and the Christmas shopping season is always a literal nightmare for retailers. To attract shoppers, retailers compete at very high levels. They will "out-offer" their neighboring retailer by having more $5 bicycles and $40 flat-screen TVs than the next guy. They make loss-leader offers to attract more people to their store hoping people will buy more of their fully priced goods. It is a well-proven fact that retailers depend on the Friday after Thanksgiving to put their stores in the "black" for the entire year.

I just want to take a moment to explain where the term *Black Friday* came from, for those who have never found this out. Forgive me if it seems to be a bit elementary. I used to think that *Black Friday* was just a darkly humorous barb at the way people act during this shopping day of all shopping days. And I still think it is. I mean, people have *died* over trying to buy gifts! How insane is that? But no, our behavior on this day has nothing to do with the term *Black Friday*.

Traditionally, accountants have used two colors of ink to signify profits and losses. Losses in red ink and profits or gains are in black ink. The red ink is in place to draw attention to the fact that there is definitely an issue with these numbers, black ink lets us know that all is well. Or if not "well," then there are at least no losses. Gains may be pennies or there may be a break-even of zero gains/zero losses but there no losses in the black ink. And since retailers depend on the Friday after Thanksgiving to put them over the top into profitability, or into the "black ink," that magical, mystical Friday is dubbed *Black Friday.*

I for one try to find the silver lining. We have elevated, crass materialism and selfishness that we guise under the idea of "giving," which is really nothing more than a vain desire to out purchase our neighbor and prove something to ourselves about how "selfless and giving" we are. The fact is that we are very selfish in our giving because we want to give the best of the best and take great satisfaction in getting the "coolest" thing for our family, our friend, our neighbor, etc. It reminds me of the biblical story of the widow's mite. The great community leaders and wealthy citizens were throwing as offerings their bags of money, coins, wealth, whatever they had, into the alms pile to distribute to the poor. They did it to be seen. They wanted praise. They wanted to look good/feel good. And that is what we have done to the "gift" of Christmas.

Because of this desire to be seen or to give the best of whatever for our own gratification, the materialism that is displayed around the Christmas holiday season is just outrageous. If there was a stronger term than "outrageous," I would use it. I have a solid belief in the core spirit of Christmas. I believe that even if you are an atheist that the joy of the Christmas season can do you some good. It is supposed to be a time of giving, but to give gifts of the heart. Sure, the first Christmas story is that the wise men brought the Christ Child gold, frankincense and myrrh. But these men traveled for a very long time, under very harsh conditions to give gifts of their hearts to a child they believed to be born under holy circumstances. These gifts were offered in humility, as a sign of respect, as a token of love. These original gifts were given in such a different spirit than we now shop for gifts that we probably don't realize how far removed we are from the spirit of Christmas.

Enter Santa Claus. Some say that he is a symbol of the ultimate good and joy. Some say that he is just another crass sign of materialism and engenders selfishness. I say that Santa is a very positive character and embodiment of good principles and that the way people use Santa determines what effect the idea of Santa has in our lives. We can either use him to foster selfishness, or we can use the symbol of Santa to inspire good. And face it…it is just a lot of fun to have joyful colors and tales of the jolly fat man to inspire happiness in our children.

In the modern world, with people becoming so preoccupied over material things that they are willing to kill over flat-screen TV's and the latest Nike sports shoe, we need to be reminded of what is decent and good. To me, personally, one of the greatest paintings I ever saw was Santa Claus at the manger, the Christ Child in swaddling, and Old Saint Nick was on a knee, with his red stocking cap in hand, smiling in adoration. So you see, I see our Santa as a type of bridge between the material and the spiritual worlds. Santa brings things, but also reminds us to be good, and I think this is vital. So yes, security professional, there *is* a Santa Claus.

One day Santa came to one of the many Anytown malls I have worked doing security, and this particular mall needed him the most. These poor folks could hardly afford Christmas for the most part, and Santa was a reminder there is a good purpose to Christmas that far outreaches the material stuff we buy. So I was very glad to see Old Saint Nick. And you know what? I even went to "see Santa" that year. It was nice, and I was quite sincere. He appreciated it.

But that being said, I was there on duty the day the Anytown mall's Santa Claus arrived. I just happened to be standing there when he came up the hall with the marketing manager of the mall. When I saw who was coming, I stood back against the hallway wall. I watched as they approached, and at just the right moment, I put eyes front, brought myself to attention, and saluted as Santa passed me. He smiled and thanked me and said, "No, no, please…," but he chuckled as he said it. You could tell the old boy, a naturally bearded Santa, loved it. I could not help but smile and I was so glad to do that for Santa.

Later, I approached the marketing manager and said, "Sorry if I was out of line, but I could not resist."

And the manager said, "Are you kidding? That was great!"

So I did a great thing for Santa Claus. In fact, I personally believe that shopping malls should do a type of ceremony for the day that Santa arrives. I think that a Santa honor guard of uniformed security officers should accompany him to his Santa chair and just kind of make a big deal out of it.

But that's just me. I'm a bit sentimental.

STOLEN FREE CANDY—FIRE HIM!

There was a time that I heard of the termination of a security officer. This officer was a good man, professional in his duties, and he was specially chosen by his security company to be trained for this particular post. The post was a high-rise building, a big one in the downtown district of Anytown. Such posts are considered prestigious by security officers who covet these positions. Often downtown high-rise accounts will include the security team, though contracted, in the company's benefits program as though they were regular full-time employees. Such benefits programs often far outweigh the benefits offered by security teams to their employees. This is becoming more common for reasons to be discussed elsewhere, but not in this book. That being the case, it was a good thing that this fine security professional was offered the position.

The client sometimes will interview the potential security employees; other times they will leave the hiring of security up to the company itself. Both approaches have pros and cons. The bottom line is that the high-rise company and the security company work together as partners and normally share a good relationship. Ultimately though, the client normally has the right to decide who does and does not work on the post. That can create some collisions between the security company and the client.

In this case, the security company brought one of their best people aboard, which the client okayed. They wanted this man to start training, so he did. This particular high-rise had cameras throughout, on every floor. Not every building does, and that depends on the nature of the business, the preferences of the company, the expenses involved, etc. Since there were cameras on the floor, the building manager could review everything that happened in the building each night.

The first night of training came and went. It went very well, as was expected. Everyone was quite happy with the new addition to the team. The trainer in this case noted in his report that the trainee was catching on quickly and everything appeared to be on track. However, the building manager, the one who hired the security company, found a problem. And in her mind this issue was so big, that she demanded the security trainee to be dismissed immediately. He was not to return for the second night of training. People were shocked, and understandably so, none more shocked and aggrieved than the trainee who caught a much-needed break.

Why was the trainee dismissed? He was fired for a cardinal sin that security professionals should never commit. He was fired for the crime of *theft*. Theft! Of all the things that security professionals may do wrong while being trained, theft is among the worst. That is even worse than nodding off on duty. Theft is practically unforgivable. Certainly, I would completely agree with the client that theft is not acceptable, and I would agree with the trainer's termination. That is, I would *normally* agree with the termination.

You see, this situation was not as it appears to be on the surface. It is true that the trainee was accused of, and in the eyes of the manager, did indeed commit theft. But was that really the case? You see, during the course of the training, the trainee took a piece of candy. The candy was in a jar sitting on the desk of an employee. The jar was out right in front of a walkway, just like jars of candy are often found. Complimentary mints, chocolates, hard candies, you name it. It is a very common practice for employees to put such things out on their desks as a free offering to whomever may walk by. The trainee took one of these, and the trainer thought nothing of it. Who would have? I certainly never would have thought that was problem.

In this case though, for whatever reason, the building manager thought that the trainee taking a piece of candy like that was indicative of his being a thief. There are many times I saw things that some of these building managers do. And I could not for the life of me figure them out. There seems to be a sort of, I don't know, superiority they believe they have, I guess. They will do things that just seem over the top and leave the security team to deal with the results of the choice they make. In this case, the security company had to try and find another suitable security professional to fill the slot, start the interview process all over again, and still try to get the job done shorthanded and racking up the overtime.

I don't really understand why people treat security the way that they do. This case is clearly one of those abusive things that was just completely unnecessary. It is not very nice to hire someone and then suddenly fire him for a very poor reason. I wonder if some of these people just have bad days and then won't back off their decision because they don't want to appear weak or indecisive. Or did the manager in this case want to enforce their will just because they could? It is truly difficult to say.

The one thing I will say about this case is that such treatment is more common than most people know. Security officers certainly take a lot of abuse. And it does not really matter if they are doing their job well, or poorly. What matters is whether or not the people like the security professional. When a security pro is well loved, they can do no wrong. When they are not liked so much, they can do nothing right. It is a very odd dynamic. Odd indeed. No matter what the risks the security officer takes, no matter how well they work, no matter who they know or don't know…if someone takes a disliking to them, they are history. It may have something to do with the fact that the security officer is a type of authority figure and people don't like authority, no matter what level they are at in the company hierarchy. Maybe that's it…it's just that simple. It is a power trip.

THEN THE RAGS STOOD UP!

One night I was on a patrol of the building exterior. This would have been in the downtown district of this Anytown. The area was known for its homeless people, and some of them were not particularly nice. There was a big drug problem in Anytown, and many of the homeless were addicted to opiates. Heroin was a big deal in this place, and when a heroin addict is denied his fix or if they are little late getting it, they would become extremely grumpy about it.

These patrols accomplished exactly what they were intended to do. Every forty-five to sixty minutes, and they varied the times to keep the bad guys from predicting a routine, a patrol was done. At least one person with a flashlight would make a complete round of the building exterior. On this night, it was me. I was out taking a look at everything; we needed to check for graffiti, litter, broken windows, human or animal excrement, and people who might be camping on the property.

Camping is a loosely applied term. We are not talking about a situation where a person has tent, mess kit, and sleeping bag. Campers, in this case, are just anyone who is sleeping on the sidewalk, in whatever state they may be in. When you work in a town that is overrun with drugs, you will find that people will sleep wherever they can on whatever they can find. Sometimes, a person will have a tent, but not usually. Sleeping bags are also fairly rare. Mostly, you will find some guy curled up with nothing or what loosely resembles a blanket. Backpacks are common, and the homeless will use them as pillows.

When I came around the corner, I found a man asleep. And he was asleep on a pile of rags. He was right in the alcove of a revolving door. I suppose that provided some scant protection. It kept the wind off a little bit, and he at least knew that no one could come up behind him with that building at his back. It made some sense for him to be there. But he still had to leave. I could never answer the question, "But where do you expect me to go?" with any decent suggestions. All I could do was to run them off the property. I had nothing else for them.

While I realize you can't bleed for them all, I still felt bad about shaking a guy out of a deep slumber. I have never touched a homeless person who was asleep on the street. I might tap them with my flashlight, or use some other means to awaken them, but touching somebody who is asleep is bad mojo. That can get you hurt bad, you can catch some sickness, you can get lice or bedbugs on you...it is just hard to tell. Plus, what if the sleepyhead is particularly jumpy? Unfortunately, we have a lot of war veterans on the street and some of these boys, or girls, as the case may be, are not only jumpy but skilled in hand-to-hand. You touch one of them asleep, particularly during a nightmare, you just might catch a case of DEAD. And dead is very tricky to cure. Especially if you are not found for a while after you get hurt.

Taking all that into consideration, I kept some distance, "three leaps and kick," as I used to like saying. That way, if my boy in the revolving door alcove suddenly jumped up on me, I had a least three long strides before he reached me. That should be plenty of time to react, even if he had a knife. Guns are very rare in the hands of homeless folks because they are usually sold to buy food, booze, drugs, or whatever else. Addicts know no bounds to their depravity, and they will sell whatever they have to get cash.

At my chosen distance, I said, "Hey! Hey! Hey, you...time to get up. I cannot have you sleeping in the doorway like that."

Suddenly the man just *leaped* off the ground. He came up ready to fight, and surprisingly quick at that. He was on his feet surprisingly fast and with him being far enough away to avoid harm, I started to speak. I identified myself to him and told him that he needed to vacate because he was on private property. He sort of just growled at me and started to try to get tough, and I told him to back off and leave or it would get really ugly. He chose to leave.

I expected him to pick up the bundle of rags he was sleeping upon. He looked at the stuff on the ground and just kicked at it and said, "Hey." Well, it was not the first time I saw a homeless person talking to inanimate objects. Then I really got a start when the pile of rags started to stir and then stood up. I was a bit taken back to discover that the pile of rags was this guy's female partner, sister, cousin, friend...whomever. Then the pair left the site as he looked back, glaring at me. I found by experience, in that particular Anytown, it was not a good idea to let the hobos have the last word. They take that as a victory for them and a display of weakness on the part of the security professional. When they start thinking you are weak, it is all the more likely that they are going to return. So a show of strength is needed.

Knowing this, I said, "Glare me at all you like, but just keep moving. And know that I am here all night long." So he kept glaring and walked away with his arm around the bipedal rag pile.

Such scenes are both sad and tragic, but at the same time it is well-known in that Anytown there are sufficient programs to get these people off the street. In fact, at one of the cash donation sites, I saw the services available to the homeless and their cost. If a homeless person takes advantage of all the services, it costs $3,000. That is just for one person, and that includes drug counseling. Now when I see things like that, it is very hard for me to feel sorry for the homeless. With that kind of support available, which at that time was approximately equal to my monthly take home pay, it is hard for me to feel sorry for them. Basically, in that Anytown, if you were homeless, it was very likely your own choice.

CRIMES COMMITTED BY THE HOMELESS

The local police of Anytown once asked our security services client for a favor. Always anxious to foster solid relations with the local PD, which was almost without exception a wonderful idea, they granted the detectives a favor. We allowed the police detectives to set up a sting. They had a small surveillance post inside our building. The building had a very contemporary design, full of glass panes over the entire face of the building, which overlooked a local park. This particular park, about a quarter-acre or so, was a suspected hotbed of drug trading, prostitution, and various other seedy goings-on.

The idea was for plainclothes detectives to keep tight surveillance on the park by using cameras and binoculars. Then after they collected the information they needed over the course of several days, they would start picking people up. The surveillance went on for the prearranged time period. The police did not interfere at all with security's routine, and we made sure our people left them alone. We did not need some "cop wannabe" from our team creating problems or messing things up for the police. Nobody bothered anybody, and everything went smoothly.

At the end of the surveillance period, the cops swooped in all at once, not doing a mass roundup, but instead making surgical busts. They removed specific persons of interest from the park's population. These people had heroin and other drugs for sale. They also found among the homeless, violent and wanted criminals who came in from other Anytowns. These were drifters who would leave when things got too hot, and the cops in their Anytown were onto them. There was also the usual thieving and other illegal activities which occur in these populations.

The one criminal I learned of was a very impressive criminal, good at his business. He was arrested for violent crimes, and when the cops took him, they found thirty-four different sets of identification on his person. This guy was a "trophy hunter." He would take the IDs of his victims, but not to steal their identity. He would take the identities as souvenirs of his crime. He was not just a criminal. He was a hunter, a predator who got a thrill out of keeping the IDs as a reminder of the experience of taking their stuff. I don't know if he had killed anyone or not, but it would not surprise me.

Experiences like this cause people in the know to lose all romantic notions of how the homeless are just victims of life who need our help. The truth is that most of the homeless out there are making victims of us, we who support their lifestyle by giving them money. The more money and help they get, the less inclined the homeless will be to get off the streets. I have met people who used to be homeless, and without exception, they tell us to *never give money to the homeless.* When we give them money, we are just supporting their drug and criminal habits.

NIKE SALES

I once worked as a phone agent for the 1-800-NIKE phone lines. I was in a call center where clients from all over the country could call in for their Nike products. When a "shoe release" was pending, we would have extra phone agents staying on the clock to sell shoes online. Five hundred pairs of the newest Nike Air Whatevers would go flying off the virtual shelves. In twenty minutes or less...all of them gone!

That has nothing to do with security, but I bring it up to give some perspective to the passion people feel for certain brands. In this case, Nike. On the retail circuit, Nike passion causes mayhem and chaos. The whole Black Friday shopping lunacy, that shopper super-madness rooted in greed, is turned loose whenever there is a Nike shoe release. Check out the internet sometime, and you can see images of how people have pushed their way through the pull-down gates the stores use at malls.

So how does that shopper madness affect security? Well, the security team of a mall is responsible for the safety of the mall. When crowds become unruly, they become a security issue. So Anytown mall, where I was working as a security trainer, would allow the shoe stores that sell Nikes to hold a special opening for the shoe releases.

The mall would agree to allow the early morning sales to occur before mall hours but with specific parameters. The people would only be allowed to line up outside certain entrances, and they could not come into the mall until a certain hour. Then the people would have to line up outside the store within the stanchions and velvet ropes we set up. So...how often would it work out correctly? Almost never.

More often than not, environmental services people would come in and out, doing their jobs. People would take advantage of the open doors and come into the mall too early. Then we security personnel would have to round them up and either put them back outside or put them in the lines at the stores. Sometimes they would complain, and we would advise them that just because we are allow-ing them in early for a shoe release, it does not mean they get to go anywhere they please. Why not? Well, because the mall is *closed*.

The tension in the air during these sales was just ridiculous. People were so demanding, so covetous of a pair of sports shoes that they were completely on edge. It was hard to believe, the attitude of these people. One time a guy got his shoes, and somebody said, "Hey, man! Can I just look at them before you go?" He just wanted to sneak a peek. The man with the shoes was very proud to show them off, and I had to hustle him out the door.

Security teams were put on the alert during these sales for potential shoplifts or even riotous behavior. Robberies were a concern too, in certain Anytowns with rougher neighborhoods. Once the people got their shoes, they were to leave immediately. We strongly opposed curbside deals in the parking lot. Cash and shoes exchanging hands was bad news. There was always a robbery potential but doing business out in the open like that practically begged someone to get out a gun to get both money *and* shoes from the customers.

There was one shoe release during which people's behavior was starting to get out of control. Fortunately, the sale was in the afternoon, so we had police officers on the site. As it turned out, we needed their help. The people really started to get out of hand, were starting to get loud and get pushy, and were not following the rules of the sale. They would not listen to the security pros that were assigned to the sale. Most of the time, if this kind of thing started, all the store managers would have to do is to threaten to shut down the sale. In this case though, the people would not even listen to the store managers.

It got to the point where it was loud enough, and people were unruly enough that the police officers on the site called in backup. Then the officers who came in were staging outside. When their presence was not enough to quell the disturbance, they put on their riot gear and started brandishing anti-riot shotguns. They were likely loaded with the nonlethal beanbag rounds they use in these cases. But whatever the shotguns had in them did not ultimately matter because the crowd saw what was happening and wisely quieted themselves and then walked away peacefully.

The best strategy to use in any security scene where the situation is not emergent is for the security pros to allow the people in question to escalate. Then security reacts to the escalation with predetermined steps that would have already been planned out before the fact. The security team or individual professional does not want to be the entity that causes the situation to escalate. But again, there should be plans in place of what to do with an escalation in these shopping situations. It is always best for the security team to know what they are going to do as individuals and as a team.

A well-thought-out plan and good training in that plan's execution are great tools to have on hand. That way the security team knows what they are going to do without looking at each other blankly while the supervisors and management teams try to work something out on the fly. If security knows ahead of time what to do, it gives them an edge, and while it may appear reactive in action, the strategy is proactive in practice. Organization and knowing how to respond to specific behaviors is key. But in this case, security could not handle it and knew that they were about to be overwhelmed. Then they backed off and turned the scene over to the cops. This was highly appropriate, and nobody ended up getting hurt.

The sale was shut down, the people filed off without their coveted holy grail sport shoes, and everyone learned a lesson about that particular Anytown mall. They just don't put up with any nonsense. Their security team gives orders and they will be followed by the shoppers or the sale will end, and nobody gets their shoes.

Funny thing about the Nike shoes…they are not all that attractive. They really are not. They are just simple sport shoes. There is only fuss made over them because the consumers are creating the fuss. There is nothing so special that warrants all the mess we see. These shoes are not that big of a deal and certainly are not worth anyone getting hurt, stabbed, shot, or killed over. I guess that the value of the shoe is in the eye of the beholder. Passion is not logical; it is emotional, and the emotions at these types of sales run quite high. *Amazing!*

POT, FIREWORKS, AND A MOTHER'S FURY

I was a new employee of the Anytown mall and had completed my security training. This story will show how things can get out of hand very quickly and change the entire nature of a call. This was a very simple matter that became very complex and resulted in three arrests and some very upset parents.

The mall had been closed for about a half an hour. It was a quiet night, so the security director started off for home. The wife had made him some beautiful pork chops for dinner, and he, being a man who appreciated food and a girth to show it, was anxious to get home. We all bade him good night, and he left in his car. Things seemed nice and normal, with a smooth closing procedure.

Then a call kicked out from dispatch that there was a noise complaint. Someone said that there was a loud racket in the men's room just up the hall from the security control center. I was the closest unit, so I went in first to check it out. I found three teenage boys, about high school age in the john, goofing off and making noise. I called it into dispatch before I approached the boys with, "All right, you bunch of clowns," I said. "Let's clear out of here. The mall's closed. Time to go!"

It seemed to be pretty straightforward, and dispatch sent two more security personnel to help me out.

Two of the kids went with the other officers, and the third brought up the rear.

The last one said, "Hey, look, I really gotta pee. Can I?"

I said, "Sure. Take care of your business."

So he went back into the john. After the other two were gone, I got a ticklish feeling that I needed to check on the third. When I went into the restroom, I saw him leaned over the changing table. He had a plastic baggy and was sweeping a green, flaky substance together into a neat pile.

I said, "Hey! What is that?"

The startled kid was jumpy and panicked. "That's nothing, sir! Nothing!"

Well, Mr. Nothing grabbed the baggy of all the stuff he could scoop up and started running toward the urinal. I stepped in front of him. He had room to stop and not make contact, but he chose instead to intentionally charge headlong into me. Now this became an assault case. And very likely a drug case as well. He was really trying to get past me, and I did not want him to destroy evidence and possibly clog our urinal with a plastic bag. So I made the choice to wrestle him because he had already initiated the assault on me anyway.

I managed to grab my radio and yelled, "I need help in the restroom, now!"

Well, the female dispatcher knew that the other security officers were walking those other two kids out the main court doors, so she was the closest unit. She responded to the men's room. She came in and found me wrestling this kid and joined the fun. We tried to force him up against the wall, but he was pretty determined and wiry. The supervisor found his way back to the restroom and joined the fray. We got control of the kid and called out that there was likely a controlled substance on the scene.

Next thing I knew, the security director was back with us at the mall. No pork chops for Daddy tonight! Crap! Not only that, but the two other security officers had handcuffed the other two clowns and brought them back the moment they heard that drugs were on the scene. So now we had three boys, all under eighteen years old, handcuffed and waiting for police. Our guys searched the backpacks of the other two and found them in possession of fireworks, which were clearly illegal at that time of year in Anystate, USA.

Then the young man who had the baggy started begging, "Come on, man, be cool! My life is over! Man, you can't call the cops! You can't!"

The supervisor responded with assurances that a little pot never ended anybody's life. By the time the police arrived, we had all three of them sitting on the floor, secured. The cops asked us to lift them up and bring them to the police substation.

We made the requisite calls to parents. Two of the sets of parents, moms and dads, visited the Anytown mall. When they arrived, we could tell that they were none too pleased to come out to the mall at 10:00 PM and pick up their kids who had just been arrested by mall security and were being criminally charged by the cops. You could tell by their general appearance that they were all settled in for the night and suddenly had to jump up and shuttle themselves out the door to go face some bad news. They seemed very annoyed with their kids. None of them blamed the authorities present for what their kid had done. None of them were mad at us and clearly held their boys responsible for what they had done. This was quite refreshing; in probably half the juvenile cases I had brought before the police as a security pro involved parents blaming *me* for their kids' behavior.

Tonight though, this was not the case. Nobody was saying, "My kid acts this way because you picked on him," or "Who do you think you are to single out my son?" None of that. It was not any fun at all for them, but they clearly laid the blame where it belonged. The two clowns were charged with trespassing and the fireworks violation. These two were very cooperative with us and did not get lippy about the charges they were facing. They were ticketed and released to their parents. Frankly, I think they would have rather spent the night in jail than to have gone home to Mom and Dad.

The last kid was a little different story. He was mouthy. He had on a Johnny Cash T-shirt with Johnny, for whatever reason, apparently onstage with his guitar, giving "the finger" to the world. Not his finer moment. But this kid was defiant and so much so that the security director, who was normally a very tolerant man, had me file a formal year-long trespass document against him, the lead jester of this band of clowns. This kid was outspoken and running his mouth, even sitting there in a police station, surrounded by cops and hand-cuffed to a bench.

While I was filling out the mall's trespass form, under "Reason for Trespass," I stated that this kid was in possession of drugs, assaulted a security officer, was in a group which possessed fireworks, was trespassing, verbally abusive, cursing, and in violation of the mall dress code with the Johnny Cash middle finger shirt. The jester tried to soften me a little by saying that he did not want to fight me and that he did not intend to assault me, that he was just trying to dump the evidence. I told him I already knew that, but he had nonetheless assaulted me, and the charge stood as written; I was not giving him a break.

He started getting lippy with us as soon as he discovered his contrite routine was not going to get him out of trouble. It was pretty easy to conclude that he was used to manipulating people.

He told the cops that he did not "accept all that stuff on the form." One cop, finally sick of his crap, told him to "Shut up!" He did. And I was greatly relieved. I wanted to smack him upside his head, the way somebody should have a long time ago.

Now, by this time, Jester was the only one left. The other greatly upset parents already left with their kids, and I am pretty sure that the parents were clued in to the fact that one member of the party, though not their sons, was in possession of some weed. I don't think these parents were very happy to hear that either. Again, I just want to state how pleased I was that the parents did not blame us or call me a "Paul Blart blankety-blank."

So Jester was sitting there and our security guys let his mom into to mall. When she got into the substation and saw her son sitting there in handcuffs, this poor lady came completely unglued. I believe that their family was from Laos; at least that was the impression I was under. But whatever their nationality, Mom was clearly in distress. She saw him and, she t *ballistic!*

"Aннн! What you doing? You ba' boy!" she shouted.

Then yelling at him in their native tongue, she suddenly charged at him with her hand up, drawing it back to slap him a good one.

Personally, I would have allowed it under different circumstances. But we were in the police station, and he was handcuffed. The cops were running the scene, and they were responsible for Jester's safety whether or not they liked it. To allow her to hit him would have ended in some serious consequences for all of us, including yours truly. So for all of our sakes, the policeman said, "No!" and grabbed her arm. "Ma'am, I am sorry for what your boy did, and I understand, but you can't hit him! He is handcuffed."

Then she started yelling at him again in Laotian, which I could not begin to understand. Whatever she was saying, it was not very kind, and he understood every word of it. When she had fully vented on him, she turned to the police and told them, "He ba' boy! He always do thing an' get on trouble. Then he tell me, sorry, Mama! I no do again! But then he do again! An' now he smoke pot? You catch him with pot? I can't do no more for him! Now he go wi' fadder. He fadder may him behave! I lef' work to come and talk to you an' to take him home! But dis time he go to da fadder! Him make boy behave!"

My heart went out to this poor lady. I mean, man! What was this kid thinking? Defiant of the authorities, making trouble for his poor, single working mother...it was just a shame. Really, it was a shame. I don't know what the full story it was; maybe the boy was angry because his parents broke up. But honestly, from the sound of what Momma was saying, it seemed that Jester was taking advantage of his mother's good nature and was doing whatever he wanted because he knew how to trick her into thinking he "be good boy dis time." Poor Mom. I never saw Jester again, and I don't know what happened with his court case. I hope Mom got Dad to take him, and I hope Jester learned to behave himself.

BULLETS VS. BRICKS

There are military veterans and then there are military *veterans*. I prefer the latter of the two. Being raised by the product of the US government's "conflict" in Vietnam, an action they finally classified as a war many years after the US retreated in humiliation in 1973. The men who fought that war were *veterans*. The people who returned from Stormin' Norman's Desert Storm were *veterans*. Any soldier, sailor, Marine, Airman, or special operative who actually saw combat are *veterans*. But when I meet some doofus who just likes to play with guns, who barely made it out of boot camp and never saw a day of fighting, it's hard for me to be around that type.

Being raised by a combat-hardened Marine and Green Beret I learned what REAL veterans are like. And I can pick out a phony "stolen valor"–type fairly quickly. Most war veterans, when they talk, have very little bragging to do. They are contrite, humble, and full of grief for their lost buddies and comrades. People who claim to be vets and love to show off or talk tough just don't impress me. I mean, my old man (RIP) would talk a lot with fellow veterans or others who understand, but they would not share much with people who don't understand. And the stolen-valor people...they have no use for at all. And these kinds had better shut up around real vets because if they don't, they will be put in their place really quick.

We had an event on our patrol team where one of our *veterans* actually had to pull his weapon. He had to pull his sidearm on some guy who said he had a gun. This guy was standing on the roof of a building and yelling at the people on the sidewalk. Our supervisor, Major Doe, was the one who took the call. When the man started yelling, Doe let it go and told him to come down. When the guy said he had a gun, Doe became understandably concerned, but when the man started throwing bricks…well, it was time to act. Bricks from that height were dangerous, and it was time to consider severe action. So Doe reluctantly pulled his gun and pointed it, finger off the trigger and alongside the trigger guard.

As it turned out, he did not have to pull the trigger. The cops arrived and got the guy off the roof of the building. No harm, no foul, no one got hurt and no one *died*. Major Doe was a veteran of combat, a man who had killed people while defending others. He knew for certain what was going to happen if he pulled that trigger, it was the same thing that always happened whenever he pulled the other trigger before. A noise happened. A loud noise. A wound happened in another person. A death happened; a life ended. And Major Doe died along with them, just a little bit. It tore a hole in his heart and mind each time the light faded from someone's eyes. He was ever grateful that he did not have to pull that trigger on that guy; but at the same time, he knew he would have.

This particular security experience is not about Major Doe. It is though about the security pro who told me that story before I learned from Major Doe what truly happened. The guy who I am talking about spent about twenty minutes in the service of the United States military. He liked guns. He made it sound like he was a real hotshot but was actually a total loser. When he told me the story, he thought it was so very "cool" that Major Doe got to pull out his gun in the line of duty. He said with great relish and a sick grin on his face that "Doe almost shot this guy in the face!" After that, I knew that this veteran was not a *veteran*. I knew that this guy was somebody whom I needed to avoid. Anybody that could tell me about another security professional nearly shooting some guy in the face and actually getting a gleam in his eye definitely had a problem. A guy like this does not belong in security.

THE TV COST TWO LIVES

There was a tragic loss prevention event that took place in an Anytown, USA, retailer. This was back when flat screen TV's were relatively new and expensive. They were high-profile items for shoplifters and other thieves. At this particular retail location, a shoplifter grabbed a boxed TV and ran out the door with it. The loss prevention manager saw the guy and could not catch up to him. The shoplifter jumped into a car and raced away. The loss prevention manager should have just copped the plate number, vehicle and suspect descriptions and called the Anytown police. But he did not do that. Instead, he called out to a cart chaser and said that he needed him to come along. The two of them jumped into the LP manager's car. And the chase was on.

This car chase involved two cars. To the best of my knowledge, the police were never called. This LP manager took the law into his own hands and engaged in an illegal car chase. As a private citizen, he had no business pursuing a shoplifting suspect across public streets and far off the property he was supposed to be protecting from shoplifters. And certainly, he had no business trying to stop someone in a speeding car by using his own car to give chase. But chase he did. And he had in his car with him a young man, about seventeen-years-old, not even a member of the loss prevention team. Neither of the pair had adequate training for this kind of action.

The chase continued off the main streets and into a residential neighborhood. This is where it got really dangerous. They were racing around, chasing a desperate man, and all for a stupid television. The police, even if they knew about the TV and the ensuing chase, could not possibly know where these guys were. So there was no way for the police to help. Eventually, the chase did end though. Tragically.

The two cars sped through the residential neighborhood until they came to a dead end. The shoplifter stopped. The LP manager and the cart chaser stopped. They got out of their car. The shoplifter got out of his car. The LP manager and the cart chaser approached the shoplifter. The shoplifter raised his hand. The hand had a gun in it. Shots fired. Two people dead. All over a television. Dead. Never to go home again to their families. One of them a seventeen-year-old cart chaser misled by an adult. And a shoplifter has now become a murderer. All over a television set. A stinking TV cost two human lives, just because an LP manager did not understand his boundaries and let his emotions get the best of him, and a shoplifter decided it was worth killing over.

The most tragic thing is that he pulled a minor into the fray with him. I mean, what was this guy thinking? Running off and doing something impulsive on your own is one thing; involving someone else's child in such a situation as "backup" is completely another. Not only was he behaving irresponsibly, but he was behaving illegally. And that illegal behavior got him and the young man he roped into this thing killed.

At any point, the LP manager could have changed his mind about chasing the shoplifter out the door, about getting his own car to chase the guy, about involving the minor, about pursuing the suspect off property and cornering him on a public street, about trying to enforce. At any time, he could have called the whole thing off and saved both their lives. And, the shoplifter could have decided to not pull the trigger. But he didn't. And now a boy is dead, will never graduate high school, get married. It's all over for him because an adult he apparently trusted influenced him to so something foolish. The boy probably thought that the LP guy had to know what he was doing. It's all just a terrible shame, and it was an avoidable tragedy, one that changed so many lives so unnecessarily.

THE STRAY DOG BIT THE SAMARITAN

One night at an Anytown Anyhotel, I was on patrol and doing my thing, "minding my own business" as usual. Then I found him, some drunken young man urinating in the parking lot.

I ran him off the property. I thought that should be the end of that. It was, but only for the night. The very next night, well, guess what? I was called to the hotel lobby, and they told me that he was back, the same guy I caught the night before. Only now, he was in the lobby, apparently drunk again and passed out in a chair.

I went over to him and tried to speak to him and wake him up. He was breathing steadily, but I could not get his attention by speaking to him. So I finally walked over to him and tapped him on the leg with my 4 D-cell flashlight. He partially woke up and looked over at me. He saw my uniform and then really woke up. He was in some trouble, and he knew it.

I asked him the standard question of, "Sir, do you have a room here?"

And to my great surprise, he said, "Yeah."

Well, that changed the whole game. He was not registered, but hotel guests were allowed to have guests in their room anytime they wanted. When you rent a hotel room, it is like renting a house. As long as you don't violate your agreement with the property owner, it essentially becomes your property, and you can have visitors.

Instead of taking his word for it, and turning him loose, I asked him to show me where his room was. He did not have a key for the room he showed me. So I told him to knock. If "his friend" was truly there, he would have him in. If his friend was not there, which is what I expected, then I would likely involve the police at that point and have this guy either arrested or cited. But to my surprise, the hotel guest answered the door. Not only that, but when I explained that this guy was caught urinating in the parking lot last night and claimed that he was staying in this room, the guest claimed him. That *really* surprised me, but whatever was going here was not my business. I told our guest that if this guy is with him, then he needed to stay in the room because he was drunk and generating complaints. The guy said that he would keep his friend inside so he would not bother anyone.

I had moved onto other things and had all but forgotten about the event. Then a call came from the check in desk. A distress call was heard by someone in one of the rooms. The caller stated that someone was pounding on the wall, yelling for help, and there was a lot of ruckus coming from that room. This hotel had the room entrances on the outside of the building, so I ran across the property and up the stairs. On my way up the stairs, a group of young men were running down the stairs. I had no way of knowing whether or not they were involved in this event, so I just kept going. Besides, if they were involved, there were too many of them for me to deal with; I was a lone security professional and unarmed. No way I could stop them from running, and I had no reason to pursue them.

I kept going until I reached the room. The desk by this time had called the police, and they were on their way. I pounded on the door and asked if everything was okay. The man inside answered but said he would not open the door. I had a passkey, but I could not open the door if a guest had it locked from the inside, to prevent me from violating privacy. I identified myself as hotel security. He did not believe me. I slid my badge under the door, and he cautiously opened it. When he saw me, he asked if those guys were gone. I told him we were safe, and he had me come in.

He told me what happened. He said that the young man I brought to his room was somebody he just met. He did not know the kid but saw that he was on hard times. He felt sorry for and was trying to counsel him about how he was living his life. The guest said that when he saw me bring the kid to his room, he did not want him to spend the night on the street because he knew that I was going to throw the young man out. So out of compassion, he assumed responsibility and had him come in to stay the night.

The guest further stated that he was just kind of talking to the young man about going to college, getting his life in order and breaking the chains of poverty that were holding him down. He told me that during the conversation he mentioned that things were going so good for him because of college that he had three or four thousand in cash with him all the time, including right now. Then the kid somehow got a hold some friends of his without the guest knowing it.

By this time, the police had arrived. They came into the room with the guest's permission.

The police asked why they were called to an apparently quiet room. The man started over again with the story and then told the police that the young man he was trying to counsel called his friends and tried to rob him. He somehow managed to shove them all out the door—how, really, I don't know, but that was his story. Maybe they only got partway into the room. Who knows? Then when they heard him calling for help and knew security was on the way, and probably the cops as well, they ran off. The reason he did not answer the door for me was because they had tried to trick him.

After they were outside, they waited quietly for a moment and then knocked on the door and said, "Hey, mister? You okay, those guys are gone."

And that was when he started beating on the walls and calling for help. The room next-door was the one who called the desk.

The police were not impressed. They were pretty cynical about the whole thing and asked him point-blank if he had any drugs around. He said no, and to this day I don't know if he did. I don't think he did; I believed the guy's story. On the other hand, that does not make me right. He could have been dealing, but I don't think he was. I think he was just an honest, sincere guy who was trying to help a stray and got himself BIT. I hope he learned something from it; he became pretty annoyed with me when I kept calling the potential robber his "friend." But really, that is just tough. He did a naive thing, and I hope he learned from it. You have to know when to be good-hearted and when to shut them out. This man's mistake, though compassionate, could have gotten him killed.

THE NUMBERS MAN AND THE PAY PHONE

This is one of my favorite stories. I was working hotel security. The Anytown hotel hosted several celebrities who would come and go. We never knew who would show up. I met Dale Earnhardt's parents before his accident. They were wonderful people. Keanu Reeves was there, but I did not meet him. John Madden was there too. People came to meet him and then stood around him like he was on display in a zoo. He just got up and left the lobby to go to his room. I met the guys from the band KORN (with a reversed R) at this hotel. One of them became an actor and played a major part in the movie *Hackers*. I am just telling you this, so you understand that this was not some fleabag, flophouse hotel. It was near a major international airport. And I don't know why this guy thought it was a great idea to do what he was doing in our lobby.

Dad had some peculiar ways about him. He was very concerned about my staying out of trouble, but he ran for a while with a biker "club," not any major criminals, but rowdy. He allegedly mighta, but not really, had some friends who mighta been rather well-known in family organizations, though we all know that he was never near any of them. And they, these guys who did not exist, and did not know who he might be, liked him because he had a very convenient memory about some things. He never saw any of them, either, not like some people would try to claim.

I want to very clear about this though: Dad was every inch a civilian and had nothing to do with anything that people who don't exist don't do because they don't exist. *Capisce?* Some guys are good to have around because they know how to fix a vacuum cleaner, a sewing machine, are "good people," and they are honest men who understand respect and how to separate personal stuff from business. They also keep the lady of the house happy with her appliances, but these same guys don't ever seem to remember being there. Where? Huh? Who? Me?

So okay. You get the picture. Well, one night when I was on patrol, I saw this really big guy who was five hundred pounds if he was an ounce. And I noticed that he was on the phone for a *loooong* time. Well, all he would do on this phone call was read off lists of numbers. Long numbers with dashes and letters mixed with numerals. I caught on when I remembered what Dad told me about "numbers" rackets. It was what people did for their gambling fetishes before the states started their lotteries. Then numbers rackets were state-sponsored, and that made it legal. I have my personal feelings about lotteries, but that's another book all by itself.

My recollection, selective though it needed to be, was that sometimes "numbers men" used insurance policy numbers to run their game. And these numbers looked very familiar. I made a call and verified what I saw. I was told by my "guy" that this other guy on the phone sure sounded like a numbers man. That being said, I went "hmmm" and thought about how to handle this. I thought calling the cops was too bold a move because I would not want to hack off a family and be swept up off the parking lot by a forensics team trying to ID my ashes. But I really did not want to approach this guy myself either, so I settled for a compromise. It would keep him outta jail and me outta the papers.

I kept my thoughts and ideas to myself, and over the next few nights, I would be sure to walk by him several times, making sure he saw me looking at him. When it became apparent that he was not going to take the hint, on about the third night, I went out to where he parked his old, beat-up car. I planned where to wait; behind a rock wall about waist-high. He could see me, I could see him, and I had plenty of room to duck, if I needed to. He did not seem to be armed, or very aggressive, but one can never tell if he has something hidden under the seat, what orders he operates under, or if he has somebody covering him from outside. I never saw anyone, and I checked, but they could still be there somewhere. The rock wall, again, was a place to duck. When Slim came outside, I made sure he saw me see him. I made sure he saw me watch him go to his car, and I made sure he saw me take out my note pad and copy his plate, vehicle, and personal description.

The message was clear:

> *"I see you, I know what you are, what you look like and I have enough information to give the cops. I could have snuck around behind your back and gotten the same information for the cops anyway, but I didn't do that. I don't want that kind of trouble. I just want you to go away quietly and never come here doing this thing of yours, ever again. You do that, and we will call it even. You get what you want, and I get what I want. I get a quiet hotel, and you get to stay on the street. No harm, no foul, no problems between us; just business. You got yours, I got mine, and we keep it that way."*

He never came back.

THE SEX FIEND ON THE PLAZA

Granted, security personnel are not well-known for their smarts. And they are not well-known for doing their jobs very well. This is something that the industry has done to itself by using low-wage employees. You won't generally find well-educated professionals who willingly work for chump-change wages. You get what you pay for, and that is one of the issues I hope to address at some point in this book. Depending on how it comes together, you might have already figured it out before getting this far.

I mention this because you might say, "Well, George, how did this situation get this far out of hand?"

Well, if you see above and understand what I am getting at, you will conclude that this person in a security role was not very wise, not street-smart, and was not well-trained. Because if she were, she would have known how to handle this guy before the situation went haywire. I will tell the story in the order of how the events happened. By the end of the story, you will see how the first contact could have ended this whole thing more quickly and easily than it all turned out.

We got a complaint call from a fourteen-year-old girl. We put out a description to the mobile patrol and the rest of the security team of some creeper who was trying to get this terrified girl into his car. He was driving along beside her, slowly keeping pace with her walking stride. He kept trying to get her to come closer, to get in his car, telling her it's not safe to be alone in this neighborhood (yeah… with guys like him out there), and so on. She shook him off, ran to the pay phone, and called us.

Well, I thought that this guy was going to be long gone. As it turned out, he wasn't. The mobile unit found him and told us that we needed to get out there because she was not going to take on this guy alone. We ran outside, and he was not there. He had gone into the mall. Mobile security described him, and it matched the guy the teenage girl had described. We finally caught up to him in the food court. There were three of us security guys. I was the smallest of the three, and at the time I weighed about 220 pounds and stood just over six feet.

We started talking to this guy, and he was getting very nervous, really fast. He obviously did not want to talk to us. But we *did* want to talk to *him*. Guess who got their way? So we asked him about talking to the teen girl. He admitted talking to her, said he could talk to whomever he pleased. One of our guys put in a call to the cops, told him he was going to stay and wait. He did not like that idea, became afraid, and then this scuzzbucket tried to bully his way through us. He came right at me, and that was a bad idea. I stopped him cold, the skinny little man. He wore half-shaded glasses and just had a certain EWW-WWW feeling all about him. You understand what I mean. He was just nasty.

Well, now that he had charged into me, we really had *another* reason to hold him for the police. But first, we had to subdue him so that he would not run off. In less time than it takes to tell, he was pushing against me. I pushed back, with a solid grip on his shirt. He twisted and wriggled and threatened us with a lawsuit, like we had never heard THAT before. We finally got him turned around, but the momentum of the three of us carried him forward. He was against the mall railing, and we bent him over at the waist. I got one of his arms up behind him in a "chicken wing" hold.

We were standing there, the four of us, and then the supervisor went to meet the cops. After a couple of minutes, my grip got fatigued, and the creeper managed to pull out. I reared up to really take him down, and he said, "No, no. I won't fight you." We offered him a chair in the food court, and we sat down at the same table, flanking him so he would not have room to break loose. If he flinched, he was going to get roughed up again, and he knew it. He sat still and waited for the PD.

After a few minutes, Police Officer Jane Doe showed up. I was glad to see her because she had a strong maternal instinct. I had seen her protect kids before. This would be good. When she got the story on our old buddy, she was hacked off! She laid into him professionally, yes, but quite thoroughly. She had his ID, put the info on a field card, and she spent quite some time running his ID. We got the Polaroid instant camera out and took the creep's photo. It looked just as scummy as he did.

Meanwhile, Officer Doe was doing all she could to find *something, anything, to bust this guy.* But nothing came back. I would have bet money that that guy had something to go in for, but he had no wants, no warrants, no prior arrests or complaints. He was clean… well…not *clean*, but you know what I mean. Finally, Officer Doe gave up, and she laid back into him. She told him off and kept telling him off! She was very careful to not actually accuse him, but she stated this or that as "opinions." He made some smart remark about how he did not know how old the girl was because she was not holding a sign that said how old she was. So Officer Doe said that in her *opinion*, he knew how old the girl was. In her *opinion*, he was trying to get her into his car for some illicit reason. She expressed a deep regret in her *opinion* that she could not arrest him right there on the spot. But she could not, so she told him that he was being trespassed by "these security officers who had a legitimate concern" *permanently* from the mall.

She had worked with us before, and we had a pretty solid relationship. I did not even have to ask her badge number anymore; I had put it on so many reports. She knew how we did things. And she did not check with us about the permanent trespass, but we certainly took her suggestion. He was permanently trespassed. And I think he knew how lucky he was to get out of there to go where he wanted with no special bracelets.

Later, we found out from the plaza security officer that this guy had sexually harassed her. This is where the "not so bright" part comes in. The plaza officer was sitting there, writing something on a spiral notebook. Now, in the first place, she should not have been writing in a spiral notepad while she was supposed to be monitoring the plaza. The plaza area of this mall was open, and there was a small sort of playground on it. Her job was to monitor the playground. She was obviously not monitoring because the creeper made his way to her without her really seeing him.

He looked down at where she was sitting and said, "Hey, what'cha doing?"

"Oh, hi. I'm writing a story."

"Can I see it?"

"Sure."

So creeper looked at the story and said, "Hey! Where's all the sex in your story? It cannot be a good story without sex."

She just looked at him, and he walked away, almost certainly pleased with himself. Now, if the security officer was doing her job, she would have immediately told this guy to leave. Or—and this is a perfectly acceptable and probably safer alternative—she should have at least called in the guy's description, had security officers come down to the plaza, and we would have introduced him to the cops much sooner. That would have meant that the girl who reported him would have never been harassed. I think of how awful that must have been to that girl. I am sure that she remembers that moment to this day and is warning other people about creepers like this.

OFFICER WARPATH DOE

There was this one cop who was tougher than tempered nails when he was working with shoplifting juveniles. I mean, this guy had no mercy when it came to some of these kids. We had some cops who were just so nice they gave the kid a reason to still "feel good about themselves" even though they just did something wrong. The whole "you're not a bad person, you've just done a bad thing." That approach was nice and all, but it rubbed me the wrong way in some cases. It seemed that the kid who was being interviewed *needed* to feel bad and to realize that they just did something that bad people do.

Now before I get too far into this, in reference to the policeman who took that "Officer Nice Guy" approach also may have been tough, but he just did not do it publicly. I just thought of this too, while I was writing:

One time, Officer Nice Guy had this kid who was shoplifting, and his brother was lying to cover for him. The brother's coat was on a chair, and when I moved the chair, the stolen merchandise we were asking about, fell out of his pocket. The kid gave verbal consent to search his pockets further, and we recovered about twenty-five bucks in today's money in stolen stuff—candy, novelty toys, just dumb stuff. Nothing of any serious value. After we filed the charges, Nice Guy took the lying brother into the manager's office of our security suite and sat with him alone. The brother was "smiling" when he went in but looked considerably "distressed" when he came back out. So...?

Anyway, back to tempered nails. I just loved working with this guy because he had this nasty, gravelly voice. It was not faux either. It was not a put on. This guy was just wall-to-wall gritty. And all the shoplifts were worked the same. We'd call, the juvie would sit there and wait for the PD—sometimes crying, sometimes hardcore, whatever. I've seen it all. So the cop would come in, red hair and moustache, overly wrinkled and just tough-looking. The first phrase out of his mouth was usually derogatory.

"Hey, security! How the —— are ya? What? You caught me another genius, another —— Albert —— Ein —— Stein? Gee, whiz you guys! What, you can't you let a cop eat his —— lunch? Wait a minute! What the—am I yelling at you for? Friggin' Einstein here started this party! Hey—Einstein? That your name? No? Well, what is it? Let's get this party started, Einstein, cuz I'm Hungry!"

"Um... I...uh..."

"You forget your name, boy? You don't know your name? Everybody got a name, even an obvious dumb butt like you!"

"John Doe."

"Well, Mr. Doe... How the —— are you? Where's your parents?"

"Um...working..."

"Oh. Both of 'em?"

"Uh-huh"

"It's yes or no, Mr. John Doe Einstien. I don't—speak—caveman, boy!"

"Y-y-es. They both work."

"I see. Your mom too? She drop you off?"

"Uh—I mean, yes."

"Well, ain't that just fine, Mr. John Doe Einstein. She's out there working hard to support your —— and you're here stealing at the mall. Well, ain't that just a fine thing. What kind of grades an Einstein like you get these days, Mr. Doe?"

"As and Bs."

"A's and B's? A's and B's? What'd you do with the brains God gave you, boy? You check 'em in at the door? They fall out of your head at the arcade? Hey, security…you got any brains left in the lost and found?"

I walked over to the shelf and checked the lost and found book, while Warpath waited, and I said, "Nope. Nothing here!"

"Nothing in *there* either, is there, Einstein?" Warpath asked, pointing at the shoplifter's bowed head. "So tell me, Einstein, what's your real name? You got any ID on you, boy? Yeah…school ID will do. All right, Mr. Doe, Johnny, is it? Uh-huh. You ever been arrested before, Mr. Doe? Mr. Johnny? No? Well, yeah, you have, genius! You got arrested before. Right before I got here! Ha! Ha! Ha! You ain't laughing, genius! Well, that's good… Hey, security!"

"Yeah?"

"You ever smell a dead body?"

"Oh yeah…you get that stink on your clothes, and it never comes out."

"That's right, security… It never comes out. Heh! So tell me, Mr. Johnny Einstein Doe, what's your hardworking mother's name? I gotta call her now and tell her how much fun you had here at the mall today, getting your —— arrested. And boy, is she ever gonna be as happy as a pig in ——. Oh…that bother you, Mr. Einstein? Well, it should! Now you just sit right there while I call… Oh, hello there. Is this Mrs. Jane Doe? Yes, this is Officer Warpath of the Anytown police station. I'm very sorry to bother you at work, but…what? Oh, no, ma'am. I'm sorry I frightened you. As far as I know, your family members are fine. But there is an issue. Yes, ma'am. I am sorry to report that your son, Johnny Doe has been arrested for shoplifting. No, ma'am, it's not a joke and I am very sorry. Can you come and pick him up? All right then, yes. I understand. You need me to talk to your boss? No? Okay. Thirty minutes or so. Don't hurry, and please drive safely. Johnny here is quite safe. Okay. Bye now."

I should note here that Officer Warpath's voice was considerably softer while talking to the boy's mother. I must say that it was moving. I felt bad for Momma Doe. I really did. And at his core, I know that Warpath did too. He came down hard on the kid so that he would not want to take the chance of running into another cop like Warpath. Or any other cop for that matter. Now I have seen other moms come to the mall to pick up their shoplifter kids, but this one was different. About every other mom I met was angry with their kid. But this mom was different. This kid was different too. His head sunk low in shame; you could feel it. And his mom approached him in *pain,* not anger. I have seen defiance, anger, rage...you name it. This mom and son did not have any of that. It was pain, all across the board. That was something to see; there was a lesson learned by the son, and you could tell he would never need to learn it again.

As for Warpath...the really tough guy... Heh! There was a write-up in the Anytown paper about him some months later. Apparently, there was some kid playing with a remote-control car in a cul-de-sac. Warpath needed to make a turnaround in his patrol car and used the cul-de-sac. He accidentally crushed the kid's remote car. What did Warpath do? He could have just shrugged and moved on. But he didn't. He stopped, identified himself to the kid, gave him his badge number, and made a field report, complete with the kid's address, parental names, etc. He left the scene.

A couple of hours later, Warpath returned to the kid's address and rang the bell. His mother answered the door and called for her son. When Warpath met the kid, *he handed him a brand-new remote-control car to replace the one he ran over.* Big, tough Officer Warpath. Crusty, rough old veteran cop with a soft, gooey heart of gold. We can only imagine what happened when that story hit the papers...as soon as one cop saw it, you know the whole precinct heard the story. A few years later, I ran into a retired policeman who just laughed when I told him I knew Warpath and I saw the paper. We chuckled for a while over big, tough Warpath. The retired cop said he was razzing him about the story, and Warpath said, "Well... I didn't see the —— thing!"

That all being said, I guess the lesson in this is that all of us, even the tough guys, we all have more than one role in life. One role is what we choose to do and what we become to the world, which is an assumed role in which we are playacting. The other role is to simply be the person who we are on the inside. It IS who we are. Warpath playacted a tough, street-hardened cop who came down hard on kids who went wrong. But the real Warpath had a big ol' heart and took the time out of his day and money out of his pocket to fix the injustice forced on a brokenhearted boy. That was one of the greatest things I ever saw a policeman do. That was one act beyond the call of duty. He should have gotten recognition for that...out of earshot of the other cops, of course.

A SIMPLE MISUNDERSTANDING / MY INTERVIEW BY THE COPS

I include this simple story not because I was a security officer, but because it shows how a young girls' smarts led her to do the right thing.

At this time, I was not working in the security field. But I was working for a company that took care of developmentally disabled persons. They had me running an independent living home. There were three young women living there. It was a fine job, and I liked the people I worked for. There was a lot of mutual trust. But one day they thought I had disappointed them. On this day I had left the house, per our normal routine, to get my dinner. I was on my way back from buying my fast-food dinner when I got a call over the Nextel radio/phone.

"George...this is Dennis. You gotta get back to the house. The Anytown PD is there, and they are asking for you by name."

"By name? Uh, yeah, yeah. Let me get there right now. On my way."

Well, I was worried now. The cops never ask for you by name unless they have information. Apparently, the boss man thought of that too.

"Uh... George, if you have any outstanding warrants, you might not want to go back."

"No...nothing like that. My prints have been run three or four times during my caregiving career. I am quite clean. I am, though, worried that there has been some accident at my house or something and my wife told the cops where to find me."

"Roger that...we are on our way too then."

I arrived at the house first and the police were outside. Three of them. That was never good news, seeing that many cops. I parked the van and got out. I walked toward them, with my hands where they could see them, but without being obvious about it. I greeted them, and they asked my name. I told them, and then suddenly all three of them were huddled around me. That made me a bit uncomfortable, but I did not flinch. I was used to working with the police, and I knew they were just trying to stay safe. They did not know me after all.

One asked if I worked there and what time I arrived. I told them. Another asked if I saw anything on my way in. I said there was a girl on a bike. They asked me to tell them about it.

I thought, "Okay...the kid was a runaway," and they wanted any info I could give them. So I told them the story.

"I was on my here, and I saw this girl on her bike, and she was riding ahead of me. She was on the sidewalk to my right. I stopped for the STOP sign. She wanted to cross the street, so I waved her across. Then I did a U-turn at the stop sign. The girl continued up the road on her bike, ahead of me again. Then I pulled into the driveway here and went to work."

"Did you say anything to her?"

"No."

Then one of the policemen started to sort of smile, and all three of them began nodding, and one finally said, "Okay... I think we got the picture now."

"What?"

"Well, we got a call from an anxious mother. She said that her daughter told her that a man in a white car, parked at this house on the corner, was suspicious. She said you were following her, stopped, tried to get her over to your car to get in. When she refused, you followed her up the street, pursuing her, but stopped at this house."

"Oh…well…no…"

Then the police were just sort of laughing. We were all relieved at the simple misunderstanding. By the time my boss pulled into the driveway, it was all cleared up. The police went and talked to them anyway, just because. They assured my boss that everything was fine and explained that a perfectly innocent circumstance was stretched out of shape, that's all.

The police apologized and said that they had to check this out. I understood perfectly. I told them to tell the mom that I had no problem with what she did. The daughter and she did exactly the right thing. I taught my daughter and wife to the do the same thing. I am not in the least upset about this and so on.

When I got home that night, I told my wife what happened. She said that I should just not try to be nice. She said it seemed that whenever I looked somebody in the eye, I got into trouble.

WHAT COLOR IS GANGRENE?

I was out on the mean, cold streets of Anytown. Frozen snow was blowing all over the place. Before I continue, I need to point out that I was in the field of caregiving for adults with developmental disabilities and I was in involved in elder care. I worked as an activity assistant in elder care in this particular Anytown. This particular night I am referring to though, I was in security branch management, and I was overseeing the function of our downtown accounts. I stayed close to town on nights when it was this cold because I did not want to end up in the middle of nowhere with a car problem or something in temperatures like these.

I was in between post visits when I stopped at Anytown Convenience store. I walked in, and while habitually scanning the store, I saw something unusual. A man was camped out on the floor, sitting on his sleeping bag. I thought that was strange, allowing a homeless man to camp inside like that. Then I recognized him. He was one of the guys I used to take care of at the elder-care home. He was a developmentally disabled adult. I used to help him play the penny slots at one of the smaller casinos we would take people to visit on certain activity days. This guy thought I was the greatest guy in the world because he walked out of the place with about eight bucks, winning fifty or sixty cents at a time. He came with $4 and walked out with $8. That is a good day's gambling, anytime you walk out of a casino with profit, no matter how small.

While I was taking this all in, knowing that this guy was once safe in a warm home, and wondering who put him on the streets again and why, I heard something.

The clerk of the store said, "You just sit right there. I have an ambulance coming."

That was when I noticed that the homeless man was not wearing gloves. His hands were black. And not because of his race either; his hands were black with frostbite.

I heard some guy in line make a remark about his hands. I said that when your hands or body parts like are blackened that way, you have gangrene.

The guy then responded, "Those hands are not green, they are black."

I was yet again astonished at the ignorance of John Q. Public.

I told him, "No, gangrene is disease, not a color. This man," I continued, "is about to lose his hands. Those hands cannot be saved, the black skin is dead tissue and cannot be revived. The hospital will immediately cut them off, or he will die of blood poisoning from infections."

And everyone got quiet, all of us just staring at this guy's hands. I wonder to this day if the elder-care place took him back and kept him this time. I mean, that guy was already mentally handicapped and homeless. Now he is a bilateral amputee of the hands. He is now pretty helpless.

I cannot shake that image of those hands. It was a terrible thing to behold.

HANDCUFF HOTEL

Some guys just should not be in the security field. Here is another experience I had with one of them. Again. We had this Security Officer Doe who worked with the Anytown Security Company, and he was posted at a hotel. Every night, somebody was arrested, somebody was handcuffed, and it was always somebody from the homeless population. In this Anytown, the homeless generally did not want trouble. That was why we had such a hard time figuring out Officer Doe.

We saw him do some pretty strange things in front of us, the supervisory staff, and it made us wonder just what he was up to when we were not watching him. For instance, we had four people, including Doe, talking in the parking lot. I was Doe's direct boss, and my boss was also present, was as well as another line officer. Suddenly, we heard a couple start fighting. This muscular Latino guy and his girl were yelling at one another on hotel property. We were being cautious as we approached the couple, then all at once, Doe bolted toward the argument.

This Latino guy was big, and he had some muscle. Doe would not have stood a chance, even if the guy did not have a gun. Two of us security personnel were armed, but Doe ran out ahead of the guns. If something went completely ape-nuts, we would not have been able to use our weapons because Doe was in the line of fire. Idiot!

My boss yelled at Doe to get back, and that alerted the argumentative couple. They saw uniforms, and she immediately grabbed her man by the hand and assured us that everything was fine. Well, we liked to see that they were in control enough to just stop hollering the moment they saw us. I love it when a problem solves itself. We told them that we were not cops, were not there to check IDs. We worked for the hotel and explained to them that we did not want to arrest anyone. Case closed. They were happy to not get arrested; we were happy they were just having a moment and solved it immediately.

Our problem with what Doe did was obvious. He ran into the line of fire; he ran toward an argument between a man and woman, dangerous in itself; and he did so from out of the dark. That guy could have thought Doe wanted some kind of trouble. If that man thought Doe needed to be knocked out for rushing out of the dark like that, well, too bad. We would not have even charged him because Doe seemed to be attacking them.

On another night in the same parking lot, Doe and I got a call that a man was screaming and beating his head on the asphalt. We answered the call and found him, on all fours, screaming and beating his head on the ground. We approached and told him to stop doing that before he hurt himself and to quiet down. He looked up and greeted us pleasantly, which was surprising. He spoke with us rationally, which was also surprising.

He did not have any apparent head injuries, so we called the police to the scene. The cops were none too happy about being called by us, and I could not really figure out why. For some reason, our branch manager was also on the scene that night. Branch Manager Doe was a good guy, very fair-minded. Sometimes too much so for the branch's own good. Sometimes, perhaps even often, the security team would suffer because of the branch manager's decisions to keep employees on the team for the sake of being a "family." But for the record, my "family" is the people I go home to every night. Everyone else are either friends, acquaintances, or coworkers. I have no "family" at work. One cannot afford to have such deep ties at work because things go wrong at work all the time, and one cannot allow personal feelings on a heartfelt scale to drive work decisions. This especially applies to supervisors. You will see why in a minute.

Getting back to the behavior issue. In this case, yes, the cops did need to be called. And for once, Doe did not handcuff him. I would not let him. I told him that the guy was not getting squirrely on us; there were enough of us, three guys, to stop him if something went wrong; and the homeless guy was compliant. There was no need to handcuff this guy. When the cops did get to the scene, they ran the guy's ID, and it turned out that he had about $5,000 in outstanding fines. That is what was listed on his warrant. Understand, that was not actually what I would call a hard-core criminal.

His criminal record was all petty stuff like trespassing, low-level drug possession charges, and public intoxication fines. Over time, the fines simply got racked up on the guy because he could not pay them. He was homeless, jobless, and probably addicted to meth. And from time to time, he'd act up, and someone would call the cops who would bust him, cite him and, he would never show up to pay the fines. After a while the courts took petty crap seriously. The cops were disappointed to announce to the poor guy that they had to take him to jail "for real." They explained to him that he could not just simply keep breaking the law, even the "little laws," and not answer to the courts. He had to go in. The $5,000 was just too much to forgive.

Doe heard that and tried to "knuckle-bump" me. I just looked at him like "*really?*" and ignored the attempt… I "left him hangin'." I was not impressed at all by Officer Doe's candor. I actually felt for sorry for the homeless guy because he had to go to jail for real. I don't think that the law was wrong, and it had to be done under law, but the cops were still reluctant to take him away. That was why I felt bad for the guy, and so did the police and my branch manager. That knuckle-bump business was unprofessional, and it made us look bad. It would have been exponentially worse if I had engaged him in a celebration of this poor, broke slob being now completely ruined. So yeah, in a rare moment of compassion for the habitual lawbreaker, I did feel bad for the guy. He went to jail. Doe was still on the job.

Officer Doe was known for that kind of outrageous, ignorant behavior. He was pretty scary actually. He was telling me all about how he grew up just "loving handcuffs" to the point that his "mom was afraid that he was going to become gay." That was a strange conversation, one based in ignorance…and what being "gay" had to do with it, I never found out. Needless to say, it gave me insight into who this guy was Doe was a strange duck. He just loved to handcuff people. He would find guys asleep on the ground and instead of just waking them up and sending them off the property, he would *arrest* them—and call the cops. The cops really started to hate coming to that hotel. Things were always stirred up there for no particular reason.

It got to the point where homeless people would hang out right along the property line, just to rile him up. I mean, think about it! These folks have nothing better to do. Security can't do anything unless they are on the property. Unless they cross the line into "disorderly conduct" or some kind of dangerous threats/harassment charges, what is security going to do? Nothing! Nothing but stand there, being taunted, pacing back and forth, completely impotent. The security officer now has achieved "Barney Fife" status. It is all very entertaining for the ones calling out Doe. He caused most of the trouble himself!

The fact is that the client was being very patient with the security company. The office had a lot going on, and the client understood. But that did not make things very easy for me. I had to keep fielding the complaints on this bonehead and he would get the oddest ideas. He would just tell people that the company was going to let him go armed. He said that if he went and got his concealed carry permit that the company would make him an armed patrolman. I knew that had to be a mistake on his part; it *had* to be an assumption of some kind… I would have stepped down from supervision if they armed him. I would not be responsible for that idiot. I approached the branch manager in an e-mail and asked him about the claim. As I figured, it was completely false. And we all had the same thoughts about Officer Doe: *If he was so anxious to punish people and handcuff them, he would probably look for any excuse to* SHOOT *somebody.* So *no*… Officer Doe was to "never carry a gun on duty for Anytown Security." And that was in writing, from the branch manager to me. Along with yet another paragraph on how we could not afford to fire him because blah, blah. Bottom line—they did not prioritize getting rid of Doe.

Finally, this all came to a head. All these conflicts and issues with Officer Doe took their toll. All the security officers, some of the more sarcastic cops, and many of the hotel staff were trying to get rid of him. *I* was trying to get rid of him. He was a troublemaker; he was egotistical and had a low opinion of anyone who tried to tell him what to do. He thought he knew so much, but in reality, he was not all that bright. Finally, one night, the inevitable happened, and we got into it. We got into it pretty good, too. The little punk tried to take me on. You can about guess how well that went for him.

Before I had even gotten out the door to hit the street, the branch manager called. He had just received a report from the hotel that the hotel manager had not seen any recent reports from Doe. In fact, there were five days' worth of daily activity reports missing. I found Doe on the site and gave him the benefit of the doubt. At first. I took him outside, telling him that I needed to talk to him. I asked him about the reports, if they were misplaced perhaps? Or if they were sent into the office by courier? Mistakenly turned in to a different supervisor? Eaten by the Homework Dog of the North? Then he told that *no, he had not written them.*

I was actually dumbfounded. I could not believe that something as critical as daily activity reports were missing over a five-day period because he had simply refused to write them. In some private security companies, if a lieutenant or sergeant comes by and finds that his line officer is behind on his DAR by more than an hour R, that security officer can technically be dismissed entirely from their job. Now, this is rarely enforced to such a strict standard; I have never seen anyone get fired over a missing hour on a DAR. I supposed it could happen, but it likely would be over a different cause and the missing hour would be a footnote in the termination papers or a "final straw" event that pushed the termination button.

Five hours, no…but five days? Yeah. This was definitely a different situation, and the conversation was to be very different than the standard tongue lashing. It went down like I thought it would. It had a different ending, but it went about as I expected. It started out with me telling him that this was ridiculous. Then he told me that he was the best security officer they had on staff, that they were lucky to have him. Oh man…yeah, that was Doe all right. The big, bad John…ruler of the stoned, homeless population, and handcuff king of the helpless. Sheesh! What a bonehead.

After a couple of minutes, I finally had enough. I told him about my experience in the security field and how I never missed a DAR. Nobody misses DARs. They are too critical for not only professional, but legal purposes as well. DARs stay with the post and the security companies long after the officers who wrote them are gone. These reports are the only proof that there was a security officer there at all. This is important for a number of reasons. One, the security company is contracted, and by contract is bound to have an officer on site. Two, if something goes wrong, then a DAR can be called up for any number of reasons. These reasons include, but are not limited to, proving that adequate security was present in the event of a lawsuit, showing that contracted services were provided, listing activities and findings of the security officer during the shift, and so on. You get the picture.

Then you know what happened? Officer Doe went off on me, telling me that I would not lecture him; that he would not stand there and listen to it. That did it! I went off on this young man, and I actually pulled rank, something I hated to do because I think that security officer "ranks" should not be used as they do in the military. I told him that he would listen to me, that my master's degree and four levels of rank *above* him were now talking, and he was *gonna hear every word!* Then a miracle happened. Heaven smiled down on me.

"Yeah?" he said, "Well, I quit!"

"Right now?" I hoped out loud.

"Yeah! Right now!"

"Turn in your gear."

Without a word, he turned on his heel and walked right back to the building. He went to the office, turned in his stuff, and complained to a few people on the way out. He said he quit because of me. Okay! I'll take the blame/credit! Just go! After he left, these people approached me and told me that they did not know why he would cry to them about me...they were the ones trying to get rid of him! The desk manager of the hotel did not care, except for being left without security. I told her not to worry, that I would cover Doe's shift personally until we could find a replacement. They smiled and thanked me, profusely...for him going away.

I called the office and told Major Doe what happened. He said that Officer Doe just proved to everyone what a little (wench) he really was. He asked if I was okay to hold the post. I said that I was glad to under the circumstances. It was just a matter of time before we got sued with the crap Officer Doe was pulling. How was the client? Oh…they were very happy with me for getting the job done. They did not care if he quit or was fired. They were just glad to see him go. No one that I spoke to that night was sad that Doe was off the post. In fact, this kitchen worker who spoke mostly Spanish said, "He gone? Good…cuz he wa' *crazy!*"

And funny thing…all of a sudden, the office could find time to get a replacement for him. Imagine that…

HOW A REPUTATION BUILDS

When you are in a smaller town, you can develop a reputation pretty fast. Some of the things that you've done becomes the stuff of legend, for good or bad. I once had a supervisor who found out from me that I worked with an old friend of his. He checked up on me. When he found out that his friend said I was "a good guy," the current supervisor immediately trusted me. Had I not been "a good guy," things would have gone differently; I am friends with both of these guys to this day.

One's reputation can really be built or destroyed by the police department of one's locality. For instance, I met a cop on a hospital post one night. We recognized each other immediately. It was a, "Hey, how ya doing?" We were glad to see each other, and maybe even a little surprised. We pieced together where we knew each other from.

"Oh, yeah…the Notell Hotel," he recalled.

"Yep, that was me. You guys had a lot of trouble out there, didn't you? With that Officer Doe guy."

"Oh man…tell me about it. He was always stirring up trouble. We had so many calls out there, it was ridiculous."

"That would explain the sarcasm. It's quieter now?"

"Sure is. And were glad to see it. That guy's gone now, I guess?"

"Yeah. I was the patrol captain. I was responsible for that stuff he was doing, in a way, but I could not really control him, either. He was dangerous. The company, Anytown Security, would not get rid of him because they did not want to be troubled with finding someone to cover the slot. Eventually, I fired him…more or less."

"More or less?"

"Well, yes. I was hoping to get rid of him but couldn't. So I went to the post one night and really got on his back for not filing DARs five days in a row. He got mad and quit."

"Excellent work. Well, I am glad to see that you are moving up in the world, so to speak. Working here at Anytown Medical Clinic has got to be better than that."

"Worlds better! Good to see you, too. And stay safe."

"You too."

This exchange that took place was a great thing between that cop and me personally. He was not a bad guy after all. I thought he was a jerk, but that was just because he thought we were idiots for stirring up the fecal matter at the hotel. This overly enthused security professional who did not have a lick of common sense in his head actually thought that he was some kind of hero. He did not understand that what he was doing was very dangerous.

When you have someone who does not have a lot of self-confidence or self-esteem, who does not understand that nearly every person has value of some kind and deserves respect of some kind, there can be a lot unnecessary problems created. Such a "someone," in this case a security officer with handcuffs and the perfect targets upon which to employ them. He was creating victims of those around him. He perceived this as "power," much the way a narcissistic criminal deploys his or her trade on the human race and perceives their own actions as expressions of power.

It made Officer Doe *actually feel good* to do this people. Now, don't confuse this with the kind of situation in which security professionals feel good about taking a real criminal off the streets. The security professional who nabs the shoplifter or the burglar, or worse, or who makes a report to the police that leads to their arrest, has justification for feeling good. Such instances are fairly rare, but when a security pro who is in the business for the right reasons such as "serving the general good and protecting people and property" does the right thing at the right time for the right reasons, well…yeah. Heck, yeah! They deserve that good feeling. They did right.

But when a security officer oversteps their bounds and starts making trouble for the client and for the police, then we have a completely different story. For instance, a security officer once felt threatened by an employee of a client. This employee did not speak English. The security officer was asking that employee questions. The employee was just trying to leave for the day. He was in kitchen garb, dirty, obviously having just gotten off his shift.

The employee was trying to get home, but Officer Doe was trying to ask questions. When the man did not respond properly, Doe persisted and started to actually harass the man. This guy, a Spanish speaker, who again obviously had just gotten off kitchen duty, left the property. In this case, Doe should have just let him and then went back inside to ask the other client employees who that was. But instead Doe pursued him off the property, into a neighboring convenience store, and *pepper sprayed the guy* for not stopping to answer his questions.

In this case, Doe should have been arrested for aggravated assault. He used a weapon, chemical agent in this case, to stop a man who had done nothing wrong. Not only that, he did it off the property, where the security officer no longer had any right or authority to even speak to this man. So you see, we need to understand as a security community that we should not arm or give arrest powers under the client's policies to people who just don't know what they are doing, or who are emotionally unstable during a confrontation. These kinds get carried away and are dangerous. They should check trucks in at a loading dock or work at some isolated construction site and never be involved in confronting the public for wrongs committed.

BONGS AND CHILI PEPPERS

Security professionals have to make judgment calls every day, just like police, medics, and firefighting professionals. This is because security pros are often the very first people to find a situation. But because they are not "public servants" and work for private agencies, they don't get the lauds and honors other first responding agencies get. The fact is that a lot of work done by security officers goes unrecognized, simply because they quietly go about their duties and just come at night or in the day, depending on their shift.

So when do security pros call the cops? When do they not? Are there things that are technically violations of the law, but often overlooked. And why is that? Well…the police are not generally going to be appreciative of 911 being called for some dude tokin' a bowl. Let me review with you, wonderful readers of my tales, a couple of pot-smoking stories. You will soon see what I mean.

One night while on patrol at an apartment complex known for break-ins, I heard that dreaded sound: *clink!* Why is this the dreaded sound? Because it was not a *clunk!* The different is that the first sound is caused by human movement. The next sound is caused by stuff just falling, being knocked over by stray cats, or it is just an ambient sound.

You see, after being on night patrol for so many years, you learn that after nightfall, there is a different "feel" to the world. The human senses sharpen, because when you fill the role of a security officer, it is not just "your job" to be a lookout; it is your personal safety on the line. After a while, in my case, I developed a kind of extra sense for being able to evaluate noises. I could tell when something had just fallen over, when a load in a truck shifted, or when a noise was caused by a person. It is easiest to tell a human-caused sound when someone tries to stifle the noise or tries to put something back in place after it fell loose. At times someone would yelp or curse and remove all doubt.

One night I heard a certainly human-caused noise. It was behind someone's apartment. It was always a little scary to approach such a scene because you were always taking a chance of being injured with a blunt weapon or gunshot. Being raised by who I was, the Grim Reaper was a close companion. I was constantly on the alert and even more so on duty at night. So when I heard that noise, I assumed it was an attempted break-in. Taking advantage of being backlit by the ambient streetlights, knowing that they would cast a shadow and cover my identity, I shone my flashlight over the fence and onto the patio.

"Who's there? Come out with your hands up!"

"Um... I live here. I'm just um...sitting on my patio."

But at that moment, the pungent odor of cannabis burning assaulted my nostrils. I saw this long-haired, blond, big dude, his eyes as big as saucers, staring at me.

"Look, man," I started, "I smell what you doing, okay? Don't try to lie to me."

He just stared at me still and swallowed hard. Crap! Busted! I could tell by this haunted look that he was out on the back porch, toking at his bowl because he obviously *had* to be at 2:00 AM. I figured he had a woman inside that threatened him with, "If I ever see you smoking weed again..."

"Listen, dude, I don't care if you have to hide out here from your old lady to smoke a little grass. That's your property, your home and your own affair. I don't have any business in or asking you questions about your private life," he relaxed. "I am just here to make sure nobody is breaking into your place."

"Oh...oh man. Thanks. Hey, appreciate you having my back and all."

"Okay...you have a good night."

I turned off my lamp and resumed my patrol. No point raising heck about that. I was actually relieved.

Another cannabis story took place at some apartments. I saw these younger adults out on a balcony with a big old bong.

They saw me coming, and someone said, "Hey, security! We're over here smoking weed!"

"Security doesn't care!" I said with a shrug.

This goes back to realizing what the limitations of security officers are. We are not law enforcement officers. No one was in immediate danger. There was no fighting or arguing. And the local police just were not going to drop what they were doing to come out and see what a bong looks like. It was not going to happen. So I managed to score some points with the local young people who understood I knew the way things worked. Was I happy about it? No. Did I think that what they were doing was wrong? Yes. But at the same time… what could I really do? My authority comes from policy and not from law and reporting them to the property owner would have been a waste of time. Some things they were just not willing to enforce. So…neither was I.

One more pot story from the Anytown hotel.

I saw some guy go into his room and leave the door open. Then he started shouting for "Jaaa-aaane! Jaaaa-aaane!"

Well, in his room I saw this hookah pipe with yellow rubber hoses coming off both sides. It was certainly an item of paraphernalia. That and the string of chili peppers they had hanging from the fire sprinkler concerned me. Something seemed just more than a little "off" about the whole situation. I reported to the front desk agent, who asked me if I thought we needed police. I thought we did.

When the Anytown cop arrived, he did not seem to be very happy with me at all. He told me that it was legal to have the hookah. I understood that because there were "head shops" all over town where you could buy exotic smoking gear. My concern was that I did not want them to start getting crazy in the room, and I had this gut instinct that they were about to do just that. The cop told me that he probably could not even get into the room, but if he did, he might be able to find some marijuana ash around the edge of the pipe or something. But he did say that he would call for backup, because you never know.

The next cop came in and looked just as bored as the first one, both of them now onboard with wasting a bunch of time with this Barney Fife. I took them to where the room was, and one went around back to the outside window in case someone tried to jump out. I said that I would "wait right here," and they appreciated that. Good. This Barney knows when to stay out of the way. Both the policemen thought that these people would never even open the door. One cop out back, the other at the front door; both were ready and the cop at the front door knocked.

Next thing I know, the door *opened!* I never thought for a minute they would open up, but I was hoping the police would at least scare them into keeping any parties low key. Well, when the door opened, the cop at the door looked to his left and pushed the guy against the wall. Then PD Officer Doe talked into his shoulder mike, and the other cop came running. They handcuffed the guy at the door. Then suddenly "Jaaaa-aaaane" got involved because the cops grabbed and cuffed her next.

Then they started calling things in and searching the room. I reported to the desk and told them what the police were doing. I said that I would stand by there, because the PD would probably need to talk to me again. I was a respectful distance away, staying out of the way, and all I could see through the window was this big tuft of matted, nasty strawberry-blond hair bobbing up and down, kind of like the hair's owner was agitated. After about forty-five minutes of questioning, I had to make rounds and check the rest of the place.

Another half hour or so passed, and the desk called me up front. The police needed to talk to me. They collected my statement and said that they found the hookah pipe I just described, residue in the pipe, then they found powered cocaine, crack cocaine, and crystal methamphetamine...these folks were gonna PAR-TAY da night away! Not only that, but there was enough drug presence there to make it a felony. They told me that while they were running IDs on Dick and Jaaaa-aaane (!), they found she was wanted on a felony warrant in another county, but they could not legally share with me the reasons for the warrant. I was fine with that.

So in one night, I hand the Anytown a two-felony bust, with Jaaaa-aaaane (!) on some kind of "really wanted" list. The grumpy police were all of sudden happy with old Barney, and they were all excited about the turn of events from that night. The Anytown Security Agency was really very happy with me in the morning. I reported what I did, the outcome, and received congratulations. Now, on the other hand, and on the other side of the coin as it turned out, the hotel was not very happy about it. They were not *mad* at me, but thought it was not the best idea.

My whole take on this situation was that these people were going to do a bunch of nasty, illegal drugs in the room. With the chili peppers hanging on the sprinkler system, a whole string of fresh, not dried, red peppers, is a pretty heavy thing. What if they had gotten stoned and started tearing up the room or bumped into those peppers and knocked that sprinkler head off? We would have had a huge flooded mess and the Anytown Fire Department on the site just because I overlooked some people who had illegal drugs.

Like I said, it just did not feel right. I have stated above my position on people smoking pot. The pipe would not have been a big deal, except for the fact that they had the peppers strung up, and he had a big mouth calling for Jaaaa-aaaane (!). That whole scene just took a weird little turn, and it did not seem right. Oh…and in the end, the police cut the dude loose, and he came back to his room. The desk manager and I thought he was gone for good, but he came back, and because we did not cancel his room, he still had access to it. Kind of weird, that was, but at the same time, he did not do anything more than come back and get some sleep.

I just did extra patrols there in case he came out to make a fuss, but he did not. In his place, I would not have either…

As for me, if I ever had something like that happen again, I would take all their clothes and belongings and store them. Then I would have the desk cancel their room key and reservation. If the party came back, I would instruct them to move on and find another room. Gross misconduct like that does not deserve a room.

I TAWT I SPWAYED A PUDDY TAT

Back in my Anytown patrol days, we had an apartment complex that housed many feral cats in its dumpsters. Now, that may not sound like a "big deal," and normally, it would not be. But in this case, the dumpster cats were taking over the place. In this particular Anytown, the climate was warm most of the year, so when "young men's fancies turn to love" in the spring, these cussed cats would just reproduce all over the place. And boy, were they nasty, mean little buggers.

Now, it is not the procreative activities of the cats that bothered us; the feral felines at least showed good taste. Better than many humans, these cats kept their business private. What happened under the cars, in the dumpsters, and behind the bushes *stayed there.* They had no need to exhibit what nature expected of them. Nobody cared, nobody wanted to know, and the cats were fine with that.

But here was the problem—territorial disputes. Cats would howl and scream and fight all night long. And naturally, since security was also there all night long the residents of this fine tenement… I mean, semi-luxury living accommodation…thought this to be our problem to solve. After all, being on patrol and wearing a shirt with an embroidered badge on it automatically made us the primary "puddy tat awtawities," right? (Okay…yeah… I am a fan of Looney Tunes and Tweety Bird…and?)

So since we were informally, or perhaps even socially pressured into an "other duties as required" situation, we handled it. We would actually pepper spray these cats. We had to quiet them down somehow, and that was the only thing we could do short of shooting them. And no, that was not going to happen. Nobody was going to *shoot* cats in the dark in a full parking lot. We did not have any information on how else to handle the cats, so pepper spray it was. And it did work, without really hurting the cats.

Although I must admit that I do wonder about one cat that wandered out from under a car finally. That ugly, rough, feral cat, mean to the bone, was just *miserable.* It was soaked with pepper spray. It just kind of limped along, alive, but hurting. And seeing that cats have to lick themselves clean, well… I did sort of feel sorry for it. But what was I gonna do? Give him a bath? Nope! So…that cat just had a rough several days is all. Besides the chemical agent that some people mistakenly refer to as "mace," is actually pepper spray and only pepper spray.

Pepper spray is made from the oily extract of the capsicum chili pepper. Very hot stuff. And being oil-based, well, it does not really wash off well with water. We discovered one day when I was a real live, card-carrying EMT on the 911 circuit of Anytown, USA. The cops doused this guy with capsicum spray. He was miserable. And because he was miserable, and docile now, the firefighters tried to help him out by pouring normal saline all over his head and face. The results were different than intended. Not only did the saline fail to

176

rinse the pepper oil off the patient's face and eyes, but some of the oil, not blending with the water, floated on top of the water and followed the cascade on down the patient's shirtless body. So now, the man's torso was being fired up, and the water did not stop there! Oh yes... yes, it did! The pepper oil kept going on down to *there!* Yes! Yes, it did! Right down over the man's nether regions! Ouch! Oohh! Owie!

Naturally, the police were turning away and laughing. The firefighters not treating the patient were groaning, and the medics who were "just tryin' ta help" realized how helpless they were to do anything about it and just apologized as they put him into the ambulance. Talk about a "fire down below"! That was just crazy.

Now, I personally have never used pepper spray on a human subject. People who think of that form of non-lethal enforcement as some kind of be-all, end-all solution are dead wrong. OC spray, short for "oleoserum capsicum" does not just affect the subject to which it was applied. It affects everyone who handles the subject, including cops, medics, hospital staff and any/all persons who touch the subject. The problem is that you don't always know when the stuff is on your hands and if you touch your eye or nose...well, it's not good.

And when the stuff is in aerosol form, like any other airborne agent, it can follow airstreams and get into ventilation systems. As a mall cop at some Anytown, USA, mall, I unwittingly walked into a pepper spray zone. Some joker turned some of it loose in a crowded food court. When that stuff hit my nose, it was like the worst allergy attack, ever! It burned, it itched! My eyes instantly welled up! And that was just what I would call a micro-dose of the mist. I can't imagine what it would feel like on my face.

Many OC spray courses require the participants to be hit with a dose of the stuff, directly in the face. They do that so that the defendant's attorney cannot argue that the cruel security professional had no idea of how much his client would suffer when the security pro hit him with the OC. On the other hand, some courses don't require it, so it is probably more a matter of opinion on how well that legal argument works than it beingan actual necessity to get hit with OC, court or no court.

GEORGE E. KELLOGG, MSSM

I also want to make a point to people who use OC as defensive weapon on the street. At best, the OC spray is just a deterrent and a temporary distraction. Don't feel "safe" just because you are carrying pepper on your person. Also, you need be sure you check with your local jurisdiction on weapons laws. Be aware of where you are deploying and be careful when you are deploying it. You don't want it to get on you. Know that it probably will get on you.

I personally would only use it if I had no other choice. And I would spray the attacker right in the eyes, and then I would run!! While this stuff will burn a normal person like crazy, you must understand that on the street, you may not be dealing with a normal person. If your attacker is on the wrong drugs, he may not feel the effects of OC. If he is truly, violently mentally ill, he either won't feel it or he will feel it but just not care. So the lesson that I would leave here is that if you use OC, deploy the stuff and get away safe. Getting away from the attacker is more important than getting back at the attacker or putting the attacker in jail.

MY MAGLITE, MY BEST FRIEND

I want to open this one with saying that I have never had to strike a human being with a Maglite. In recent years, other brands of big ol' honkin' flashlights that are the perfect legal tool for any security officer to carry have also become available. An Asp collapsible baton is a weapon. A billy club is a weapon. A nightstick is a weapon. A small bat or other club is a weapon. But a flashlight is a flashlight is flashlight. And you can accurately report, "Mr. Badguy lunged at me with a knife, and I sidestepped and knocked him to the ground with my flashlight."

I used to carry my Maglite, the 4-D cell battery size, up my sleeve when I was a plainclothes training manager. I would for a time, hang the light from my belt on a specialized holder. But after walking around all night with that thing bouncing off my leg, I would actually develop bruises, so I quit doing that. Then I realized that with my long overcoat on, or even just my sport coat, I could carry it up my sleeve and it would not show. With some practice, I learned how to silently let it slide down my sleeve and into my hand.

So here is how the scene would play out. I would be walking up the street, on the sidewalk in Anytown, USA, to check on accounts. My job was to be sure that the security officers were on duty, healthy, a good fit, getting along and as happy as could be expected under the working conditions which were not always optimal.

I would be approached, usually for money. And I don't like being approached for money because I knew from people who used to be homeless that the ones asking for cash usually spent it on booze and drugs. Not only that, but it would get old, and half the time the people who approached me had already given my guys on post that night a hard time. I was not going to pay them for doing that.

They would see me walking, empty-handed, and then they would make the approach. As soon as I saw the approach, I would stop walking and make eye contact. Then while they were watching my eyes and telling about their wife's seizure, or how they are an unfortunate veteran, or how they had not eaten in three days but were still obese, I would slide my Mag into my hand. Then when they were just about to ask me for cash, I would simply raise my hand and show it to them. This two-inch thick round, eighteen-inch-long iron bar was enough to make them say, "Oh. I see."

When they saw, and I knew they saw, I would bid them a good night and tell them to never approach me again. It was none of their business what I was doing. I would not explain myself, I would simply let them come to their own conclusion about the who, what, when, where, why, and how of it all. After a while, homeless people would just skirt around me. Word got out that the guy in the suit or overcoat was not a friendly.

As I said before, I never had to hit a person with my Maglite. But there was an event that was sort of oddball. Somehow a cat had gotten into the Anytown hotel, in the basement. Clearly, the cat was feral. And a nasty black cat to boot. Now Kitty was about twenty feet from the exit door but would not move. I stepped out of the way, to let Kitty out. Kitty would not move. I got behind Kitty, but Kitty would not move. I "shooshed" Kitty, but Kitty would not move. I stepped closer, and this time Kitty *did* move.

But when Kitty moved, it repositioned itself into a posture that indicated a fight was about to happen. Kitty started to yowl, but when it became a deep-throated demonic *growl*, I had to act. As the cat reared back, I reached in, and with a sweeping arc, *clink!* I popped Kitty across its knucklehead. I kinda felt badly about that right then. But I also knew that the cat was going to attack me because it was a wild animal. This was not like Halloween, TJ, Pickles, or any of the other cats (and dogs) I have lived with over the years. This was a nasty cat. And it had to go.

I don't know if the Kitty ran off of to die or found some feline Excedrin PM to sleep it off somewhere, but I am pretty sure if Kitty lived, he had a headache.

9/11: A TIME TO REMEMBER

When I was a security officer, I was also an EMT. I kept the certification up to use in the field. At the time, EMT/Security was kind of a thing. I don't know what the trend is now, because I have been clear of the actual security field for a while, but back in those days, it was a fairly popular thing to do. The reason for that was that it takes a lot of the same personality traits to be a security officer and/or an EMT.

First of all, you cannot mind the odd hours. And I do mean *odd*. The hours, the lack of sleep, poor diet, all of it can happen to both the EMT and the security pro. Plus, you must be able to respond to bad things at the drop of a hat. You need to go from possibly sitting still or just walking to action without even really thinking about it. It also takes courage of a sort to deal with things firsthand. Both positions are a type of first responder position. This is one of the main things I want the reader to remember from this book.

The stories range from funny to shocking, but all of them together reflect the true nature of the security professional's job. With so many similarities between the two types of workers, EMT and security blend very, very well. This is partly because, as you have seen, security professionals at the officer level can very frequently come upon medical issues or other situations where medical training can be of great value.

On this particular job, I was an EMT, and I was trained as an incipient stage firefighter. Before you get too impressed, all that means is that I could put out a trash can fire and/or contain a fire and wait for the real firefighters to arrive and save the day. We had fire gear, the heavy coat and pants, the SCBA mask and tank, and we even a small fire engine. I must say that it was a ball driving a fire engine. I did like that part of the job.

Well, after some time the nature of the post and the people started to get to me, and I ended up leaving the post. I could not handle the crude locker room conversations and generally uncouth behavior of my coworkers. Leaving was easier than trying to change the others. For that place to become comfortable enough for me, so many guys and gals would have had to change their habits around me and I surely would have become unpopular. Then I would have been eventually forced out socially. It is very dangerous to not be socially popular in a place where your safety may lay in the hands of that guy sitting across from you.

But that aside, I had been on the job only for a couple of weeks or so. I went home at the end of the night shift, as usual. I went to bed. After my several hours of sleep, usually four or five—and poor sleep it was—I woke up. I went out to the living room and found something very unusual. My children were home from *school*. And it was only 11:00 AM. Then I saw that they could not be "hooking" school because my wife was sitting there with the kids. They all had the same dumbfounded expressions on their faces. Their eyes wide and mouths were about half open; they would not look up from the TV.

"What is going on?" I asked, greatly concerned.

My wife looked up. "I did not want to wake you, because you needed some sleep, and there's nothing you could do about this anyway."

"What are you talking about? Something on the news?"

"The United States is under terror attack. They hit the Pentagon, the Twin Towers in New York have been destroyed, and I think they got the White House.

"What? What is this?" I stood there for a moment, trying to take it all in. "It's like the movie *Independence Day.* I gotta make a call. I called a buddy of mine who had some loose ties to the FBI. He went aside at his job as a security manager and quietly told me that no, the White House did not get hit. The plane that was on their way to hit it got taken down by our own people."

At the time, we both thought that our "own people" were the US military. But later we learned about, "Let's roll," and how passengers on the plane tried to take the plane back from the terrorists, who then grounded the plane into Pennsylvania soil rather than to be completely defeated.

I knew that we would need to put in overtime at the post. They would need more people, and we would need to replace some folks, as people almost always have to go out of town during a crisis like this. Sure enough, there would be plenty of OT for a while. But I did not fully understand why. Then after I arrived at work for a double shift, I was told by the shift supervisor that many of our employees on the post were retired NYFD. I almost puked. The shock of all this was bad enough, but to see that the guys I worked with and for were going to go help retrieve the bodies of their friends, or what may be left of them, it was almost overwhelming.

For a memorial and show of support, I put in the back window of my car "*NY (SPACE) FD*" and in the space, I put an EMT sticker that was basically a rectangle, but rounded at the top. The overall and unintended effect was chilling. In the back window of my car, when the sun was coming through the window just right, the shadow cast over my car's rear ledge made it look like a headstone from Arlington National Cemetery between the NY and the FD. It was a stark reminder of how things could change.

Things were still up in the air, as to what really happened. But what we did know was that we were all Americans, we had suffered a terrible, intentional tragedy, and somebody was going to *pay*. The White House still stood, our country still stood, though many lives were lost. America would be changed forever; we the people are resolute.

In the weeks that followed, we found out from near daily reports from our friends who went to New York that several of their own had been killed. Some bodies, or at least portions, of our friends' old comrades at arms had been recovered. These were the bodies of the NYFD personnel who rushed into the buildings before anyone knew that the towers were about to collapse, also killed, and these people were given some mention but not as much, were two medics who were in an ambulance at the scene when the big collapse occurred.

I cannot say enough about this event and how lives changed. The 9/11 attack also changed the face of American Homeland Security forever, and with that changed an entire industry. The private security sector started to be taken more seriously. Shortly after 9/11, they began offering college courses and even advanced degrees in security management. *Counterterrorism* became a big buzz word. I did now know how soon the MSSM would become available, so I did not really consider looking into the schooling at that time. I looked afterward, when the program was entrenched with a solid curriculum, and I went to school then.

Speaking of 9/11 itself and not so much about the post, I have often reflected since then on how the inspiration for the attack came about. There was a book written in 1994. It was written by late author Tom Clancy. The book *Debt of Honor* was the tale of a Japanese airline pilot who, for some reason, blamed the United States government for the death of his son. The pilot commandeered a passenger jet airliner, its tanks full of fuel. He did so by cutting the throat of his copilot and just outright stealing the plane before its passengers boarded. He then, just like the "divine wind" (kamikaze) flew the plane into the US capitol building while all three branches of the federal government were in session. The result was that the entire government was dead. All except for the main character of the book. He was, I think, secretary of Defense, and by default, suddenly became the president of the United States.

Now, since Osama bin Laden was once a US ally of sorts, and was educated at Harvard University, I wonder how much he read

Tom Clancy? I will just leave it at that. Certainly, Tom was an excellent author, the most technically correct military author ever to write in the United States, and I *do not* hold him in any way responsible for that tragic day in US history. If there is no connection between the two events, there is certainly a coincidental correlation.

And I have learned during my career that when things seem to neatly fit together, they usually do so for a good reason. The perfectly interlocking pieces of a jigsaw puzzle are simply not cut by accident.

REALLY EXPENSIVE COLD PIZZA

During this whole 9/11 event, while the entire country was still reeling from the effects of the terror attacks, I ended up switching jobs after the NY firefighters came home from Ground Zero to the firefighting security post. I was given an offer from my FBI-connected friend. I went to work with him at another EMT / security post, one where I could wear a shirt and tie. I really liked that job.

Due to the nature of the heightened alert and various factors that caused concern, our post was big on the standardized color system. Different colors would equal different levels of threat. It would go something like the following:

> Green = Low
> Blue = Guarded
> Yellow = Elevated
> Orange = High
> Red = Severe

And the company I now worked for really was into that whole color-coding and loved going ape-nuts over the colors.

On this one sunny and lovely day, we happened to be at terror-alert level orange. Now, understand that everyone who worked there was drilled over and over on how the color chart worked. Therefore, everyone with a pulse knew that "orange" was serious business, and they knew that there were things you just did not do during that color's alert status.

Basically, all the rules that the company normally had would be subject to stricter enforcement. For instance, everyone was required to wear a company ID badge. This was especially important during orange alert. A forgotten badge would normally be a "wear it next time" reminder from a security team member. But during orange alert, it meant a trip to either your supervisor or to HR if your supervisor was not available. See how that works? Everyone would get all upset over it being an "orange," day and things would be enforced at a higher level.

That being said, I was watching the cameras and *ZOOM!* This car came roaring across the parking lot. Speeding across the parking lot was forbidden. Oh, let me mention one thing too; the security team was required to enforce parking regulations with paper tickets that the company would issue. When someone messed up, we'd write a ticket, leave them a copy, and give a copy to the bosses. The bosses then decided if the employee would be forgiven or if they would have the ticket taken out of their paycheck that period.

So anyway, here went this car zooming across the parking lot. The driver parked in a handicapped parking space, crossways, so his car was occupying two spaces. One handicapped parking, one not so designated. Then he jumped out of his car and ran in through the main entrance to the building. He did not stop to badge in at the door, instead doing a classic "piggyback" maneuver by letting someone else badge in ahead of him, grabbing the door and entering without using his own badge.

At this point, we were not sure of this man's identity. We could not see him well enough by the camera to recognize his face or see if he had a badge. I went outside with one of my officers, we got in the security SUV and jetted over there. We parked outside the building, right by the car, and I got out. I didn't recognize the car. I could either go in myself or send the other guy. I was just about to go in when we see this young guy smiling and waving at us.

"Hey! It's just me!" he exclaimed. He was holding a flat cardboard box.

"Who are you? Do you have an employee ID? May I see it?"

He then handed me his badge. He said, "I just wanted to run upstairs and grab this last whole pizza before someone else got it."

"Well, you know we are on a code orange terror alert status, right?"

"Yeah."

"So you know that you are not supposed to speed or piggyback your way into the building."

"Yeah...and?"

"Well, human resources may or may not opt to talk to you about this."

"I don't care..."

"Okay, sir, thanks for your time. I fully understand."

My next couple of hours were spent creating an airtight case for everything I did. I wrote an incident report, and I also wrote him a ticket that read like a shopping list:

Parking in Handicapped/Restricted Space...$75
Speeding...$30
Invasive/Over-the-Line Parking...$40

This ticket was about the biggest I had ever written—$145 for the whole thing. And my report read, in summary, that this young man did not have respect for the rules. While he was not rude, he seemed indifferent to his employer's concerns over terrorism. His closing remark when I told him human resources may or may not decide to contact him was, "I don't care!"

Now had this kid been at least apologetic, it would not have gone so hard on his paycheck, but he flat-out stated that he did not care for the employer's rules. And I believed him. I knew that he did not care, and so I wasn't going to waste any of my time trying to correct him or warn him. I figured I would leave this one up the HR staff to handle. I wrote the report and stapled both copies of the ticket to it so that HR could give him a copy when they interviewed him. I thought that I would let them have that honor instead of my dropping it into his mailbox.

Word got back to me, and I found out that the employer was not messing around. They not only brought him in for an interview, but they also suspended him for three working days. Then he brought up the ticket, and HR told him they had nothing to do with that. He had to go talk to security about it. Seeing that security was the department which referred his nasty self to the HR department, he was not likely to find a lot of mercy. He didn't. Security management decided that they would not back off any part of that ticket. Not after he did what he did.

This was actually a classic case of what one's attitude can do in a situation where one has been caught. In this particular situation, had my young friend expressed any contrition, it would have probably not been quite so hard on him. The punishment he received was pretty harsh, and it was surprising. He did some things wrong, yes, he certainly did, and he incurred the maximum penalty the human resources department was willing to dish out. Normally, they were not so hard on people. In fact, I would say that a lot of times they were fairly forgiving.

In this case though, they had to make an example. Why? Because in this case, he violated security protocols that the client took very seriously. They lost several good people during 9/11 because when the Twin Towers fell, it took one of their main offices down, with all hands aboard. *None* of their employees who went to work that day ever saw the light of day again. The company had a very employee-dedicated culture. They loved to coddle and spoil their people. They were a tight-knit bunch. The 9/11 losses were devastating. And for this young man to blatantly break rules which he clearly understood and then to say "I don't care" when I told him he might be approached later by human resources? Well, that could not go without some kind of response.

I added everything up that happened to him, and it cost him over three hundred bucks. This is a prime example of letting the emotion of greed over one's reason. This caused him to lose dollars to save pennies if you do the math. He lost $30 for every $10 he saved. A three-to-one loss ratio. His investment in this case lost him 300 percent.

That was *one expensive cold pizza!!* I hope he enjoyed it.

FORGIVE ME, I'M A KLEPTOMANIAC

One day, in Anytown mall, we were having this nice "normal" (is there such a thing?) day. Then we got a standard shoplifting call from the little knickknack shop. Okay, that is fine. We report to the store and the clerk says that she saw this lady pull something off the shelf and put it into her purse. She watched her throughout the store, and when the lady was about to leave, she stopped and tried to get the thing back, but she would not admit she had anything. Pretty standard, blah, blah, blah. It looked like a good catch.

Well, the manger did not really have a back office in her shop, so we had to now march down the middle of the mall. Two of us security personnel, the alleged shoplifter and the store manager. Yay! The other merchants in the mall just sort of nodded knowingly when we walked by. They've all seen it before; every store was familiar with thievery. It always looked the same. The manager was usually grim and aggravated. The shoplifter solemn and either contrite or defiant. Security looking like, "Yep, we got *another* one. Another genius on their way to either fines or jail, depending on what happens."

We all walked into the security office and the police had already arrived by the time we trudged our way there. The cop gave the usual "So what's going on?" routine. We said that the manager was the witness and we backed out. It was her show now. In a few seconds' summary, she told the cop what she saw.

Then the policeman looked at the suspect and said, "Okay, let's see what's in your purse."

The lady opened her purse and started pulling things out: wallet, keys, change…and then that thing we were looking for. The knickknack. Okay, open-and-shut case. We had the witness who kept their eye on the person, the witness saw the selection and concealment of item on their person, and saw the person pass by the last point of payment without stopping to pay and was clearly on their way out of the store before the witness stopped her. Good catch and a solid case. The cop was about start processing the shoplift and had his ticket book out and ready. I was getting my trespass form out to start my report.

Then we all stopped. Something happened. She reached back into her purse. What was she reaching for? Out came another knick-knack. Then another. Then three more. Then a handful. Five, ten, fourteen…more than *twenty* items were in her purse. Now it was time for the camera. The top-of-the-line technology for its day. A Polaroid Instamatic camera. Point, click, and *bzzzzzt!* Out came the picture that developed in the open air, right before your beady little eyeballs. Seriously! That was how these cameras worked! Google it!

So we took the photos and the evidence and started a report. We needed the lady's ID and so on. We had to also start tracking down the stores these things belonged to. Some had price tags right on them with the store name, some things were not so easy to identify, and we had to try to recall where she stole them from. We had to call the stores to come pick up their stuff, but that would happen soon after the investigation was completed. The worst part was that *every* item had to be accounted for…individually. It was going to be one long report for me. At least a couple of hours' worth of my time to process all this stuff. Great.

In the midst of all this surprise and aggravation, she suddenly made the announcement that no report was going to be necessary. *What did she say?*

We all stopped and looked at her.

The cop asked her, "What do you mean, 'No, report is necessary'? We have to file reports on this."

"No, there is no report because I am not guilty of anything."

"You freely admitted that you took all this stuff."

"Yes."

"So what do you mean by saying you are not guilty?"

"Well, I have a paper here," she pulled a slip out of her wallet, "that says I am a kleptomaniac. It is from my psychiatrist."

The policeman did not even look at the paper. He did not care, and neither did we.

"Look, ma'am, even if that says you are a kleptomaniac, and even if it is from your psychiatrist, it does not give you the right to just go around stealing stuff. You still committed the crime, we still have to do our reports, and you still have to get the ticket. You can appear before a judge, and they will decide in court if you are guilty of a crime or not. And…by the way…these people here are going to process a trespass against you. Correct, security?"

"Yes," I said, "you will be trespassed from the mall for a year. And for what it's worth, lady, if I knew I had a severe problem with alcohol and my doctor said that I was an alcoholic, I certainly would not go hang around in a bar. You *need* to stay out the mall. We are probably doing you a favor."

So she took her ticket, we got the stolen stuff back to the stores as best we could, and that was that. I never got a call to appear in her case. I don't know, and again really don't *care*, about how justice was served. I did not see her again in that mall and was all the happier for it.

The thing is, though, in cases like this, there a lot that goes on behind the scenes. It takes a lot of time and man hours to go through all the stuff that was stolen. The more individual items there are to log, the more time it takes to complete the process. The items must be individually logged. You may do some grouping, say, "Five Snickers bars, three Hershey bars with nuts, and a Butterfinger were found to belong to Rottenteef Candy Store." But you cannot say "Various candy bars, thirty in number, were found to belong to Rottenteef Candy Store." Everything had to be accounted for properly to make the case solid. The exception would be truly piecemeal things like screws or hard candies

Then all the calls had to be made to each of the stores who had things stolen from them, so they could send someone to pick them up. We did this as a courtesy. We did not have to do it, but we wanted to get the stuff back to the proper owners. One might think that the other stores would want to press charges, but that is not the way shoplifting works. If the individual was not caught in that store, then they did not get to press charges. We just treated it as lost and found and they came and picked up their stuff.

BLUE JEAN BLUES

I learned that shoplifting can actually become a very serious matter. In fact, it can become felonious in the extreme. The law, justly, sees a kid grabbing a CD out of "record store" (do they call them that anymore?) differently than it sees an organized shoplifting ring. I learned the difference when a man in a wheelchair, who was unfortunately afflicted with brittle legs due to a form of dwarfism, was tagged by the cops. There was a loss prevention agent at one of the big retail stores who caught this guy on video taking blue jeans and stuffing them under the cushion on his wheelchair. This looked like a normal shoplift, but the guy was out the door and off the premises before they could anyone to respond.

Well, they thought..."Okay, that was that...one got away." But then the guy *came back*. He did the same thing. This time they got the police involved and the cop said to just let it go and see where he goes. Get a plate number. I don't know if the police had a case working against this guy, or if the cop present had a gut feeling, but they let him go just to see what he would do. He made several trips back and forth from the store to his car, from the car and back to the store, each time taking more and more pairs of blue jeans.

Finally, a police officer followed him out to his car. He saw all the jeans in the open trunk, as the man in the wheelchair was loading more jeans. The man suddenly noticed the cop standing there and slammed the trunk shut.

"You're too late. I saw in the trunk already. You had it open. I need to you to come with me please, sir. Right now. You, sir, are under arrest. Don't try to leave."

The man in the wheelchair, now an alleged shoplifter, came back into the mall with the police. Since the event had spilled out into the mall property, the mall security team was involved fully. I was called down to the security office to take the report. I thought it was going to be another mundane, plain ol' shoplifting case involving a ton of paperwork and time, but this time, the case actually became very interesting.

There were actually several police officers involved in this case. We had the loss prevention team of the anchor store involved directly this time. That was not usually the case, but they made the initial call, tracked the shoplift, and called the police themselves. The only reason mall security was involved was because, as I had mentioned, the alleged crime had spilled over into mall property. The parking lot was outside of the anchor store's "tenant lease line," which is a legal boundary; this boundary determines where the store's property ends, and the mall property begins. Since the parking lot was the mall's property, and that was where to cops tagged the suspect, we got involved. There was only one store and the parking lot involved in the case. More stores would have made the case more complex, with more accusers and more merchandise to process.

When I arrived at the scene, the police already had custody of course, but they were using our office as a matter of convenience. We certainly made all our resources available to them. The cops in this mall actually had a certain kind of respect for our particular mall security team, because we handled things the way police would in as many instances as possible. This was because a retired police lieutenant was running our security team. That was both good and bad, but we will review the reasons for this in a different section of this book.

On scene, there were a couple of people in plainclothes. You could always pick out the cops. They have a different look about them than loss prevention. The police always look less naive, or something like that. There is a certain, special kind of "tough" that veteran police have with their mannerisms. The police were interviewing the suspect and loss prevention stood by quietly as I did, speaking only when spoken to. Answer the question simply, comply with the request, and then shut your mouth. Nobody wanted to say anything to blow this bust.

It was of an especially sensitive nature, this case, because we had a handicapped or disabled individual on our hands, in our custody. This man was about thirty years old, had a normally proportioned torso, and a normal voice. He was a good-looking Latino man with the customary thick, black hair and a thick moustache. He was well dressed in some expensive-looking casual, athletic team jersey clothes. He wore an attractive, and thick, gold necklace which was unmistakably real. Very colorfully dressed, poised, and calm, this man's only abnormally striking feature was his legs. Those legs, that poor guy was born with, were stumped. His legs were "dwarfed." His feet were small, I was almost sure, but he was wearing normal-sized, very pricey, athletic shoes.

In a very calm and deliberate manner, he described his crime to the police.

He said that he was here at the mall, and yes, he knew he was under arrest for shoplifting. He stated that he was willing to talk to the police. He said that he did not want a lawyer present at this time. He told the police, everyone in the room really, that yes, he had taken the jeans. He had taken them for resale. He would not relate who his buyer or buyers were, but they were for resale. He said that this is what he did for his living and this is what enabled him to "dress this way" and own what he owns. He was very matter-of-fact and appeared to be unruffled by his arrest. Maybe he was just accustomed to it; maybe he expected it, who knows? But he did not appear to very upset by it.

The police took his statement, writing it by hand. When the suspect was finished talking, they closed the statement. They asked him to sign it. He refused, kindly, to sign it. The cop said that it was not a big deal to him whether or not he signed it because they would just write "REFUSED" on it and it made no difference to them. Naturally, they would have preferred the signature. You always hear on the cop shows about the "signed confession." The signed confession is always preferred. Makes the case go easier for the prosecution, I suppose. But in this case, they were denied a signature.

The suspect then turned the conversation to *why* he was doing it. I was interested in hearing the reason why he was doing this for a living. He told us that in his medical condition, he could either go on Social Security and live a crummy life on a pittance or do whatever he had to do to make his living. This was a bright and good-looking man, obviously capable. Certainly, there must have been other avenues for him to pursue besides *theft* for a living. Just not being able to walk certainly did not justify his shoplifting for a living. The why of it does not matter in court. The judge really does not care *why* you acted the way you did. The judge is there to deal out justice, according to the laws that are on the books. I have never heard of revised statutes in any of the fifty states, which said, "Oh, by the way…everything in this shoplifting/theft statute? Yeah, you can forget about that if you had *really good* reason for doing it!"

The police were finished with him and asked me if I had any business with him. They knew we normally liked to trespass the shoplifters. Most juvenile cases we trespassed for six months, unless they were really nasty then we gave them a year. For a kid, not going to the mall was like getting a prison sentence. We knew that, but we wanted to teach them a lesson. Sometimes, my boss would give a kid less time or even forgive a trespass if the parents came in and reasoned with him. By "reason with him," I mean that they came in to see him, were generally embarrassed, were willing to understand why the mall security did what they and made a promise to supervise the kid at the mall from now on, if he would lift the trespass. Sometimes, if he believed the parents, he would let the kid come back, but only if Mom or Dad were there supervising the child.

In this case though, because he was not only a shoplifter, but kept coming back into the mall to steal and was unrepentant, he was trespassed for "life." He was to never return to the mall. We rarely did that with shoplifts, but this was above the norm. It was over the top and this cat's attitude was pleasant enough, but he said, "Don't worry homie… I will be back. Whenever I want to, I will be back."

I reiterated to him the nature of the trespass, and that if he did come back he would likely be arrested. I never did see him again, whatever the case.

The police, on their end, were going to up the charges from simple shoplifting to "burglary." I don't know if they succeeded or not. I never heard back. The reason they were citing burglary is because this guy left the store with the jeans, came back, loaded up some more, and came back. I don't know how successful the prosecution was.

This was really something to see though. It truly was. How many people can say they helped prosecute a *dwarf* for burglary?

DURING A FUNERAL? SERIOUSLY?

We had this young man who returned to the mall after he had been trespassed. But the thing is, that in the rush of everything that happened, he never signed the form and did not realize or maybe forgot that he was not supposed to come back to the mall. Anytown mall had its ups and downs and kept things pretty quiet. But they ended up in the papers over this one. The mall itself did nothing wrong, and neither did the security team, but the fact that it happened on their property made this one a story for the papers. Let me explain.

I was absent on the day that this event occurred. There were a couple of young men who ended up being prosecuted for trespassing and for a stolen vehicle. The trespassing charge was not issued by the mall, but it was issued by a church. The church was of a Christian faith and we know how common funerals are in Christian churches. Well, the church ended up getting involved in a police chase. Like the mall, they had done nothing at all wrong or incorrect. The Anytown mall and Anytown church were both victims of circumstance.

What had happened was these two young men decided that on such a beautiful day in the mall parking lot, it would be a wonderful idea to steal a truck. They did not look around very well. If they had, well, they would have not picked that moment to become truck thieves. Somehow—and I am guessing that the owner of the truck and the cops just happened to be in the same vicinity at the same time—because somehow, the owner of the truck managed to call the police and the police managed to catch the thieves in the act before they were able to leave the mall property.

When the two men saw that they were being chased by the police, they decided to ditch the truck. Once they ditched the truck, they of course ran from the truck and went any old way they could go. One of the men was caught right away. The other managed to run a little further and he got onto the property of Anytown Church. Then, truly desperate and banking on the idea that no one would look up, he got on the roof of the church. But there were two problems.

First problem, the church was roofed in red clay tiles. These tiles were shaped like half-pipes. They were not made to be walked upon with any degree of stealth. So, when that panicky young man was running across them it made a noise that could be heard throughout the building. And you know what else? You guessed it! The church was not only occupied, but it was occupied by mourners attending a funeral.

That was the part emphasized in the papers, the funeral. The fact that all of these events came together just right to create the perfect storm is just amazing. The fact that one of the car thieves returned to the mall was even more amazing. He had been charged with a felony, and I guess that he was out on bail. But whatever the reason he was still on the street, he was back in the mall. We saw him, matched him to a photo in our "Rogue's Gallery" and brought him in on the trespass.

The cops did respond and because of his good attitude toward it all, they did not haul him in. The police did not see any point in arresting him, unless we wanted it done for some reason. We really did not. This was the first time I had seen what I could call a "real" criminal on the street, especially one who was in the newspaper. He was a fine-looking young man, he was very frank about what he had done, was calm, amiable, very friendly to us. He was so far removed from what I believed a felon to be... I was new in the security field at this time. I had not seen any real criminals other than shoplifters and vandals up to this point.

I thought this "felon" was going to look mean and nasty, have a tattoo, a sour disposition, curse every other word, etc. But this young man was kind and polite. He understood that we had a job to do. He was sorry that he had caused such a fuss just by showing up again, unaware of his trespass. He was quite contrite and regretted what he did. It was more of a theft of opportunity thing for him and his friend; it was not a chop-shop kind of crime. He was not a serial thief. Now that I think about it, I think he and his friend were runaways or something like that. He said that they were walking, they had been walking for a long time, and they found that truck with the keys in it. He asked his friend if he was tired of walking, and that was how they ended up stealing the truck.

He said that he was sorry the moment they did it, and even more so when the police were chasing them. Then, when he ended up on the roof of a *church* of all buildings, and to end up there during a *funeral?* That was just the worst. He really felt bad about it. He was about the most sincere and introspective person I ever busted at the mall. This guy was a criminal, yes, and needed to be punished, yes, but I don't think that he was going to make a career of it. I don't know where he is now, of course, but I do wish him the best.

GUNSHOTS AND STABBINGS

One night, when I was on call, studying for my master's and working from home by monitoring the phone and responding to any calls that came out in the dark of the night, something happened. I heard the distinct *pop, pop* of gunfire. I instantly and rapidly moved to my window. The blinds were down. My wife was telling me to not go out there, and I firmly assured her that was not my intention. I could tell from the sound that the shots were very close to our apartment and I wanted to be certain that they were not in our parking lot. I had my phone in hand, 911 already dialed, and carefully peered through the blinds after turning off the main living room light.

I saw, out in the middle of the street at our main intersection, a man lying in the crosswalk. I saw someone standing over him. I was not sure if I saw a gun or not, but I gave the description of the scene to the operator. Then, suddenly, blue and reds lit up the entire scene.

"Wait! It looks like you've already got a unit on scene!" I said to the 911 operator.

"We have unit on scene?" she asked quizzically.

"Apparently, yes. I see red and blue lights and it looks a police officer."

"Let me verify that… Okay, yes, we have a unit on scene."

"Do you need anything else from me?"

"No, but thank you for calling in."

I don't know all of the story behind the shooting. I don't know the motive, other than one man obviously had some kind of issue with the other. The shooter did not see the police officer's patrol car behind him when he fired the shots. The papers reported in the next day or two that the victim was hit twice in the abdomen, but he did survive. He lived through being shot twice at nearly point-blank range. I have no doubt that the man survived in part because the police were right there and able to get medical attention right away for the victim, plus the fact that the shooter did not get a chance to finish the job by putting one into his head while he was on the ground.

Another violent incident I witnessed was a stabbing. You see things in movies or on the TV, but television and movies really cannot capture the moment. Not truly. They imitate it pretty well in their screenplays, but the real thing is completely different. When you are not in the safety of your home or a movie theater…more on that later…it is just…*different*. For one thing, you know that you can get killed. You are there. You are seeing it real time, and brother, let me tell you something. It happens so fast. It just does.

One night while on patrol, we decided to get into our car and cruise the perimeter of the construction site we were securing. It is always a good idea, to get the lay of the land whenever you are in a security position in a strange neighborhood. That way, you can see the areas where problems may potentially arise or from where gunshots could be fired in rougher neighborhoods, etc. This helps in particular with larger sites and limited security manpower. You can figure out the best and safest places where security may post to prevent problems and keep your men from getting hurt at the same time. You want to establish the tricky balance between staying safe and still keeping the property secure.

We were cruising nice and slow, working the area, looking things over and we saw two vehicles parked in the road, facing each other. Two groups of people got out of the cars, dressed in normal civilian clothes. No gang colors or any other apparent indications of trouble. The groups confronted each other, and I to this day don't know if this was drug deal gone wrong or some kind of confrontation, but we saw one guy suddenly lunge forward, make some kind of quick motion with his elbow and his group hastily retreated to his vehicle. We thought that was odd.

Then we saw why the lunge and escape took place: the second group grabbed their man, who was holding his belly and sagging to the ground, wincing. They grabbed him as a group and quickly hustled him into their van. They shut the door to the van and sped off. My partner and I looked at each other, our mouths open. We had just witnessed a stabbing! We had no plate numbers or anything definitive to tell 911, and it was not on our property. Nothing to report, no evidence, off the property…well…we just let it go. It would have been a waste of time to make the call. That was a pretty strange thing. It truly was.

When I reflect on this night, and the event, it seemed surreal the night that it happened. It is frightening to consider how quickly the whole thing went down. In and out. Man collapses. That was it. Just that fast. That lightning-quick motion and someone's whole life changed, right along with everyone else involved with his life. Friends, family, co-workers, acquaintances…everyone "knows that Freddy was stabbed." And how bad were his injuries? We had no way to tell, of course, because we were in a car ourselves and they rushed him off so fast that we were not even sure of what we saw until we pieced it together. But when I realized what it was, and considered what I know about abdominal injuries, this was potentially life-threatening. It all depends on where the blade hit him, what kind of blade, what organs or blood vessels were hit, whether or not the knife was all rusty and dirty, etc. There are a lot of things to consider with that kind of injury.

I hope his friends got him to the hospital, and did it fast.

HUFFING GOLD ON THE CURB

One pleasant, sunny day while I was just patrolling the Anytown mall, I decided to do a foot patrol outside along the front curb just outside the plaza. I did not see anything unusual, but I did *smell* something odd. I caught a whiff of paint. Spray paint. I followed my nose to a particular spot on a curb. The spot was colored golden, and I reached down and touched it. Fresh, all right. Recently sprayed. I became concerned. I looked around quickly to determine what else may have been marked by the paint. Gangs were big on tagging various properties in Anytown and I was concerned that we might have a new gang in town using gold as one of their colors.

But seeing no such evidence, I did see a girl standing near the curb, watching me. She was dressed in Dickies flannel, pants and boots. This was common gang attire at the time. Then I noticed something strange. She had gold paint near her nose, and on one of her hands. Was she so desperate for a buzz that she was using the space between the sloped curb and the pavement to huff paint? It was pretty obvious what was going on from what I saw. So I asked her where that gold paint came from. She looked away from me, trying to turn my attention, but I would not fall for that. Turning your head away from someone you are confronting can get you killed. At least two security professionals I know of *died from head shots by looking away*.

I kept my eye on her and her hands. Good thing too, because I noticed a bulge in her sleeve. When she made her hand motion, I heard a very distinct *clink!* I adjusted my position to a forty-five-degree angle toward her. This gave her less surface area to attack, less access to my vital organs, and a better angle from which to defend myself from any direction. Whatever she was carrying, if it saw the light of day, she was gonna get put on the ground. HARD. That may not sound very nice of me, but now I was dealing not with a teenage girl, but with a suspected gang member who might just have impaired her judgment by huffing paint.

She saw my posture change, and with it, the whole flavor of this particular scene. It was now a dangerous scene with at least one chemical agent present, a potential gang member, and only Heaven knows what up her literal sleeve. It got a little tense, and I called this situation in on my radio. I called for a backup officer to come to the plaza area. We cannot forget that not only could she have some of her "homies" nearby, but she was a minor female. Being a male adult, one preparing to take to custody of a minor female, I could not take any chances or leave any opening for her to make claims of covert fondling or inappropriate behavior on my part.

Now that backup was on the way, I told her rather firmly that she needed to reach up her sleeve very slowly, with two fingers only, and remove from her sleeve whatever object was there. She slowly and carefully removed a spray can of gold paint. Bingo! I caught me a huffer. Now what to do with her? We could let her go, but considering the whole situation, I was not going to become liable for whatever she did by letting her go. For instance, if she were to take her paint can, leave and then huff again, I could be legally responsible for her dying or getting hurt because I knew what she was doing and did not act on it after she was in my custody. I was not going to let that happen. And even though my first thoughts and concerns were for my own welfare and liability, I did also believe that it was in her best interest to get caught and maybe become discouraged about huffing paint. It was a very dangerous practice and she needed to stop this before it did kill her.

So we took her to the office, with me carrying the evidence. Then she started crying and begging for us to not call the police. It was too late for that though. The die cast, the call was made. The cops were en route. No calling them back now. We took the girl to the security office and waited for the PD. She probably got her way a lot by crying. She tried that with us but got nowhere. The cop who came, a strong female, could not care less about the pretty girl's tears. Along with the tears, our little gangsta got a new set of silver bracelets to go with those hoop earrings and she was carted off to jail. I hoped that the girl learned her lesson and got away from that huffing business. That was a very nasty thing to do to her brain. Case closed.

On a sidenote, I did once see a kid huffing spray paint on a bus stop bench. He hit the paint and fell back, with his eyes rolling into the back of his head. That stuff is mean, and it really does some bad things to the brain and central nervous system in general. I guess the high is not very long lasting, and the unintended effects are just pretty awful. Huffing paint can kill you; it says so all over the can. I hope that the kids finally wise up a little and start realizing that their brains are not there for them to destroy.

GEORGE E. KELLOGG, MSSM

LOOKING AWAY, TRYING TO BE NICE

There are two instances in which I know of security professionals have been killed while trying to perform a public service. I guess it can be argued that everything a security pro does is a public service. We may do it for a company, and that company may dictate the living made by the security professional, but the position that the security officer holds is one that serves both the public and their client. The public depends on the security to know and do their job. Part of that job is for them to protect the property and part of their job is to help the public be safe and feel protected as well. But what about the security professional's duty to self?

Sometimes, or most likely, most of the time, security professionals want to believe that people are out to do the right thing. We want to believe that people are good at heart and that when someone says they are in distress; they are coming to us for help with true intentions. We want to help them and do the right thing on the assumption that they are also doing right. We want to believe that the people we are trying to serve are truly innocent. We want to believe that they are the victim, and they need our help.

There are a couple of cases where security people have been killed, trying to do the right thing. One security pro was distracted from the street by averting his eyes to assist someone with a normal query. Two young ladies approached this security professional with a very normal, decent question. The kind of question that would seem oh-so-routine. They were asking for directions. The security pro obliges them, naturally, and takes his eyes off the street around him. He is now engrossed with the questions, with helping these girls find their way around. He does not notice the figure step away from the building against he was perhaps leaning,

Suddenly, there is the crack of gunfire. A single bullet tears into the security professional's head. He drops to the ground, dead. All because he was in a uniform. All because he was trying to do his job. All because he paused to assist someone in need. Now that man is *dead*. Killed, as it turned, by some evil creature in human form who had become so predatory in nature that he rebelled against all authority. In that authority, he somehow began to resent human life, the right for someone he does not like to live. He deprived that person of all his rights, of his right to ever go home again to his family, of his right to simply continue to live.

That person may have been caught, may have been prosecuted. But what does that matter to one who lost his life? What would it matter if that predator was even imprisoned and after due process, *executed* for his crimes? It does not matter to the dead. Not in any way that we actually understand fully. The security professional has been denied another day, another hour, another breath, just so someone could make a name for himself. Somebody who wanted to be a tough guy, wanted to show the world that he could sneak up on "The Man" and burn a cop. This predator, this would-be killer, wanted to kill a police officer, but instead, he killed a decent civilian who happened to be in a uniform. He did not burn "The Man" after all. He went to prison for nothing, because his killing was cowardly and did not do anything to advance his "street cred."

Another case of some hapless security professional being "nice" to the public and paying the ultimate price came in a little different form. This young man was on patrol outside of a holy structure. He was walking around, checking for vandalism, flowing water where water should not be flowing and that kind of thing. His job was to make sure that there was no one on the site who could do damage or harm. His job was to guard the building in and out; a decent enough job, one that a person could reasonably expect to come home from every night. After all, only the innocent hang out around holy places. Only decent people, or those seeking help, will be near a sacred structure, correct?

Well, that seems to be the thoughts on the mind of the security professional, the last few minutes that he was alive. During his patrol, he must have heard noise in the bushes that surrounded the structure. He stopped. He probably looked more closely this time and realized that he saw a person in the bushes. He called the young man out of the bushes, and likely asked what his business was being in that place at that time and how he might help. After all, a public

servant serves, correct? He wants to do the right thing for the innocent person he just met, right?

The young man who just came out of the bushes told him that
it was terrible! Men were chasing him! He needed help! The security
professional, wanting to do the right thing and suddenly assuming
that this young man was telling the truth about being chased, turned
his head toward the perceived danger. But he turned his head away
from the *real* danger. He did not consider the neighborhood that
he was in. He did not consider the kind of people who would likely
be roaming around at that hour of the night, and that one of them
might actually come that close to a holy place.

It seems in this case that perhaps this young man put too much
faith in the religious structure's power to attract good and repel evil.
We will never know. We won't know because we cannot ask the young
man what was on his mind. We can only assume that he trusted the
young man who came from the bushes to tell the truth. For whatever reason, this young security professional turned his head away
from the real danger to scan the horizon and his surroundings for the
group of dangerous people that were supposedly chasing the "victim"
to do harm. As soon as the security professional turned his head, the
young man from the bushes put a gun up to that turned head and
pulled the trigger, the roar and fire of a gunshot pierced the silence
and lit up the night for an instant. This gunshot did not nothing but
startle people and drop a young man to the ground. That young man
never knew, in all likelihood, what hit him and why.

Do you see the common element in these two scenes? The most
obvious commonality is also the one that is the most overlooked.
In these two cases, both men took their eyes off their surroundings.
They looked away from the real danger and tried to help. In both
cases, they were killed after turning their back to the real threat. They
each took a bullet in the head for believing that the person in front
of them was innocent, and not a threat. The two girls in the first
instance could have been innocent and the predator hiding near the
building was just was just waiting for his chance.

Or the girls who asked the question could have been asked,
could have been paid, could have earned points with the local gang

for doing this whole thing. What I am saying is that they could very easily have provided the distraction for the gunman to slip up on the security.

SO WHERE'S THE FLAG?

As I write this, I am steeped in grief for one of our Anytown's police officers who was just killed last night in the line of duty. Ours is a smaller Anytown and a smaller department, naturally. So the chances you know a police officer personally are greater than in a much larger Anytown. I did not know personally this police officer. I did not know his family. But he did leave one behind. I have the greatest sympathy for this officer, for our city council who is directly involved with the police, and for the officer's family. This particular Officer Doe actually attended a Veterans' Day celebratory breakfast we held in the gym at our church building. I was too busy cooking and serving to meet Officer Doe, but I am deeply touched at his passing. He seemed like a good man, to take his time to visit us; he was a Marine and combat veteran.

The most tragic thing about this is that he leaves behind a young wife and their infant daughter of four months. I am in tears as I write this. I am, after all the years I have served in the public sector in crime prevention, detection and response, feeling a kinship with that police officer and his family. The police will never respect me as one of their own, nor should I expect them to. Nonetheless, I do feel this in my heart. I am very sad about this tragedy. Officer Doe is the first Anytown police officer killed in the line of duty. The *first!* I cannot imagine what the department must be going through right now. They are a smaller department and thereby naturally a tighter-knit department.

Police officers, veterans of the US military services, and other public servants are rightfully buried under a flag. I have been honored to have carried to the grave a fine soldier, bearing with five other pallbearers his flag-draped coffin. I have seen the news footage on police officers killed or dying on duty. I have seen former presidents of the United States and other politicians with a flag over their caskets, and rightfully so. They are, after all, public servants.

I was once partnered with a paramedic, a nice-enough lady. She was pregnant and very family-oriented. We got along okay. Shortly after I left the ambulance service where I held the position of a field EMT, I found out that she had been killed in the line of duty, in an ambulance crash. It was quite sad; I was deeply touched by the outpouring of respect from the community. The Anytown Fire Department saluted her burial by sending two ladder trucks to extend their manlift ladders, forming an archway at the cemetery for the funeral cortege and procession to drive beneath on their way to the gravesite. That was a classy way to send off a public servant. I was impressed.

Another time, I was an incidental witness to a funeral procession of a firefighter who had left his home state to go and fight wildfires in Anystate. I say that I was an incidental witness because I was just sort of there. I was attending to some religious duties in a different part of Anytown when I noticed upon my leaving the services that the street was lined with people, and lights...flashing lights and vehicles all lined up in an orderly procession. I knew it could not be an emergency scene; it was far too orderly. This looked more like a community parade, but there was no holiday or event to celebrate. When I looked closer and saw all the fire department colors vehicles, I knew what it must be.

It was an amazing outpouring of support for a firefighter who had died tragically while fighting fire in a state not his own. I saw that this was not the actual funeral, but it was, in a sense, a parade for the firefighter coming home. This was the procession lining the road and following the hearse that brought him back to his hometown from the airport. His body was shipped back to his own people and this was his return home. Some of the vehicles were civilian cars and trucks. Many of the drivers and passengers were wiping tears from their eyes. This was a true hero's welcome and I was glad to see it. He would be honored by a flag-draped coffin.

No one plans to die when they get up to go to work, but death always haunts people who are in some kind of public service where crime or disasters are concerned. Police officers get shot, stabbed, beaten or run over in the line of duty. Firefighters can die tragically in the very fire where they were saving lives and property. Paramedics and EMTs can lose their lives to careless or overly fatigued driving; or they too can get shot while trying to help the people of the community. I once knew an EMT who was shot at a hospital by a demented elderly lady who was armed with a gun and thought somebody was going to hurt her.

There are many ways to die in the public service sector, whether in the military, police, fire, or emergency services. Any first response type of job is risky business for the employee of that particular service. The risks of police, fire and military are obvious; the risk of medical first responders is a little more subtle, but the risks of needle sticks, contagious and deadly diseases, traffic accidents while driving code 3 (lights and siren) are just as real as more overt dangers and they *are* public servants. At times, ambulance service personnel are even members of the International Firefighter's Union and get the benefit of a Firefighter's Union sticker on the back window of their car. Cops automatically respect that sticker and the job their fellow first responders perform on the same streets where cops fall.

But what about people who serve the public good in the private sector? The Civilian Service Recognition Act allows for the family of a civilian employee of the Federal Government to receive a US Flag if the employee dies under certain circumstances. For instance, if someone is texting and walking but not paying attention, accidentally trips the mailman causing him to tumble over a railing and die of sudden impact three stories later, he can become eligible for a flag. But if that same mailman is texting and talking on his phone while driving his mail truck and misses that hairpin turn, pitching himself and all our Hickory Farms gift boxes over a cliff, he does not get a flag.

So a mailman who is accidentally killed on duty gets the honors of receiving a United States flag. One who dies by just being stupid does not get a flag. Okay, fair enough, I guess. But I am left to wonder why the mailman who delivers mail gets the same right and privilege as a military vet, cop or firefighter? Somebody tell me if I am wrong, but isn't there a little different element of risk in the mailman's job? Think about this for a minute…military personnel, police officers, firefighters and the affiliated medical personnel are out there on the streets or on battle fields of foreign lands intentionally, willfully placing themselves at risk. They are being brave, putting themselves on the line. They work horrendous hours. They sacrifice much in their families' lives and know that they are doing so for the good of other people who sometimes, oftentimes, actually, take them for granted and don't even appreciate them.

The mailman has fairly regular hours and is taking no more than the usual risks any other person takes to get back and forth while doing their job. The mailman does not go out into public knowing that he might fall through a roof or get burned to death. There is no expectation that he could meet on the street today some guy who is a mad-dog killer and might have to shoot him or be shot instead. The mailman does not have to tolerate being shot at by gang members who were just trying to kill the person being fixed up by paramedics. And yet, the mailman has a pretty fair chance at being buried with a flag draping his casket. Or at least having a flag presented to his survivors in his name, by approval of the president of the United States (POTUS).

To me, and if this is only me, then fine, it is only me who thinks this. But what I think is that men and women who are intentionally taking extra risks in the name of their fellow countrymen, are the only ones that deserve the flag. They are, after all, in a very different public service sector than the mailman or the mayor.

Now… I am going out on a limb here. Security professionals are TRUE FIRST RESPONDERS and this is the main inspiration for this book. There are reasonable arguments on both sides of this idea I am about to present. I am willing to listen to all of the arguments and look at both sides of this thing. I am willing to be reasonable and change my mind about it. It would not be the first time that I have vacillated on this issue. I have been on both sides of the fence over the years. There needs to be some reasonable compromise somewhere. I have to ask myself in all fairness, too…what if I am the one who is wrong in how I view this issue?

Currently, my view is this: we see soldiers fall in the line of duty and they get to have a flag-draped coffin and a flag presented to their family. My mother received my father's flag while I was in the course of writing this book. In fact, I wrote part of it in my brother's living room while I was in town with my son to take care of Dad's funeral. Dad never did have much of a career, for reasons I will mull over some other time, but he was certainly a military man who deserved a military funeral. He was buried in the Arizona National Memorial Cemetery. Look it up sometime. He's there. But I digress. The funeral was well-deserved because he fought for his country, to battle the communist menace in Southeast Asia. And we have men and women who are fighting other menaces all over the world. These people deserve to be buried under the nation's flag.

We see police officers fall in the line of duty. They have their widows or widowers mourn them. Children are often involved. Families suffer terribly. I have even heard stories of police officers who have been shot and lived to tell about how they dreaded going to work that day because they "knew something was going to happen." These men and women go out on patrol, every day, knowing that they are the thin blue line between civilians and chaos. They know that they are out there facing people who would love to just put a bullet in their head just because they have chosen to take a stand against evil. They take a terrible risk just putting on that uniform. Their spouses and children know that too. They know that Mom or Dad may not come home that night. And they know too that who-ever harms them will do it intentionally, knowing that they are hurting a cop. The police officers and their families are all in this together and the stresses are tremendous. Police don't show up because something good just happened in that household at 0217 hours Friday, the sixteenth of Anymonth. They are there to deal with the angry, the stupid, the drunken, the drug addict, the pimp and prostitute. They do not show up unless there is something wrong. Their lives are given in service to their community and sometimes those lives given freely are taken from them for severely unjust reasons.

Firefighters and medical first responders don't have the easiest lifestyle either. While the average person never knows if their "number is up" on any given day, firefighters and ambulance personnel have an even greater reason to believe that "today is the day" than the average person. They often show up on scene for the same reason cops do. They are not there for good news. They are there because something ignited and burned out of control. They are there because people have hurt other people. They are there because of anger and rage. They are there to solve problems for others which these cannot solve for themselves. The first ambulances were hearses; the hearse would go to the car crash and then take survivors to the hospital. Then someone thought that on scene medical help could save lives. Ambulances were then born. Firefighters became involved with medical calls soon after this, and then they became EMTs and paramedics. And now we have ambulances that appear on scene with the firefighters so they can just rescue fire or crash victims and haul then straight to the hospital.

These fire and medical personnel have shorter life expectancies because they are often sleep deprived. They are shaken out of their bed to go see something terrible at o-dark-thirty. Or maybe it is just to put the widow Doe back into bed because she had fallen out of it for the third time and still can't get up. It is not an easy lifestyle for them or their families, either, because they are facing much of the same things cops face. Granted, the cops take on the greater dangers present at crime scenes, but the firefighters run into the burning buildings that the police are escaping. So yes, these service personnel all face their risks.

Now, maybe first response medical personnel don't face the same dangers as the police or firefighters, but they do see the grinding car crashes and terror of the mutilated crime victim. They also get shook out of bed at all hours, often working the same schedules as the fire team they are assigned to assist on scene. So yes, all of these people get to say they served their fellow man and I feel they do deserve recognition and an American flag at their funeral to represent their service. They are not considered, by the way "civilians." They are something more because they are paid by the public trust as city employees. Or maybe they work at the state or federal levels depending on the type of job they do.

All this is bringing me to this touchy and very specific point: *all* individuals who have served with decency, honor, and distinction in any first responder capacity deserve an American flag at their funeral. *All of them*. The issue, as I understand it right now, is that not all first responders are considered public servants because they do not work for a federal, state, county or city's government. Therefore, they are not entitled to an American flag at their funeral.

Please understand… I do know the difference between police/ fire and military versus the service provided by a security professional. I am not suggesting that security professionals deserve to have Taps or "Danny Boy" performed at their funeral. But I suggest that all first responders, whether they work for the government or a private enterprise, who risk exposing themselves to the general public, including security officers, EMTs, paramedics, flight nurses, ambulance attending nurses and any other personnel who place themselves at risk as first responders in a public capacity of any sort, deserve an American flag at their funeral.

The first response may be to ask, "Why?" Well, the answer is simple: I recently volunteered at a police station where a good cop, who was on the job for less than a year, was killed in the line of duty. We are pouring out our support. We are decorating the police station with blue twinkle lights and blue ribbons. We decorated his old patrol car. The police are receiving a great outpouring from us because this family man, leaving behind a widow and an infant, died in public service. And we should behave this way. Absolutely.

Now let me tell you something. You may not like it and I don't care if you don't like it. It's my opinion and anyone who wishes to convince me otherwise will have a hard time changing my mind. Maybe someone can, I don't know, but nobody has been able to do so yet.

I have been in the company of security officers for a very long time. About half of my life, really, and I know what a lot these people put up with. In many cases, the security officer does their job with the idea of protecting others in mind. A lot of former cops become security officers as a form of retirement job or, in some cases they did not work out as a police officer. It sometimes happens and it is not always because they were inept or incompetent. Sometimes, the police officer's role was just a poor fit.

There are a lot of former military personnel who become security officers too. Sometimes, this is just a springboard for them to get into another job. Other times, they settle into security as a career. A lot of former military just like security work because they are just put together that way. It is simply who they are.

The point I am making here is that there are a lot of former cops and military personnel who are now in the security field. Generally, it is a sense of selflessness that provides these people with the motivation and drive to continue in the field for years. Sometimes, not. Sometimes a person just needs a job to get them through school. Not every security officer, soldier, or police officer is motivated for the reasons of selflessness. But regardless of their motive, these people are putting themselves at risk to protect the property and lives of other people, and to me, that says something about them.

I have looked up images of funerals for security officers. There were some who had special honors, yet many did not. The flag-draped casket in all the cases I could find were for security officers who were former police or military personnel. Not one casket of just a plain old civilian security officer was draped with their country's flag. I have put in my study and there is no statute that prevents a person from having his or her coffin draped with the US flag. In fact, it says that any patriotic American may have a US flag on their coffin if they so desire, and a mention at the funeral should be made that the flag represents this person's patriotism.

In these cases, the funeral flag should be of the regulation funeral size. But instead of the military or other government agency providing the flag, the family or friends should pay for it. I have no issue with that. I would just like to see to it that security officers or their family members have a chance to choose to have their coffin draped with a flag as a symbol of their patriotism, as the suggestion has been made. And I would like to see their service in security mentioned during their funeral.

There is something significant about security officers' willingness to put themselves at risk. Even if they see this as just a springboard type of job, even if they don't intend to make a career of it, the security officers' service should be recognized. We, as security professionals, do place ourselves at risk in our communities. We are the front line of defense for the entire staff of the given building, business or property.

I have titled this book *Security Professionals: True First Responders* because that is precisely what we are. As I have inferred in many of the personal experiences I and a few other security professionals have seen and lived through, security professionals are often the first ones to meet the bad guys, to find the trouble, to discover the fire, etc., and we are never really given credit for it. There is certainly something to that. Yes, there is. And sometimes it gets our security professionals killed.

My old man, noted in my dedications as "Doc Whitey," taught me that the vital function of the security officer is not overlooked by military tactical trainers worldwide. Security professionals, if they are armed or not, are the first targeted group in a tactical engagement. When the decision has been made for soldiers or mercenaries, as the case may be, to move in, the first people they kill are security professionals. The reason for this is that the attacking force fears *communication*. They don't want anyone to know they are coming, and the attackers know that security has all the means they need, hopefully anyhow, to communicate with the higher authorities and tell them that their bit of occupied real estate is under attack. It is then a very simple matter to stop communications. You simply kill the security officers. They are the first target that tactical people are going to hit. Shut down security, shut down communications, and you have more time to carry out your objective. Time is everything to a tactical operation, whether they are the "good guys" or the "bad guys," whether their objective is military or a robbery attempt. They will *kill* security.

People don't really look at that side of things, now, do they?

SECURITY WORK
VS. PAUL BLART

The general public, the American society, We the People, generally see security professionals in a negative light. Popular culture does nothing to help this either. I seem to recall some quote from Kevin James, the comedic actor, the man who played the lead role in the comedy movie *Paul Blart: Mall Cop*. The quote, I paraphrase, was that he made Paul Blart to raise public awareness about security professionals and how important their role can be. *Well, guess what I can call on that one?* Malarky! Baloney! Horse hockey! Camel sputum! And so forth.

Public awareness, Mr. James? Truly? This from the guy who plays a read role in "Grown-ups?" Yeah, you know, that movie series all full of doo-doo jokes? Just the guy I want to have representing my career choice! Come on, man! At least admit what you did! You made fun of mall security professionals all across the country! And you know what? It was pretty accurate in some respects, that movie. I cannot get around it. A lot of the stereotypes in that movie were true. I even use the term *mall cop* in my book, in these very pages. I don't deny the stereotypes exist. And yes, mall cops are a very easy target. Poorly trained, hungry for power, too lanky or nervous or in poor health to become "real police"…there are many mall cops out there that are like that. So just admit it, Mr. James, and say that you made the movie because people like to poke fun at mall security professionals. You did it, and yes, I actually enjoyed the movie. I saw it for what it was. A humorous stab at security people.

But let me tell you something. Not all mall security professionals are like that. And when a movie like this is made about security personnel, pop culture just eats it up. Every stereotype you can think of was there. They had them all. In fairness though, I will say that they made Paul Blart the hero. He saved the day and did things that no one thought he could do. But it was pretty disappointing that he ended up turning the actual police job down and stayed at the mall. He had the talent to better himself but chose not to. It could be argued that it was a happy ending because he was doing what made him happy. I was not crazy about it, but there you have it.

On the other hand, though, we had the following stereotypes of security officers, many of which I heard about from people mocking me…*before I even saw the movie.* These are not all necessarily applicable to the character of PB himself, but to all the security professionals in the movie:

1. Overweight well-meaning, naive people on the security team
2. Not confident during a confrontation about "citizen arrest" laws
3. Clumsy, poorly attentive
4. Police academy washout
5. Single, miserable, bad at relationships
6. Old, nervous, unable to handle a firearm
7. High school dropout who could not get a better job
8. The ever-present Segway transport device
9. Inept, unknowing, wannabe cops
10. Not very bright, but overly enthusiastic.

Do such people exist in the security field? Of course, they do. But there are not as many as you might think. The ones who are this inept, naive, etc. usually do not last very long because the security personnel who know what they are doing will not tolerate them for long. Their peers and supervisors will normally force them out, eventually. I have seen cases where such people were kept aboard for reasons of compassion; the boss felt sorry for them. In these cases, they try to give these people low-level assignments where few decisions must be made, and the employee still gets to have the idea that they are a security officer.

The harm that can come from movies such as "Paul Blart" exists in the fact that the younger generations won't respect the security officers when they see them. No one looks at the movie showing PB as the hero whom the cops wanted to hire in the end, the guy who saved the day. No...all anyone ever brought up to me was the hypoglycemic, fat-butted wannabe cop who couldn't cut it in the real world. And no, that movie was not the real world either.

THE REAL WORLD
OF SECURITY

The real world of the private security officer is a tough one. It is tough because as the true first responders, they may come upon any kind of crisis at any time. Security officers, particularly those in the highly public posts, often encounter life or death situations, and they are needed to respond. Part of the security paradox is that no one wants security around until something goes completely haywire. The other side of that paradox is that when it does go bad, the security pro *had better perform* or there will be big trouble for them if they don't. Then, after the crisis is over, the security officer is relegated again back to the lower echelon status of humanity until they are once again needed.

Security plays a vital role in society, filling a gap between people who are not watching out for themselves and police who are either not willing to do security work, or charge too much for the well-being of the property owners. That gap is where the security officer fits in. Security officers are private duty, but they *do* have authority. People who say a security officer has no authority does not understand the role of security. When a citizen is hired on to a security team, they have all of the authority over the property where they are working that the owner of the property has. Security is limited only by the laws of the land, like everybody else, and by the policies of the property owner.

People forget that certain constitutional rights are suspended on private property. For instance, free speech is not applicable as a "right" on private property. A person cannot come onto a mall's property, for example, and just start preaching religion, or touting and promoting their own privately-owned business and so forth under the constitutional rights of "free speech." Why? Because someone who owns the property says they cannot. When you are in a person's place of business, you must understand that they have the right to state the rules. If they say you cannot wear green shoes in their place of business, you cannot wear green shoes. If they say that you cannot play the harmonica for money in the mall, then you have to comply. Private property is private, and that is all there is to it. Whether it is someone's home or their shopping mall, they get to make the rules. And if someone who is either the property owner or the agent of the property owner tells you that you must leave, with or without cause, you must leave or face trespassing charges.

The security professionals in mall settings need to understand that their "authority" is not given to them by law but is instead given to them by the written policy of the property owner. Just so there is no question, many shopping malls post the rules publicly, in plain sight. That is the "law of the mall." And security officers *do* have the right to take a suspect into custody as long as they can show that they had good reason for doing so. The best way to think of it is that visitors to the mall are in the security officers' living room of their house. As representative agents of the property owners, the security team will enforce the rules of the mall any way they see fit within the parameters set up by the property owners. As long as the parameters are within the confines of the local laws, then security officers are within their rights to enforce the rules.

Security officers may, for instance, issue moving violation tickets that must be paid by the person receiving the citation, if the property owner says so. If the property owner wants to enforce a rule that drivers will pay $50 for running the STOP sign on the owner's property, then so be it. The security officer may issue a citation, and it must be paid at the discretion of the property owner. If the violator refuses to pay the fine, then the security may trespass that person and not permit them to legally return to the property. So you see, security officers do perform some of the same functions as police officers, as long as they are security officers assigned to that property and they are acting within the wishes of the property owner.

So yes, when there are matters on private property to be handled, security professionals may perform the same functions as police, but for that property only. In fact, security officers have more authority on that property than do the police in private matters such as STOP sign running, reasonable rates of speed and appropriate parking practices. The only time that police officers have more authority on private property than security is in matters where actual laws are broken and police are called in. Can a city cop come into the Anytown mall parking lot and issue a ticket to someone who ran a STOP sign on private property? No. But can they issue a ticket, on mall property, to a driver who ran a STOP sign on a public street, and the violator happens to pull over into a mall parking lot? Yes.

We start to see here some of the similarities between police and security work. Both positions are uniformed and authoritative presences. Both are held to standards of professional conduct by their respective employers. So in their own sphere, both are expected to take certain risks. The differences though are striking. The police officer, in the first place, has a lot better and more training. Police also have different and much better equipment. Police have the powers to enforce the law, not just the rules or policies of the property they work for. Because of their ability to enforce law and take people to a real jail under charges that will stick, police fear and respect the police. People often do not fear and respect security officers the same way.

But under certain circumstances, security personnel can have a lot of influence and make things tough for people who get too out of hand. This normally occurs when police and security people are working in a partnership on the same property. Security officers in these circumstances often have pepper spray and handcuffs, and have been trained in their use. Personally, I have never seen security officers in a direct relationship with police on the same property carry firearms. I am not saying that is never the case, I am just saying that I have never seen a case of security people carrying firearms while police are working on the same site.

Regardless of how they are armed, or if they are unarmed, the security teams normally work very well side by side with the police officers. Most police officers do respect the security team in such circumstances, though they also understand the glaring differences in their training. The police I used to work with at one of the Anytown malls used to say time and time again, *"Security! Learn a phonetic alphabet!"* And I agreed with him on that point with all my little black heart.

My teeth would be set on edge to hear, "Um…license plate number 1-2-3…um…alpha… Robert…um…uh…*keychain!*" or "Macaroni…dandelion…um…zombie…1…3…yellow…"

Argh! I hated that.

Usually though, the PD will get along with security because they have to. The client demands that police works with security, and if the police want to make the extra bucks they signed up for as overtime or whatever, they will have to learn to get along. They don't necessarily have to like security or care for the idea. They do have to work with it.

Many times, I have teamed up with cops and it worked out very well, and most of the time, they will tell the suspects that they must respect the security team and do as they say. Otherwise, the suspect will end up dealing with the police in a most unpleasant manner. I have found that if the police officer trusts the security officer then things go smoothly. I have also found that this trust must be earned. The police know who they can trust, generally speaking.

That trust goes two ways though. I have seen security teams favor some cops over others. Why? Because some police officers just don't respect or like security and won't answer their calls for help. These police officers will usually end up becoming so dissatisfied with their job that they will leave the situation. Other times, the police have a solid relationship with the security pros and things go very well. It is especially funny when someone is giving security a hard time and they say, "Go ahead and call the cops. I'll be long gone before they get here… Oh! Crap! I'm sorry! I'm sorry! I didn't know *police* were right here! I'll be good…"

By then though, it is too late, and the police are on the spot, taking them away in handcuffs.

The perception that the public seems to have is that the security professionals are hated by the police and never can work well with them. This may be true in some cases, but there are more and more cases where there is a very good working relationship between the PD and security. When it does work well, it surprises folks, particularly when they are doing something wrong and assume that since security is present that the police are not. It is funny when a cop suddenly emerges from nowhere and lays hands on the guy who really needs to have his attitude adjusted.

$700 CASH STOLEN AND RECOVERED

One particular case comes to mind where PD and security really worked together. We had kind of a unique situation involving some property lines. I will explain that in just a moment. It all started when this nice young lady, in her early twenties I suppose, approached me with her husband. They were coming out of an anchor store in the Anytown mall. They were clearly distressed.

She said to me, "Someone stole my $700 in cash."

That got my attention right away. I really wanted to help her out, but cash was so hard to recover. She gave the rundown of what happened. She was trying on some clothes. She left her wallet in the changing room. She saw some teenagers leave the dressing room area. When she rejoined her husband, she mentioned that the snap on her wallet was open. He told her to check for her money right away. Nope! Not there! It was gone.

Well, I knew what I would have done if I had just made off with $700 in cash so close to a mall exit. I would have left the mall immediately just in case someone saw me. I explained that cash was very hard to recover unless she saw who took it. I expected to get the usual "I did not see them" routine. Then I would just go on about my business because there would nothing I could do. But when she told me that she thought she saw the ones who did it, and I became *veeeery* interested! I called this out on the radio, and when they heard the words "$700 in cash," that got the police and the security director for the Anytown mall very interested too.

They came down to join us. I outlined what had happened, and the lady said that she knows who did it. The police naturally wanted to know who it was.

"Over there...buying athletic shoes."

And sure enough, there was a group of straggler kids trying to get some Air Whatevers. Now remember how I was discussing the different rights of the police and security officers on private property? This was a little sticky. The cops could not go in because it was a private store, and they did not call for the police. But...security could go in there because the mall had it in the tenants' contract that security officers could enter stores at any time when there was a reasonable belief that something was amiss, or to deliver flyers or messages of some kind from mall management to the unwashed masses. In this case, something was amiss.

I stepped into the store and approached the store manager to let them know what was going on. Now, technically, she/he could have ordered me out of the store. But then, it would have just become a matter of our waiting outside their store for the police, anyplace past the "lease line," which is the effective property boundary of the mall "tenant," or the business on the mall's lease contract.

That turns, potentially, into a game of cat-and-mouse with one side versus the other:

"I can wait out here all day long for you to leave the store" versus "I can stay in this store as long as I like."

Those standoffs are awkward and usually end with the manager speaking up and telling the customer that they don't know or care what the problem is with the security team and/or the cops, but the customer must *now* leave. Having cops and security hang around outside your store is bad for business. In this case though, the manager had good relations with us and allowed us to escort the customer out of the store.

Once we were outside, the police intervened and took over the scene. Now this was their turf because the mall hired the cops to help with security, and there was no longer a lease line issue to contend with. The police were now answering a complaint from a citizen who claimed that these people likely stole her $700. Did she actually witness the theft? No, but apparently the police officer felt that he had enough to go on to at least investigate what was happening. He started asking questions and determined that these folks did probably have the money on them. He was questioning one girl in particular. Past history, maybe?

Whatever the case, the police officer asked security to remain on the scene, and then he made the girl an offer she should have taken him up on. He said that all she had to do was to give the money back, and she would only get a ticket for the theft, have to appear before the court on the given day, but she and her group of friends or family could just go on their merry way. And...she refused. The girl said that this was "all stupid" anyway. The cop agreed and said, "Yeah, it was stupid all right, because now we are going to run everybody's ID."

We had to take this group of four to the security office, and while there were some items among them, none of the items were stolen, and one young man was even turned loose completely. Apparently, he was absent at the time of the alleged theft. In the end, after all the pockets, purses, and wallets were emptied; there was the money, in the amount and the denominations that the reporting party had originally claimed. The girl who had resisted the idea of just being written a ticket, who opted to have her ID run by the police, was the one who had the most to lose. That girl had a warrant out for her arrest and immediate incarceration in the county jail. She had skipped out on something—I never found out what, but whatever it was, she was going away for a while. Honestly, I just don't understand why the bad people don't just admit to what they do when they are given a clear path to tell the truth and take the lesser punishment.

When all the smoke cleared, the one girl went to jail. Two others were fined, and the last one had nothing happen to him because he was searched, yes, but then cleared of any wrongdoing. He was the only one who went home free of damage. I don't know what he was off doing at the time of the theft, but whatever it was, it helped him stay out of trouble. The woman got her money back. There is also something noteworthy here...her husband was the one who told her to check for the money when she noticed the snap was opened. She did and that led to them contacting me. I just "happened to be in the right place" at the right time. My career is actually riddled with my finding out things I needed to know to prevent or solve crimes. I wonder if this is special gift of some kind; it happens so frequently.

CREEPER WHO FOLLOWED MY WIFE

One day, at an Anytown mall, my wife was walking along the upper floor. She was doing as I taught her and kept her head on a swivel, all eyes around all directions. Then she noticed him. Some guy about twenty-five years old and poorly dressed. His appearance was not the problem; this particular Anytown mall was in a rougher, low-income neighborhood. She was there only to talk to me; she was not really shopping on this particular day.

The thing that bothered her about this guy was that he was fingering his groin while walking several feet behind her. He would stop when she stopped; he would go when she went. I taught her that when you *feel* like you are being followed, you usually *are*, and to never ignore that inner sense. It will warn you of danger, even when you cannot see it. So after two or three times of her stopping and him following suit, she did the ultimate test. Mind you, she was not panicking at this moment because she had a plan. She knew what to do. I had trained her; she understood the training, and now she was using it.

What she did was to *duck into a store where the guy following her would have no business entering without it looking really weird.* You see, a creeper like this does not want to get caught. He does not want to draw undo attention, whether he is there to steal a purse or sexually attack someone. And going into a store that looked out of place for him was going to attract attention. Since my wife wanted attention on the situation, she ducked into a store that sold trendy women's boots and high-heeled shoes. If he followed her in, she had him and could call security on the spot. If he walked on left her alone, maybe she imagined the whole thing, or perhaps he simply lost interest. But in this case, she was able to confirm that he was following her because he stopped right in front of the store and waited. So she called security, and I got his description.

Since I was on duty and in uniform, and I just got a stalking complaint, I was obligated to act on it right away and I had to act on it *properly*. That was the quandary for me. I knew that I could not act on this and stay objective. I was taking this very personally, and that is a bad thing for any officer who is taking any kind of call. It is tough for any type of first response team of any kind when a family member is involved in some kind of incident. I decided that it was time for me to involve the police. I contacted the first police officer I found, and he told me that, yeah, I was right to come to them. They understood that I needed to stay out of it and were glad to keep me out of it so they would not have to arrest *me*. That would have been very, very bad for a number of reasons.

They took my description of the suspect and the location of my wife. She was still inside the boot store, and he was still outside the place, presumably waiting for her to come out. The cops did approach him, and they took his ID and ran it. Then after determining that he was just being a little too creepy, and nothing more, they released him, without arrest. His background came back clean too, which kind of surprised me. I thought for certain that he would have had some kind of prior arrests for similar crimes. Alas, he did not.

My wife handled this situation perfectly. She did just what I taught her to do. She was alert, aware, and handled him without confrontation. She noted what he looked like, what clothes he was wearing, and she also verified that he was following her. There was no denying it. He was tracking her. What a scumball. While I don't expect this guy to change, I do expect him to be a little more cautious next time he decides to fondle himself while he's following a woman through the mall. That was just a disgusting thing to do. It really was. But because of my wife's smart handling of him, it all ended well and that was the best thing I could ask.

DISCOURAGED THE PURSE SNATCHER WITH A STERN LOOK

This experience did not occur on the job, but it illustrates some solid security principles and skills. This was a very simple occurrence that no one even knew about. No fuss was being made, there was no actual confrontation and no one but me and the other guy even knew what was going on. I was in an Anytown Grocery Store with my wife. Everything seemed normal, no cause for fear, no real need for concern. But isn't that when crimes are always committed? On days that seem just like every other day? Well, of course they are! One does not generally wake up and receive a message telling them, "Watch out! Today is abnormal! You're to become a crime victim today!"

We were at this grocery store, and I was minding my own business as usual, which means that I was watching everybody around us. I became uneasy, because I realized that we were standing right next to the exit. People were starting to crowd in a little because it was in the evening when everybody gets off work and rushes to the store for that rotisserie chicken and bag of rolls to take home for supper. I knew this was a prime set up for a purse snatching. And against my advice, we all know how often our own families ignore our advice, my wife did not have her purse slung diagonally across her shoulder to her waist. She did not have it on one shoulder with a firm grip on it. This was a problem in a crowded store when you are standing right next to the exit.

You see, a purse snatcher has to move fast. He has to act fast. He has to grab the purse quickly and disappear quickly. This is why we call it a "purse *snatching*" and not a "tactical cat burglary-style theft of a purse that took three days to plan." The snatcher looks for a loosely held purse, one draped over a chair not being watched, etc. And he looks for the exit. The quickest route for escape. He also looks for a way to disappear. And a crowd is the perfect way for the snatcher to simply melt into a homogenous sea of faces. If he acts quickly and moves fast enough, the victim won't be able to describe him to police, except in the most general of terms.

Certainly, right by the exit, there were cameras. Well, big, fat "so what" on that. The cameras contain footage, yes, but the majority of thefts I have seen on camera are useless in an investigation. The only way camera footage helps in a petty theft is when someone grabs the thief and then the camera proves that yes, this man we grabbed was the thief. But you must have the dude in custody because even they have a crystal clear image of the man who stole your purse, unless he is already known on some law enforcement data base somewhere, or unless you happen to know that this is your Uncle John Doe who lives at 123 Anystreet in Anytown, USA, it does not help. The majority of petty thieves are not going to work the same areas long enough to become known on any data base.

Getting back to the story, my wife unwittingly set herself up perfectly for a snatch. She had her purse loosely looped over one shoulder with no extra hand on it. She was standing right next to the exit of the store. It was crowded, and her purse shoulder was positioned perfectly for a guy to breeze right past her, pull the purse off her shoulder and run right out of the exit and into the dark parking lot and off to the races! These guys often have a getaway car waiting for them too. But in this case, things were a little different than he thought.

He thought that I was not with her because I was looking away from her and did not speak to her. That was often the case when she was shopping; that was her time, and she did not like being bothered with things like personal safety, securing her purse, watching her surroundings. She was *shopping*, doggone it! With that in mind, I did not bother her about this until later that night at home with the groceries all put away. Then I told her what happened...or *didn't* happen, in this case.

Recognizing that she was a prime pigeon, I was watching all around. Then I saw him. Tall, white male, dark hair, jeans, tan leather jacket, black footwear. He was eyeballing her purse. I could see the wheels turning while he calculated the odds. He was discreetly watching the purse and then I could see the "Uh-huh, oh yeah" light come on. He started to make his move. I saw him posturing toward my wife's big, white leather purse... I think she named this one "honeypie"…and then…CRAP! He saw me turn my body toward his chosen trajectory, covering her purse. He looked up at me, into my eyes, and I gave him the meanest, tight-lipped look I could muster up, and I slowly shook my head.

He knew he was busted, and he relaxed, backed off, and melted into the crowd, and no one was the wiser. That is how these things often go. We see it in the movies all the time. A private drama being played out between predator and prey. The spy versus the mark. The cop versus the killer. These adversaries always communicate in subtle ways not perceived by the untrained eye, but the communication is quite clear. One lets the other know "I am onto you," and the other just backs away. No one in the area, on the street, or in the bank or wherever you can imagine, is any the wiser. Something bad was averted, and like the *Men in Black* movie, "Folks get on with happy lives none the wiser." That was exactly the case with my purse snatching friend. A crime was prevented, and no one else in that store knew what was going on. They did not know that a predator was spotted by the prey; they did not know that roles reversed when the prey became predator and saved the day, yet again.

Later, when the groceries were put away, I debriefed with her. She had no idea.

Why is purse snatching still performed? Because it still works. Why does it still work? Because people just don't pay attention. It is that simple. They just don't look at their surroundings and recognize the hazards in their environment.

PING! PING! HUH? WHAT'S THAT?

Part of my duties at the Anytown hotel was to keep an eye on the liquor. I am not a drinking man, so that did not bother me one way or the other. I may as well have been watching and counting cans of paint. Actually, the paint would be a greater temptation, particularly if it is blue with shiny stuff in it. But that's another story for another time. On this particular night though, the booze check took a crazy turn. Everything "seemed normal"—but again, that is always when stuff goes down. Everything "seems normal," and *BAM*! You're head-first into an incident. Sometimes you get a warning from nature. Some people get a premonition. Déjà vu, a noise, or maybe the li'l hairs stand up on your neck. On this night…no such luck.

I pushed the chain-link gate open. The whole cage was made of chain-link fencing. The walls and ceiling were made up of chain link. And the whole thing was held together by fence parts. The metal fence post and caps held the thing together. It was a fairly sound design, and I never had any issues with this cage or similar cages I had dealt with in the past. The idea, I guess is to design a secure, effective, but cheap cage. The chain is handy because it allows you to see through it, it allows for plenty of ventilation and it does not create the challenges that a permanent room might cause if things, for some reason need to be shifted around. In a hotel basement, this could happen frequently.

That being said, I pushed open the door like normal. Then I heard *ping, ping*! In an instant, I thought, *What th*——? and then *WHAMMO!* I was hit right on top of the head! I saw stars, and my neck now hurt. My every survival instinct was suddenly slammed into full throttle. I was knocked to my one knee, and my back was bowed over by the blow, but I was still able, through the pain and stars, to spin around and confront whoever it was that hit me on the head.

Nobody! Nobody was there. Not a person, not a sound. The room was exactly as it was when I first passed through it moments ago. No sign of anyone or anything directly behind or in my periphery. Well, *something* certainly was not right. And I did not drink any of the liquor, so it was not like I was waking up from passing out during an all-night bender. No blackouts here, Jack. This was a near knockout, but not a blackout. So…what the heck was it? My head hurt like the Dickens! Right on top! And well, that was my first clue. My natural belief was that someone was hidden, I missed seeing them, but that was rapidly disproved.

Still, something in my immediate surroundings was not right. Something hit me on top of the head. Nothing had fallen to the concrete floor around me or on top of me. So that meant that, whatever it was, it had to be still up there. And not wanting to meet whatever that was again, reacquainting my head with it, I carefully looked up. And it was a good thing too. Directly over my head, right where I would have stood straight up into it again, was the chain link ceiling drooping down. Boy, did my head hurt. I was not knocked out, but I wondered why not, because it was certainly heavy enough to cause me serious issues. I got lucky I guess.

I did get checked out at the emergency room. They x-rayed my neck, and all the bones of my skull, just to be sure. I had no signs of concussion. I left there with a doctor's note for a couple of days off work. Then I went to my EMT class, where they pretty much left me to rest after I explained to the fireman instructor just what happened. He kept an eye on me for any signs of concussion or injury while he lectured class. I don't even remember what the lessons were that day.

After thinking it over for a bit, I realized that the pinging noises, two distinct sounds, were the fence posts slipping out of the metal caps. I opened the door and the ceiling, poised to fall, did so as soon as the posts pulled loose. That was nuts! I could not believe it. Hotel management got my report, including a briefing on my injuries, which amounted to a stiff neck for a couple of days, and photos of the scene from their electronic camera.

The night of my return to work, I walked back down to the booze cage, now named "Ping, ping," and before I opened the door, I checked to see how soundly it was put back together. About every six or seven inches, they had that ceiling wired in place with what I thought was coat hanger wire. Whatever it was though, it worked! I never had that ceiling fall on my head again.

ALWAYS LOOK UP

When I was growing up and even continuing into adulthood, Dad would constantly look after everybody's safety. This was a part of what I strongly believe to be his PTSD issues. He would not admit it, but he was having some serious problems. And what came of all that? Well, I certainly learned how to watch my back. That is something that has been valuable to me over that years. It has saved my bacon on a number of occasions and is probably the main reason I never ended up on somebody's list of statistics.

There was this story that he used to tell about when he was in Special Forces training. He was in school, and he got sent on a "mission." The exercise was for him to get out of their training barracks, into a different building. Inside that building, he was supposed to find a pop machine and buy one can of Coke for each of his guys. The point of the whole exercise was for him slip past the sentries of that building to get in and out without being seen. The reason they wanted him to buy cans of pop was so he would have to make some noise. Moving quietly was child's play to those Special Forces guys, even at that early stage of their training. They wanted something for him to do that was simple and harmless, but challenging. The challenge would come from the noise. The coins clinking through the pop machine. The push button activating the dispenser, the cans dropping through the machine and the noise from taking them out of the machine.

To top it all off, the sentries in that building were told to expect something, and it was their job to catch Dad. This was the equivalent of a spy operation where the opposition was clued that somebody was going to break in. All the advantage was with the guys that were in the building, which is how it would be in real life if some kind of operation was compromised and the enemy forces knew that someone was on his way in.

For Dad to get into the building was sponge cake. Nothing to it. He knew how to break into a place. So that part he did without getting caught, as expected. The tough part was going to be getting the six Cokes out of the machine, and then out of the building without getting caught. The pop machine noise was going to be the absolute signal that he was in the building. While the sentries did not know what to expect, they should know that anything out of the ordinary was a clue to the "spy's" whereabouts. Six sodas being bought at 2:00 AM was about as unusual as it gets.

Here, now, is where it gets interesting. Dad knew that the noise was going to draw the sentries like ants to a picnic, and time was his enemy. He knew he would have just one shot at getting all six Cokes, because once they heard the first noise, they would activate and come after him. So he had to take the time to get all six Cokes and five was not an option. All *six* had to be brought back to the barracks for his guys to have a Coke. Any less cans of pop meant that somebody was going to be left out, and they were a unit where nobody ever got left out. All or nothing.

So he broke in, slipped in, moved quietly, found that pop machine and went to work. He rattled and clanked his way through buying six Cokes, frosty-cold. The sentries heard the sound, and knowing that they were expecting trouble, they keyed on the sound and rushed to the scene. They thought that they had him for sure. They knew their building very well and they blocked off all the hall-ways so as to seal him in. They organized, they moved in, they sur-rounded that machine and— *Aha! Gotcha!*... Umm... Nope, they didn't get him. But how the heck did he get away? They had all the exits blocked, all the hallways covered, no way out! But no "spy"! He was gone! They milled around a little bit, confirmed that yes, they did hear the noise, they were at the correct pop machine, etc. Well... he's gone...somehow...and they finally gave up and went back their posts, tails between their legs and scratching their heads.

Meanwhile, Dad slipped out of the building after everyone cleared the hallways. Oh...but wait...before he could get out of the building, he had to use the floors to walk on. To walk on the floors, his feet had to be in contact with them. To be in contact with the floor, he had to jump down...from...*off the TOP of the pop machine!* When he got back to barracks with all six Cokes, the team cracked them open and *psssht*—they had a good laugh, at the expense of the sentries. When all six cans were purchased, and the sentries coming, with the agility they trained into him, Dad lifted himself onto the top of the machine, positioned himself back in the shadows as far as he could, and just stood perfectly still. He saw all these guys looking around for him, eyes dead ahead, eyes on the floor...but *not one pair of eyes looked up*! All they had to do was look up and they would have caught him!

That story stuck with me for the rest of my life and has become very useful in my security career. I have seen things that were hazardous, found vandalism, noted broken windows and spotted suspects, all because I never failed to look up! Our natural tendency is to do what life has taught us to do. From the time we were toddling around on the floors of our parental homes, we learned to watch where we were putting our feet. We learned that we needed to watch out for things that we can trip over. Watch the ground, watch dead ahead, even look around for other things with our peripheral vision. But we don't look up. Why? Because our feet aren't up there. Things to trip over are not up there. So it is not natural for us to look up. But what can be up there of any concern? Well, let me tell you…

I have avoided falling broken glass, I have found hazards in a factory setting, I have seen people in upper floor windows watching me, I have found vandalism and other issues, all from looking up. If you are ever in a situation where someone seems to have disappeared, start looking up. Check rooftops, trees, scaffolding, etc. for your suspect, or for evidence of where your suspect could have possibly gone. And you never really know, either, just what could come falling down on you if you are in a construction site or other place where work is being done. Look up, down and all around. Check every direction and always remember to look up!

SECURITY OFFICER FATALITIES

This is very difficult topic to address. Truly. I have spoken about the idea of flag-draped coffins for security officers, particularly if they die in the line of duty. Or dying on duty is about the same thing. It may seem that there is no difference at first, but if you look at it honestly, they are different.

Because security jobs are often taken by elderly people who use security during their retirement, and also because of the odd hours that they work, compounded by what can be very long hours, it is not unheard of to lose a security officer to a heart attack. This type of death, not directly related to job activity, is what I would consider to be a "death on duty." The other kind of death, which is very heart wrenching, would be caused by some work activity. A security officer may be struck by a car, shot, stabbed or beaten up by a suspect, killed in a car crash, or may even fall prey to a hazardous condition on the job.

Let me tell you some things that have happened to me on the job, and then some things I have seen or heard of happening to others. After that, I will address what I think of how these deaths occurred and how I believe matters of such tragedy should be handled where security officers are concerned. The fact that most security officers work for private companies, excluding sworn peace officers or other officers of the government, works into this. I will explain why. It is truly quite simple, but let us cut our teeth on some of the experiences I have seen or heard about, firstly. Then we will get into the heart of the matter.

The very first security death I ever heard of was with an Anytown Security Agency. This company was large and had to defend its reputation. They wanted to become a primary security contractor, a well-known name in the field. Finally, they did. That aside, this private company had a post which was fairly dangerous. The danger was not presented in the form of criminals trying to do harm. The danger was not a matter of toxic environments or physically hazardous buildings. No, this post was dealing with some vehicular traffic. I don't know all the details but the security officer who worked this post said that she was dodging cars for her entire shift. She was afraid that one day she would be hit by a car.

I was a supervisor on a different post, so I could not help her directly. She mentioned this to me a couple of times as she was subbing to fill a slot at my post. We talked about the situation and I suggested that she go to the office about it. She told me that she had gone to the office about it already, but they would not give her the time of day and just simply blew her off. That being the case, I did not know what else to tell her. She was reporting to the correct people and I was powerless to help.

Well, one day while we were attending a lecture at a firearms class, the lecturer, a younger man who was now affiliated with the police department in some way, gave us some wise advice. He told us that the company's policies as written would hang us out to dry if we ever fired our weapon and shot someone in the line of duty. If we ever pulled that trigger on someone, we had better be able to prove that we had no other recourse, including just running away. We had better be able to prove that we were on the ground, helpless to fight back, and had to pull the trigger to save our own life.

Given those restrictions, it was far better to simply allow the bad guy to do what he/she was about to do. Just step out of the way and let the criminal have at the client! That way, well, I would not go to jail. And think about it…that lecturer might just be correct. It would be best to have a lawyer on retainer anytime that we as a private citizen, as security officers are, to turn to for immediate defense. There is a great organization that provides this very service for armed Americans, by the way. They are called The United States Concealed Carry Association, or USCCA. I have bought their insurance that provides a covered private citizen with a lawyer immediately upon their arrest or at the moment an accusation is leveled at them. There is a considerably large amount of liability coverage you have with this membership. I think that they are a great organization. However, they do not cover their client if they are paid to carry the gun they use in a defensive situation. Back to the business at hand.

While were sitting with the instructor in our outdoor classroom, enjoying a break, it was a classic mentoring moment. We were all on the grass talking about the risks of participating in a shooting event. Then, as usually happens in these situations, the subject of *death* came up. And the mentor told us that someone who worked for the Anytown Security Agency was killed. They were in the line of duty; they were struck by a car and they were killed on site. We never heard about it because they, the powers that be, were keeping it from the security officers. That was so wrong, but very typical.

Another death that occurred on duty, with a different company, was at shift change. A security professional pulled up in his car, just like any other night, and put it in park. His guys were waiting inside the guard shack for him to come in so they could brief him and be relieved for the night. And they waited. Then, finally, someone decided that this was too long, and that something was wrong. The security officers went out to the car and saw their relief man sitting there with has eyes closed and head bowed. *Praying? Really? At this hour?*

After a moment or two they noticed that this guy was not moving. They somehow got into his car to check him and somebody called 911. I was told that the security officer was sitting there, dead, *with his hand still on the gearshift lever.* This was a case where he died on the site but did not actually get killed in the line of duty. This was a situation of natural causes where a heart attack occurred so quickly that he was dead before he could even take his hand off the gearshift lever. That must have been very spooky, seeing your coworker and possibly a friend of yours in that position. This was very difficult, indeed.

There was a security officer who was shot at an Anytown convenience store. A fellow security officer just happened to walk in on a scene of a crime. The criminals were already off the scene, but the fallen security officer was not. When he determined that Officer Doe was killed, lying on the floor in a pool of his own blood, a police officer came on the scene and ordered Doe away from the body. The cop had his gun drawn because apparently, he was in pursuit of the suspect that shot the man on the floor. When Officer Doe explained who he was, the cop eased up a lot and called into his radio, "Officer down."

The details of this death did reach the papers. Now whether Security Professional Doe was telling the truth about being the one on scene at the shooting, one can never really tell. All the details he got for his story could have very easily been found in the newspaper stories.

I will stop right here with the examples, because you get the picture. Some people die on duty; some people are killed on duty. Death comes for all people. There is not any avoiding it. It will get us all one day. No matter what we do, or don't do, death comes for us all. It is, I think, especially tragic when the security officer is on duty and loses their life taking some extra shifts or other risk that put him in harm's way just because he needed the overtime. That is just so sad, to see families suffer like that.

The hardest part is when the company just denies the whole thing happened. After all, they have a business to run, right? They simply cannot allow their good name to be besmirched by a tragic event like this. After all, these security pros know the risks they take when they sign on, right? And we cannot have anyone just up and quit their job upon hearing about the death of a coworker. This is the literal attitude of some private security companies. There is no camaraderie between employees except for some personal alliances which occur naturally between people who get along. There is no real reason to believe that the other guy has your back. Not like the cops or the firefighters. Not like the real heroes. Security officers take the same risks with virtually none of the support. Undertrained, underfunded and working for some company that sees only their bottom line.

Sometimes, yes, we will see a special memorial, but that is usually because the security officer was a police officer or military veteran who happened to become a security officer after the fact. Then the company has no choice but to make a fuss over the security professional's death, because it has already been made public and it would seem to be in very poor taste in the public eye to not recognize this veteran police officer, soldier, or both who was tragically killed or died in the line of duty.

It may seem that I am being too harsh on the private security firms. But the facts are the facts. Honestly, how often do we hear of the death of a security officer? Almost never, unless it is a death already connected with some high priority case. How can I say that? Well, let me tell you how I can say that. An organization called Private Officer: Voice of the Frontline Protector has listed at their memorial page for private officers (see: *http://privateofficer.org/ officer-down/*) for details. *As of June, 2020, one hundred and twenty sixty-four private duty officers have been listed as killed in the line of duty.* They also say at their website that "THE NAMES LISTED HERE DO NOT REFLECT THE TOTAL NUMBER OF OFFICERS KILLED IN THE LINE OF DUTY. THIS IS A PARTIAL LIST. Although we have a full time news and research department that tracks security and private police officer injuries and deaths, the total number of deaths is unknown due to a lack of accurate agency reporting, media omitting names, and misclassification of job titles."

This is the hard fact, my dear people. This is the hardest fact of all to bear. The Internet is rife with stories of people who have lost loved ones in the security industry. Some of the fallen are working in night clubs, bars, construction sites, doing patrol work, working at hospitals with difficult patients and so forth. These names are the names of security professionals who died trying to do their job. The complaints from family members have covered the gamut of reasons for the deaths. Included are some of the things, which I have listed here in this book. A lack of training. Insufficient personnel. Unsafe working conditions. Failure to properly arm the people who do security work. Lack of practice with weapons. And so on. One security professional was even shot and killed by a police officer as they responded to the same scene. He died in November 2018 even as I was writing this book.

I read one story that says Jemel was clearly wearing a SECURITY ball cap and was responding to the same shooting as the police. I cannot actually judge the cop who was on the scene. I was not there at the time. A wrongful death suit was filed. I understand why. The police call this an "accidental shooting." Well, no kidding, Sherlock! I would hope that that a cop would not intentionally kill a security officer. May I risk a glib moment here? It is not like the police officer is going to say, "Hey! Security! Look over here! Yeah, you!" *BANG! BANG!* The question that may be asked in court is the resounding *why* did the officer fire his weapon? That will be the big question and will prove or disprove the wrongful death. Not if the police officer shot Jemel, but why did the officer shoot Jemel. And how much training did Jemel have in responding to a crime? How often did he interact with the police? Was race an issue? Did Jemel hear "Stop! Put your hands up!" but never in a million years would he believe that a police officer would tell a first-response security professional to put his hand up. After all, he was one of the good guys.

And was the police officer's perspective? Another fine question. What was the cop thinking when he shot Jemel? Did Jemel do something suspicious in front of the police officer that made him think his own life was in danger? Did Jemel have his weapon out? Did he turn the wrong way and mistakenly appear that he was going to fire on the police? And what about that SECURITY cap...was it visible in the lighting conditions? Personally, I really don't know the answer to all of these questions because I have not yet researched this. There is something very disturbing about all of these security professional deaths: *THE MEDIA DOES NOT NAME SOME OF THEM!* I counted at least fifteen names of the fallen security professionals who were listed "Unidentified Officer," "Unknown Security Officer," or "Unidentified Security Officer." This is an outrage! An insult to their loved ones!

In the quote listed above from "Private Officer," we also learn that some security professionals are not properly recognized because their job at the time of their death is not properly classified as a private officer or a security professional. And I am certain that security agencies leave the names of their fallen employees off the public record or classify as them as "office staff" or some other benign title because they don't want their company's precious name or reputation dragged into this. They don't want people to know that their company has a tendency toward hiring employees whose spouses are left to sit at the table, supper getting cold, fuming and wondering why their husband or wife did not come home with that gallon of milk as promised, only to find out they were killed and the company did not bother to call.

My experience with death on the job has been limited, but sufficient to understand that while some companies may send a management team to represent the company at a security professional's funeral, many do not. Many just want to wash their hands of the whole thing to keep their company's reputation out of the mud. My guess is that they also don't want hard questions to come up concerning training and education levels of management, and the continuing education of the employees who are daily put at risk. The short of it is that they don't want anyone discovering their dirty little secrets of how they need to shave off training and equipment overhead costs to keep their bottom line at levels which please investors. They don't want anyone to know how little they pay their officers and how little training they give them. They don't want anyone to know that they work their people into the ground and past breaking points. They don't want anyone to know that their loved one was shot in the back of the head because they were overworked and nodded off, or just plain were not alert.

There are plenty of arguments for the standardization of the training of security officers. There are people who advocate for the United States to put federal standards in place that each state must meet if they are to have security or private officers working in their state. And they will need to clearly define what a security or private officer actually is, because it would be too easy to call someone a "lobby attendant" or an "usher" to scoot past the rules and laws governing private officers.

We have already examined some stories, experiences and news reports in which security officers are put in a bad light because they have said or done some highly inappropriate things. They have even behaved dangerously. There are some people in that industry who just don't belong in the field. But the way things stand right now *almost anyone* can become a security officer. Most companies don't do profiles on their people. They may do a background check, but that is about it. The only reason they do even this much is because they are forced to do so by whatever laws or rules do exist. That and they wish to avoid liability. We need to regulate this industry to prevent people from entering the field who will likely create dangerous circumstances. I believe that there needs to be basic requirements in education and training. Psychological testing should also be in order, particularly in the hiring of armed security personnel. "You got a gun? Do you know how to use it?" should not be the only qualifying question for someone seeking an armed position.

I believe that armed security personnel should be exposed to a battery of testing, similar to police officers. The testing should be similar because the jobs can put both security and police in similar situations. There should be scenario-based training and "shoot, don't shoot" training. Security personnel should know something about de-escalating situations. They should, and this important, have some clear guidelines on what situations to engage and which situations they need to stay out of and just hang back collecting information. Basic things like "don't get yourself killed" should be covered to give a security professional a clear option of not engaging in a situation they feel is too dangerous. That is what the police are trained and equipped to do. They have the military-style gear and training necessary to handle situations that security personnel simply don't know how to safely or successfully engage.

So why has this kind of thing not happened sooner? The trouble seems to be that the security industry has gotten too big to try and reign in. And regulations of the security industry are not going to be popular because they will be difficult and expensive to implement and maintain. Such standards would probably force a lot of security companies out of business. That all may be true, but we need to do something because this situation is simply a travesty! I happen to know that in Anystate, USA, there are absolutely no state regulations of the security or private officer employees within their jurisdiction. The cities have to license security professionals, and that is only if they decide to do so. There is no training regulations and the security officers are not required to learn any law whatsoever. The result is security professionals who don't even know or understand their own boundaries. The result of no federalized training standards is security officers who don't know what they are doing, and it is getting both security professionals and individuals the security personnel deal with killed!

Something has got to change before this gets any further out of hand!

A BORED SECURITY OFFICER

There are times when the lives of people on the job get very, very boring. This is true with every job. Even first responders get bored. There are quiet days at fire houses and police precincts where just nothing happens. That is good, because everyone needs a break. This is especially true for first responders because a person's mind and body can only take so much. Some people respond better than others, but evidence of what first responders do for a living will take its toll. There is no need for first responders, including security officers, to crave or to seek excitement. Plenty of excitement will come their way, if they are in the business long enough. Being a well-seasoned security veteran, I can attest to the fact that *every* security professional will get their day in the "cool/exciting/interesting story" category.

There was a case in the Anytown Security Agency that I found particularly troubling. This young security officer called out to his dispatcher that there were two men in ski masks emerging from behind a dumpster. He was ordered very specifically to *not* engage, but to wait for backup to arrive. He was ordered to only observe the situation and report his findings as the situation unfolded. He was not allowed to go into this thing alone. His response was that dispatch needed to get someone there because he was going to approach these men right now.

Dispatch had only the radio traffic to go on, so they ordered security officers in the area, who were in vehicles, to proceed to that area immediately and police were also called. This security professional was armed, and more armed security and police officers were on their way. Then suddenly, the call all dispatchers and security officers dread hearing from the field, "Shots fired! I'm hit! I'm hit!" Police stepped up their response to code 3, lights and sirens blazing and blaring, and the security personnel, not authorized to light up, did step up their response as much as they could. Medical personnel were summoned, and this brought an Advanced Life Support engine company into play. This was now very serious business and security professionals all over the city held their breath. Was one of their own about to die tonight for his ten bucks an hour?

When all of the units converged on the scene, it was the customary chaos. Lights, lights, and more lights. Personnel apparently running amok, but actually responding with the controlled form of chaos with which these things are handled. Units were coming in from all over the place. Some police officers were searching for the suspects, using the security officer's description. Other police units were securing the area, marking the crime scene with yellow tape, getting ready for the big investigation to begin. They were searching for evidence, overseeing the welfare of the security officer and asking him questions as permitted by the medical personnel.

The paramedics had removed the security officer's bullet resistant vest, which did show evidence of two shots having been fired into it. The vest held, the trauma plate did its job and stopped the bullets from penetrating it. The security officer was taken to the hospital by ambulance for evaluation. Family and loved ones were notified of his potential injury and were at the hospital. This was a scene filled with all the jazz and excitement a guy could want.

In the course of the investigation though, things just were not adding up because of the position of the bullets in the vest and the lack of bruising or cracked ribs on the officer. The evidence on the scene was just not matching the story, either. Finally, a break came in the case when police detectives met with the senior managing owners of the security company and talked things over. Then they brought the security officer in to discuss the findings of the investigative team. At that interview, the security officer broke down, finally, and told the truth about what happened. The lie had gotten too big and he could not cover himself any longer with any stories that made any sense.

What had actually occurred was that he got bored. He got bored and wanted to stir up some excitement. So he took off his vest, laid it up against a tree, called in a phony story about two men in ski masks, and then fired two shots from his duty weapon into the vest. He put the vest back on and…well, we already have the rest of the story. Needless to say, his license which was required by his Anystate, USA, security rules and laws, was revoked and he would never work in that industry as a licensed officer again. I hope, personally, that criminal charges of false reporting were filed. They should have been, because this was just over the top ridiculous. How much money, time, gear and man-hours were wasted investigating this phony report? How many police officers were taken off patrol just to answer this call?

This is the kind of thing that more careful screening of security officers would help to reduce. You may not prevent all abhorrent behaviors, but this kind of thing can certainly be reduced significantly. I am sure there a lot more stories of bored security personnel stirring up "excitement." This is the only one I have, personally. It may not be the only one, but I think you would have to go a long way to find a story to beat it. My thought is that the guy who did this probably did not think it clear through. He just got this crazy idea, which turned into a fantasy and he just ran with it. The truth had to come out sometime, and I guess he probably did not think about that part.

I WAS GIVEN A BREAK BY MY SUPERVISOR

I once worked in a medical facility where I was putting in seventy or more hours per week. I worked the overtime because I needed to make my living. I was not able to support myself on straight time alone. I had to work the overtime to pay the rent and light bill. It was a tough time because I was struggling, and my family was falling apart. My wife separated from me and the children were not so much as talking to me. It was tough, also, because this happened right at the holidays. The only comfort I had in my life at that time was my religion. My supervisor knew of my convictions, and he knew too of my tough situation. He also saw how much I was sacrificing to try and live well. He was impressed that the worse things got, the closer I turned to God.

We could not have any kind of situation that overtly showed favoritism because of the sensitive nature of this particular post and its internal politics. There are people who are just ready to create a scrap at the drop of a hat, even if the situation they are willing to fight you over is just plain *none* of their business. This attitude for some reason ran rampant in this particular team. I think it was a combination of most of the team being young, aimless and loving drama.

I approached the bosses about some of the people they were hiring. They understood what I was talking about, but there was not much they could do because they could only hire from the people who were applying for the position. So there we had the problem in a nutshell. We could not hire quality people because there were no quality people applying for the job. We were stuck working with whatever best of the worst they could find who was willing to come in and do the job. Or not really *do* the job, but at least show up for work. There is something to be said for that...just getting people through the door sometimes is a real challenge.

So with that being said, my supervisor realized I had some needs and being the good guy that he was as well as recognizing my value to the team and how often I pulled the team out of the fire, he helped me out with a religious need. I wanted to take what churches commonly call Communion, sacrament, the Lord's Supper, etc. and they offered that service at this facility. It was not a matter of me taking a lot of time or anything like that. I just needed five minutes off the floor. That in itself was not an issue, but the boss could not look like he was playing favorites because for something even as small as five minutes; someone would call him out on it, and then there could be potential legal issue.

His plan was to make sure that I was on patrol at the hour the service was convened. I just needed discreetly slip in, do my "religious thing" and slide out. I just could not be seen by the public or other security officers while doing it. The church people would see me, of course, but it was very unlikely that they would rat me out. I mean, that would be truly rotten and they were nice people. So they were glad to help me. So every Sunday at the appointed hour I would take my five minutes aside, unless of course there was trouble, because the job indeed came first, but in that five minutes I found a bit of peace in my otherwise chaotic life.

I greatly appreciated that, and it really helped me through a tough time. I am writing this not to preach religion, but to preach *humanity*. I would reach out to managers, supervisors and fellow security professionals to remind them that all people have problems and sometimes they need a little help. Now, a religious moment may not do it for the one who struggles, but maybe a quick side stop to the snack bar might boost their morale. There are times, even to this day, that I will give a break to a security professional and bring them a slice of pizza or treat them to a moment of conversation if it is not interfering with their duties. A kind word can really make someone's day if they are having a bad time.

I just want to say here that security pros put themselves at risk and know that when crazy comes to visit, they are likely going to run toward it while others run away. It never hurts to show kindness to security personnel because they are people too, and they have lives and families to go home to. Or maybe they go home alone and don't have much of a life. Regardless of what life they may or may not have, it is important to be kind. Something as little as a cup of coffee or a bottle of pop can do wonders for some poor chap that just can't catch a break.

So I appeal to security bosses and anyone else who is in a position to show a kind gesture to their security professionals, please just do it. Just show them that you recognize them and appreciate what they do. Those who have never done this work don't know just how crummy and thankless the job can be. It is downright discouraging when the very people you are working to protect don't even appreciate what you do every day. So when you see the security pro at the desk, even if they don't look all that professional to you, recognize their sacrifices and just cut them a little break now and then.

EXHAUSTION AND ITS EFFECTS

Tom Clancy, RIP, was a great military writer. He was often lauded as being one of the most technically correct authors in his genre, if not the best. One of the things that I love about Clancy's work is that he did not try to romanticize the work of a soldier, marine, airman or spy. Instead, he would tell it like it was, even down to small craft pilots messing their flight suits on long missions. If it was just a "fact of life," Tom covered it.

I like how he would go into detail about the different sensations people would experience at different times. Dizziness, disorientation, panic, euphoria are all part of life and military personnel, as often as they may claim or otherwise, are subject to the sensations of life and the weaknesses in their bodies. After all, if our honored service people did not have weakness, they would be invulnerable and could not die. Sadly, this is not the case.

I bring this up because I have learned over the years how hard I could push myself. I have since determined to never push myself like that ever again. I have gone as long as seventy-two hours without sleep. I was a much younger man when I did it, and I was never in the military, but I did do it. I was working a couple of different jobs and I was night shifter at a shopping mall on the security team. The job though is not what I wish to focus upon. It is what a person's body does when one becomes bone tired and the benefit of sleep is denied them.

I realized that first, my emotions would start to disappear. I could not spare the energy to feel happy, sad or angry unless some external stimulus jumpstarted me. I would just start to feel less and less emotionally. Then my suggestibility would increase. I would become susceptible to ideas or suggestions that seemed to come out of nowhere. I would get "great ideas." I would start to write gibberish if I was filling out a report. Then my heart would start to beat out of rhythm.

If this went on long enough, I would start to get emotional again, but I was very cranky.

RED SOCK, GREEN SOCK, TRIPPED ALARM

I was on duty one afternoon at a uniformed and armed account. The client was a high-end jewelry store in Anytown, USA. The store was located in a high-rent district and very exclusive. I was making my post-closing perimeter door checks, required after all of the employees left for the day. I checked a plain exit door at the back of the store, and when I tugged on it, I felt it give, and immediately I pushed it closed. I did not open the door fully, but any hopes of not triggering the alarm and settling the matter without an uproar were completely shattered a split instant after I closed the door and winced. I did not want a scene. I truly did not. But well, a quiet resolution simply was not in the cards.

The audible alarm, a traditional clanging bell, very loud, was the first event. I immediately called my lieutenant on duty, and as soon as he heard my voice and the background racket over the phone, he started laughing. Not that he did not take the thing seriously, but he heard me say I was okay, no event was in progress, and he knew immediately what happened. He knew I triggered the alarm with an unlocked door. We followed procedure, and he called the store owner. Meanwhile, the cops were en route but got canceled by somebody along the way, so I did not have to put up with a half dozen cops going through the building to clear it of any wrongdoers.

The problem was this: that alarm did not have an automatic cancellation of any kind. It did not time out. It did not silence. It just kept on clanging rapidly, hollering on and on like a neighbor's obnoxious dog at 2:00 AM. I'm thinking, "Shaddup already!" But no, I was stuck, standing there on my big, blocky cellular phone, one of the older types, trying to settle this thing. Something I observed as I was making my calls was of interest. The older guys in the neighborhood who drove by looked at me and nodded in my direction to make sure I was okay. I indicated a kind of "thumbs-up," and they were assured that I was fine. The younger people who drove by were smiling and laughing, staring at me like they were hoping to see some doo-doo hit the fan. Idiots!! If they thought there was some kind of danger, they should have stayed out of the area. Of course, that was not the case because everything is like a movie or video game to the younger set.

With that being said, I finally quieted things down. People got bored and stayed away, even though the alarm would not stop barking. The owner of the store was away at a birthday dinner for one of his employees, and they were aware of what happened, that all was secure even if it was a bit noisy. So they were in no real rush to get back to the store to press the necessary buttons and silence the thing. I was ready to silence it with my 9 mm, but I resisted the urge. Bullets are just too expensive anyways (tongue in cheek).

So there I was standing around and waiting for the owner to come by after the baklava and terminate the alarm. After about a half an hour, somebody showed. But…it was not the owner of the store.

This was some alarm-response truck. I stood there as he parked a short distance away from the scene. I expected a uniformed professional to approach me. What I got was a bit different than expected. In fact, it was a living, breathing picture of an unfortunate security stereotype. This young man was about 120 pounds soaking wet. Now, that I could live with, but the rest of it, not so much.

This young man, of about nineteen years I supposed, got out of the truck. The first thing I noticed was that his uniform shirt had likely been dug out of the bottom of a laundry basket. There was not a square inch of it without a wrinkle. I mean, it was that bad. Then I saw his nice navy-blue pants…which came up past his ankles about three inches. This was just wrong…but that was not where the story ended. He wore bright, red socks and on his feet, just to be clear, he wore *green* Converses! ARRRRRRGH! I could not believe what I was seeing. And then to add a cherry to this nut's whipped cream, to complete the sundae, *he got out of the truck with a big smile on his face and pulled a Maglite and rhythmically swatted his palm with it as he approached me!*

I thought to myself, "This guy has got to be kidding."

Here I was, dressed in my leather jacket with a shield embroidered over the left breast, a knit cap that said "SECURITY" across it, and I was about twice or more his size. Even if he did think I was a bad guy, what was he going to do with that Maglite? Hit me? Throw it at me? If he did not know who I was, he should have stayed in his truck at a safe distance, watched me, and called the police. But no, he made this dramatic approach like he was gonna just tell me what was what and scare me with his palm-swatting. I think he was a big fan of redneck sheriff movies or something. I mean, did he really think that I was going to take him seriously in that get-up that he called a uniform? So I let him get only so far from his truck, and then I folded my arms across my chest and raised my clearly marked leather jacket to expose my duty gear, including my sidearm.

He stopped, froze for a moment, ran back to his truck, put his Maglite inside the cab, and rushed back over to me. He had this big, excited smile on his face and asked me what happened. I explained it to him, using carefully measured and little words, as he soaked it all up like a sponge. Then he thanked me and returned to his truck. He left the scene…thank heaven…and went on about his duty. I hope he was going to the dry cleaners, but I doubt that thought had even occurred to him. I don't think he had so much as a clue about how foolish he looked and how foolish he made our whole industry appear to the world. My guess is that he did not last long on the job. Guys like that tend to get bored very easily, and they just sort of fade away into the fast-food business after a while.

QUIDADO, MIJO!

I was working at Anytown mall. A young Mexican fellow approached me. He was with two young ladies; one was a family member, and the other was probably his girlfriend. He stepped up to me, flanked by the two ladies, and he started in with Spanish. He was talking to me and telling the most awful things about what kind of doo-doo I was made of, questioned my parentage, called me a "stupid animal," which was a grave insult in Mexican culture, suggested obscene things I could do to my own mother, etc. He finished up, and he was just giving me as broad and friendly of a smile as he could. I was smiling right back like I did not know what he was saying. As soon as I knew he was finished, I said back to him:

> *"Quidado, mijo. Entiendo su español perfecta-*
> *mente. Mi esposa es mexicana!"*

The thought I just conveyed translated into, "Be careful, little boy! I understand your Spanish perfectly. My wife is Mexican!"

So not only did I understand the mechanics of the language, but with my wife being Mexican, I understood the culture. Plus, he knew that I understand all the subtle subtext to everything he was saying. I knew how gravely he had just insulted me. His reaction was immediate; he closed his eyes and said, "Aw, man!" and his ladies started laughing at him, saying, "Oh, he got you good! He got you!"

So understanding that not only was he clearly embarrassed, but I had just embarrassed him in front of the two ladies, one a relative, I just looked at him and told him that I would let it slide, but I wanted to never hear such language at the mall again. You see, his humiliation was exponential because the girls probably warned him to not mess with me, but he did it anyway, like a little macho *gallo* (rooster) who was going to tell the *gringo* Paul Blart just what was what. And I know that when they got home this was immediately published to the whole family how Juanito just got his butt handed to him by some *gringo* who understands and speaks Spanish. Not only that, but it would be no surprise to learn that he was still getting razzed to this day by his cousins.

The lesson here is that peer pressure is a valuable thing among young people. I could have been a real jerk about this whole thing and sent all three of them out of the mall, possibly even trespassing them for a while. His language was as filthy was could be, and that was a serious infraction. But knowing that his peer group would take care of him, I let him off with a friendly warning and a few laughs. I learned something valuable here too, and that is if someone is sufficiently embarrassed in front of their friends, the friends will often take sides against the offender. They don't want to have to leave the mall; they don't want to get into trouble, so when I have a situation like that, I use the peers to keep control of the friend. I tell them that while I should throw all of them out right now, I won't do it if they promise to keep their friend in line.

Sometimes it works, and sometimes it does not work or even backfires, but I prefer to keep things at the least amount of enforcement as appears necessary to diffuse the situation. If behavior will change without throwing people out or taking any further action, then why go any further? As long as I get compliance, I don't care if they actually get punished by me or the cops. There are some moments when you just need to have a little fun with people and show some understanding. This may work and stop trouble before it starts. Other times, well, you just won't have control, and you will need to resort to using enforcement measures including police involvement.

HOT MIKES AND PHONETIC ALPHABETS

I was on a security team at an Anytown mall. They had a police officer come in and give a quick rundown on why they did things that we might question. There was a case where a shoplifter got turned loose by cops after they recovered the merchandise. The security pros understandably questioned their judgment in that case. After all, security caught the guy, likely handcuffed him, held him for the cops, but then the police called "no harm, no foul" after getting the merchandise back to the mall tenant. It would ultimately be up to the tenant whether or not to press charges, but PD convinced them not to. It was a little upsetting in that case, but it turned out that the shoplifter bargained for a no charge in the shoplift because he had some information on a homicide. I don't personally agree with making deals like that, but not being a cop, I don't know how things work in that part of the world. But… I must say that if given the choice between a shoplift or homicide prosecution, I would rather see the murderer taken off the streets.

During this same training session, the cop mentioned something about radio etiquette. I completely agreed with him. He told us that we needed to memorize some kind of phonetic alphabet, be it the NATO "alpha, bravo, Charlie, delta, echo…" or one of the city PD phonetic lists of "Adam, Baker, Charlie, David, Edward…" This is important for security professionals to do because other made-up phonetics sound unprofessional or even clownish on the radio. Compare the following:

> *"Dispatch this is Sierra 1. I am monitoring a vehicle that is leaving the property at a high rate of speed after picking up an assault suspect police were chasing on foot. Copy license plate alpha, delta, Romeo, 6, 4, 2. White Toyota Sedan, four-door, Missouri plate."*

> *"Dispatch this is Sam 1… I am monitoring a vehicle that is leaving the property at a high rate of*

speed after picking up an assault suspect police were chasing on foot. Copy license plate Adam...uh... Detox...um... Red Rover, 6, 4, 2. White Toyota Sedan, four-door, Missouri plate."

It kind of sounds silly, doesn't it, when you make up things like "macaroni" or "cockroach" to use rather than a solid and confidently pronounced phonetic arrangement? It is true that we have gotten away from a lot of the 10-codes other than 10-4, which is universally understood. The reason for dropping the exclusive use of 10-coding is to improve communications between different agencies. In the Phoenix area alone, I recall knowing at least three different phonetic alphabets and 10-code sets. When 9/11 hit us, we had all kinds of interagency support to the World Trade Center, but they could not communicate well over the radio because they never considered that 10-33 might mean distress to one agency, but it might mean to another agency that they were to maintain radio silence. If a fireman gets hurt and calls 10-33, the firefighters working for the other agency might be standing by, wondering why he called for radio silence when the first guy is lying there hurt. He in turn will be wondering why the heck nobody is responding to his distress call. Imagine such awkwardness and confusion between several different agencies on a multi-event, interagency scene! Different agencies and individuals interpreting the same exact 10-codes differently will always lead to unadulterated bedlam.

Another facet of radio communication is to take care of the radio and to not "hot-mike" it. A hot mike occurs when the radio transmit key is depressed and held down without the user knowing it or it may stick in a position that allows for transmission without the user being aware. You can hot-mike by sitting on your radio and having a seatbelt buckle or other obstruction depress the key or the mike can stick open because the button does not fully release into the closed position.

I once heard a story about some Anytown, USA, cops who were riding in a police patrol car. They had just left some kind of big meeting with the department. These senior and some ranking officers were not very happy with what Chief (Doe) or Captain (Anyone) had to say. They were cursing and swearing, saying really bad things about their leadership, making personal remarks and so on. Well, they had left the property, called in that car such and such was leaving and going to so and so, but the hand mike button did not fully release when the officer put the mike on the retainer.

There is no way to know about a hot mike until someone tells you vocally. There is no red light on the radio that warns you, no tone to alert you and no automatic disconnect that kicks in to somehow end the transmission, and when you are on a city frequency, there is no way to interrupt you. You can sit there on top of that mike all day long and every word you say, every belch and belly rumble, every sound in that car or near your hip is transmitted to every person on that frequency all the day long until you or someone releases that transmission key. These cops did not know that their key was depressed, that their sounding off in great torrents of profanity and general disrespect were being sent to the whole department until another cop car pulled up alongside, the officer in that car holding his radio mike and tapping it, then pointing to them. It took a second, but they got the message and somebody released the transmit key…about ten minutes too late because *everything those cops were saying, every word of it, got transmitted to the entire city.*

Apparently, the officers who held rank over the ranking officers in that patrol car were not amused. There were some disciplinary days and actions taken such as black marks on records, demotions and even termination, as the department saw fit. Radio communications are taken very seriously, and great care needs to be exercised.

On the lighter side, not all hot keys are this serious. Sometimes, they are just remotely embarrassing. There was a security patrol officer, armed, who was assigned certain accounts in Anytown. Officer Doe had pressed his handheld transmission key against his seatbelt and was overheard talking to himself while on patrol:

"Oh…look over there…driving around… la-la-la…wait…no, that's a scary-looking place.

*I'm not paid to go into a scary-looking place..." (Or
similar statements.)*

Now, personally, I thought that this guy should reconsider what
he was doing for a living. After all, we were an armed patrol unit. We
were security officers. People do have the right to expect a certain
amount of courage from a full-grown man who wears a gun and
works in the protection business! But he was allowed to continue
his service with the company, and he was just really quite careful
about not transmitting his lonesome conversations with himself to
the whole company. He did quit though, finally—another guy using
security as a springboard to better things. But not much better. I
think he went into apartment maintenance.

OH...just one more radio foul up to report before I close this
particular topic. At a mall, there was a police force stationed on site.
Many shopping malls throughout the country have police substa-
tions in them, since calls for help are very common inside shopping
malls. Having the police right there in their own well-marked police
station may also act as a deterrent to wrongdoings, but maybe not...
the point to the story is that even well-marked and established police
can make mistakes over the radio.

There was a particular tenant of the Anytown mall, this was an
Anystore, very common to malls, which happened to sell clothing.
Normally, our worst retail problem there was when kids would get
into the store to shop and then would invade the display area where
they kept the mannequins. You might think that the kids would steal
clothing or vandalize things in the window, but all they would do is
to pull the mannequins' shorts down around their ankles and leave
them that way, in public view. Personally, I thought it was hilarious
when I would walk by and see that in the window. I would have to
then suppress my smile and tell the store manager what "the kids
did...again," and they would immediately thank me and fix the
problem. No harm, no foul. That, however, is not the point of the
story.

The real issue at hand was that the franchise owner was not
right in the head, or was perhaps just lazy. Whatever the issue was,

the I-beams behind his store were rusting over, and it was getting worse with time. Somehow, the word got out to security, and then to the police that the guy who owned the place was urinating in the back service hall, and that was what caused the beams to rust. The problem was that nobody could catch him at it, and naturally, he would not confess to doing that thing. Of course, it was obvious what was happening. The odor, the rust on the beam, the dried appearance on the floor—all these were clear evidence.

Well, one night, the cops finally caught Mr. Doe urinating in the service corridor. He was right there, hosing down the I-beam. I guess that this had been ongoing for some time, years even. The cop who caught him practically shouted into the mall radio:

> "Hey, everybody! We just caught Mr. Doe p——ing in the hall!"

Unfortunately, the mall did not provide the security team with ear mikes, so that transmission resounded in the ears of the general public, in front of some parents with small children. A few of our people got stern looks from some of the parents who were in the company of small children. Our people had to apologize for the policeman's excited proclamation. After all, Mr. Doe was a repeat offender of many years. It does not excuse what the police officer did, but it does shed some light of understanding upon the whole situation. We were a bit embarrassed, but in the end, all was well, and Mr. Doe finally got his just desserts. Dare I say he was caught red-handed?

PTSD AND THE SECURITY PROFESSIONAL

We hear an awful lot about PTSD and first responders, and we really should. We should hear about it; people should know about it; people should do something about it. I agree entirely that this is a big challenge and that it should be addressed. This is also one of the reasons why I wrote this book. People need to understand that cops, firefighters, EMTs, and paramedics are not the only first responders out there. The first response of the security professional is often overlooked. The blood that security personnel see is not often reported. The shots that are exchanged between bad guys and security professionals go largely unheralded in the papers. When a security officer gets killed in the line of duty, the community does not know it. There is no flag-draped coffin; there is no special service; there is no outpouring of support in the community. You never see the mayor of the town thank the widow/widower, and children left behind for their sacrifice. You see all these happen for cops, firefighters, and EMT/paramedics, but you never see this happen for the security professional.

Why? Well, I think it has much to do with the fact that security professionals are private assets. They are not public officers; they are not dedicated to protecting the community by a governing body. No, they are just employees of some company who tragically lost their life at work. Just like any other death at a private company, the death is passed over, and there is no fancy funeral. Not unless the security professional happens to be a former police officer or a military veteran. Then they get the flag and the heartfelt thanks at their funeral to the ones left behind. This is both proper and right; such service must be recognized.

But what about the private security professional? Every day many of these people, my brothers and sisters who have opted to go out there and place themselves at risk to protect other people and property, who choose a career where they are taking the burden of guarding individual lives and property off of the police, who cannot be everywhere, are rarely recognized when they die on duty or in the line of duty. Now let me explain what I mean by "on duty" versus "in the line of duty."

When I say that someone died on duty, I mean they had a heart attack, a stroke or some other unfortunate medical event that happened to kill them while they were on the clock. When I say that someone died in the line of duty, I mean they died performing some function that directly caused their death. They may have been hit by a car while protecting a parking structure. They may have been shot while on patrol or standing in public watching a train station. They may have been stabbed after approaching a trespasser. They may have been thrown over a railing and fell to their death at a shopping mall. These things all happen, and they are all a very real part of being a security officer.

I believe that these deaths are often kept secret because the security companies are trying to avoid the public eye. They don't want people to understand how dangerous security work can be. They don't want people to know that security professionals have died in the line of duty because it would be difficult to replace "assets" who are killed in the line of duty. While you cannot ever really pay anyone enough to die on the job and make the money "worth it," because the money is never "worth it" when you see your loved one in a coffin. And does the flag really make a difference?

Well, yes it does. It did for me anyway. The flag on my father's casket said to me that someone recognized the sacrifice that he made when he went to Vietnam, that this old, gray-haired man who now lay dead of a stroke was known to have done something in the service of his country. So yes, that gave us some consolation. It is important to recognize that sacrifice because it gives the grieving family something to hold onto. It helps them to know their loved one's life meant something to somebody else, that they served a greater good sometime during the course of their lives. The families of combat veterans deserve that with a special recognition; for when the soldier suffers, all suffer, and in my case, here, *soldier* is an all-encompassing term for all combat veterans. I will save the rest of this soapbox speech for another day, maybe even another book.

My point here is to cause people to understand that there is a real danger and traumatic element to the security professional's job. They see stuff that the average Joe does not see. Granted, they are not continually called to deal with crime and the underbelly of society quite the same way that cops are called upon; that is not the assigned function of the security officer. But security personnel do see their share of evil in this world, and they take a lot of grief for it. Security people do not have the same respect as police officers because they do not have the same authority to enforce law and they do not have the same training. Granted. Understood. Copy. Over and out. But security personnel *are often exposed to dangers that police are not!* Because security people are not respected by citizens and criminals alike, the bad guys don't fear security. Citizens don't respect security. That alone adds an element of danger to everything security people do. And don't get me started on liability! Oh my stars, the potential liabilities of a security officer who shoots someone while he is on duty are tremendous and more often than not they have no legal coverage or protection from their company!

Security personnel are often left with nothing but their own defense when they fire their weapon. The cops have the advantage of being immediately defended by the umbrella of the community they are assigned to protect. They have legal rights to defense and they even have special rules that protect the statements they are required to make. As private citizens, security professionals have no such rules; they wear the uniform, but their company will usually downplay the company's own role in the shooting; and the professional is stripped of their uniform and left to their own designs. They have no umbrella; they have no special protections; and if they have an attorney, it is either the one they can afford to pay; or it is an overworked, underpaid, burned-out public defender who is going to just plea them out.

All this weighs on the minds of the people who go to work in the security field. Then they get to see the nightmare that really exists on the streets firsthand. The security personnel on any site are the first line of defense. They are the ones who are exposed to the garbage first. They get the first whiff of the body that has been lying there for days. They are the first ones who meet that armed sociopath. They are the ones who smell the smoke and pull the alarm. The security person is the one who finds that bad guy and calls the cops. They are the ones who are first exposed to the situation. They see that danger first, and it takes its toll.

I was fortunate to have a company with an EAP to help talk me down after some of the stuff I saw, but not all security officers are that lucky. Many times, they just have deal with it their own way. Not that there is anything wrong with "dealing with it," in fact, we all need to deal with it, but counseling can help us find ways to deal with it more effectively, and it takes the security professional's family out of the loop. They don't have to find a way to talk Mom or Dad down from that adrenalin rush. They don't have to listen to the story of what happened. They don't get the burden of knowing what they are sending their loved one out every day or night, day and night, to face.

My point is that security professionals are faced with dangers that can suddenly push them from a quiet walk through a building or on the street into a pedal-to-the-metal full-blown, life-endangering situation. We keep hearing about how this takes its toll on first responders. Everyone assumes this means cops, firefighters and medics only. No one considers the "Paul Blart-Barney Fife-Wanna-Be-Ignorant-Untrained-Fool" who just saw that burned body, that man who he used to work with whose head now has a hole in it, that kid who was just mercilessly beaten by their parent or who just had his life threatened by a deadly weapon in the hands of someone who was willing to use it. No…no one considers them at all, because no one understands the heroes that these people truly are.

The security professional is left to go home to their family, shower off the dirt and blood, wash their uniform, and go back to their normal life until they are on duty again. The problem with that is the security pro never really goes *off* duty, unless they learn to deal with the things they see. There is no real support network. They have no thin blue line. In fact, they are often and openly mocked by the boys in blue. I do understand that position, because of the poor training and bad-boy attitudes that some security people portray. I get it. I understand…but society and police officers need to understand too that the security professional faces the same risks. Not as often in some cases, and more often in others. It all depends on the type of job they are doing and in what neighborhood they do it. So my plea is for the public and law enforcement to please understand that security is the "eye that never sleeps," sometimes literally, and they go home with many burdens that people just don't understand, and they do so without the advantage of being in blue. Or red. Or having any colors that anyone truly respects.

The security professional goes home to try and sleep. He has nightmares. He gets grouchy. Sometimes he cannot sleep at all. It takes a toll on relationships. Spouses and children don't get it. The husband does not understand that the wife just saw a suicide victim and has to come back home to try and sleep after police interviews. The wife does not understand that some punk pulled a knife on him tonight or that he just had to wrestle an angry drunk with a broken bottle. The family does not understand that their parent was just accosted and threatened by a homeless gang. And true to form, the one in uniform often does not care to share it and just bottles it up inside.

It does come to the surface eventually, though. Maybe not today, maybe not in a year, but I promise that if it has not been properly handled, that mentally, emotionally, and physically exhausting trauma will surface. It may likely surface in negative ways, just like it does for any first responder. This is why I titled the book as I did. I want to honor the sacrifice that security personnel make, sometimes with their very lives. Does that sound too dramatic for you? Okay, let me tell you why I know it is not.

A lot of security personnel, such as myself, develop something called "shift sleep disorder." It is akin to narcolepsy and is very common among anyone who works all night or during odd hours for extended periods. When it goes untreated, it can stop the heart. That is why firefighters have a shortened life expectancy. They not only have the disorder, but they are often awakened suddenly during what sleep they do get. Cops have the same issue, but they are not on duty twenty-four hours; they work a forty-hour week on the average, and they put in overtime. But security people often have to work sixty or more hours trying to make ends meet because of poor wages. Add financial stress to their lives, and you see the recipe for disaster. And this is not trying to take away from law enforcement and fire departments that are understaffed and underpaid...but I am trying to inform people of what sacrifices private employees in the security field make.

Security professionals suffer if they stay in the field long enough. They suffer plenty, and so little is said about it. So little is done in the public eye. Maybe it's time for all that to change. It is changing, slowly, because there are some organizations that are there for security personnel. A Google search can reveal them to you. One of the biggest is ASIS. Have a look. And find others. I encourage all security professionals to seek all the support you can while you are in the field. It's quite worth it.

CINEMA MANAGER AND PENGUIN MASK

One of the funniest burglaries I ever heard of was also a tragedy for the perpetrator. I have no idea what motivated this guy; maybe he stripped his gears or something, but he did generate a good story.

At Anytown mall, on a weeknight, the toy store was burglarized. The security team was alerted by a clanging audible alarm. They responded and found a man inside the toy store, trying to gather up merchandise to presumably steal. He saw the security officers, knew he was in trouble, and then ran out of the store with some of his stolen goods. I don't recall how much he was trying to take, because I was not on scene for this event. But the things that he did try to run off with were girl toys. I will explain why in just a moment.

They knew this guy was no professional because instead of breaking into the toy store with a disguise in place, like any action movie fan would know to do simply by watching and absorbing, he donned his disguise in the store. The choice of disguise is what gave him away as an amateur. If you recall the Batman movie series that started in 1989, you will know that each movie featured different (and truly campy) arch criminals. Remember the Penguin as portrayed by Danny DeVito? Long nose, pasty-white complexion, loved to eat stuff that made his mouth turn black and gooey? That version of Penguin? Well, this burglar, in desperation, snatched a Danny DeVito's Penguin character eye mask, complete with the long rubber nose, from a shelf and wore it to make his great escape.

He ran out of the store and down the main mall. He was met by other security people and a cop. This was yet another criminal mastermind who thought he could outrun both radio and camera signals. People don't understand, sometimes, that security and police forces have radios and cameras that can pass on information much more quickly than they could ever run. But they have to try, because they do not want to get caught. Now, this guy really did not want to get caught because he had more on the line than the average toy store burglar. Not that I am an expert on toy thieves, but you will see why I am saying such a thing in just a minute.

So this guy is running down the main mall with an armload of goodies. I don't know how hard it would be to run with your arms folded over some toys, particularly if you have put on a few pounds as this guy had. Add in a Penguin eye mask with the big ol' nose flopping around on your face, and you have a pretty accurate picture in your mind of why this guy could not outrun much of anything, much less a radio signal! Finally, cops and security catch him. He just gives in, out of breath and extremely embarrassed. As soon as the guy composed himself and the cops took his mask away, the security team could not believe their eyes…they all *knew* this guy!

It turns out that the Penguin toy thief was none other than the manager of the Dollar Theater on the lower plaza of the mall! What the heck was this all about? Well, it turns out, as things cooled down and everyone's emotions quelled, the theater manager started to tell his tale of woe. Sometimes the people who get busted will come clean with their motives, even when you don't care or don't want them to. In this case, security was really curious because they knew the guy that was doing the crime. Not only did they know him, but he was a manager of one of the tenants and a well-liked man on top of it all. That makes it tough, when you have to bust someone you know.

Well, he told his story. And it was pretty sad, really, why he did this thing. It was his little girl's birthday, and he wanted to get her a gift. Instead, he got arrested. Some present. And not only did he get arrested, but he went to jail for a bit. Shoplifting is normally a ticket, and you are set free to go home, but in this case, the guy was in the place after hours; he broke in, he stole stuff, and then he tried to evade capture. Not a good evening. I do feel for a guy who wants to provide for his little girl. I had a Li'l Princess myself. I know what it is to not have enough to give all you would like to give her. But I never felt the urge to rob somebody. Apparently, he just got desperate and did something really stupid.

The tough part of this particular gig was that this guy was a good man. We liked him. We helped him get rid of little miscreants who tried to score free movie tickets, sneak into the theater, let their friends in, etc. We helped him with stuff. We even had a complaint where the cops got involved because someone thought they spotted a wanted criminal in the movies. The man came out into the light of day and talked to the cops. He was not their man, but it was still an event where police, security, and the theater manager worked together. So you see, the team had worked with this guy before. I was involved in that event where the guy got pulled from the movie, and I helped more than once with running kids out of the theater.

The bust was clean; he had it coming. This one bad evening though ruined his life. For the sake of one birthday, he completely wrecked his career. When the theater found out what he did, they immediately terminated him. They did not want to, but they did not feel they could trust him anymore. This was tough for them because they were counting on him to take over a new theater they were opening. This was a big deal, and now he completely ruined it all. I don't know what finally became of him, but I know I never saw him on the property again. I hope that he eventually put his error in judgment, his crime, behind him and was able to return to the theater business. He seemed to be really good at it.

Watching people mess up their futures over some small event, some seemingly insignificant act, is very common. Full-grown adults with kids, family people, have at times been arrested, cited and released after shoplifting $4 items. Can you believe that? They have to appear in court and jeopardize their jobs in some cases, over a $4 trinket. That is usually at some costume jewelry boutique for teeny-boppers.

We saw a mall custodian, really a great guy and good at customer service, lose his job and get reinstated eventually. He lost his job because he got caught trying to steal a carton of smokes, and they forgave him. Hopefully, the theater manager was eventually forgiven also. I hope so.

There are people who are intentional criminals, who make a career of being bad actors. There are men and women who just don't get it. They constantly hurt themselves with their actions, and they have arrest after arrest after arrest. This guy was just someone trying to be a good father and who did something desperate and foolish. I do not believe that he was a career criminal. Not at all. So sometimes people deserve another chance. I hope he got his, and I wish him the best of luck.

But a Penguin mask…really?

FIRST TIME I WAS CALLED AN OLD MAN

Working downtown in any of our nation's Anytown's has challenges. One of those challenges is dealing with homeless people who think you owe them a living. I understand that people may NEED a hand UP once in a while. Life can throw you some hard curves, and you can end up on the street. Every town I have been in have sufficient resources to get people off of the street if they want to be. This is especially true if you are young and strong. They have educational and financial resources to help people. But you have to WANT to be helped. Some towns even post signs asking good people to PLEASE NOT give money to the homeless who beg for it, because this just encourages them to be homeless. More often than not, the money just goes to the drug trade anyway.

There are towns where the drug dealers have homeless people who are not their "clients," who cannot beg on the streets without their permission. To get the drug dealers' permission, the homeless people have to turn over a certain percentage of their funds to the dealer. I don't know how they work this out, or how they know that homeless people are paying them enough protection money, but the whole deal is just rotten to the core. And it serves only to make the poor that much worse off.

When I was working nights in several Anytowns in Anystate, USA, as an account training manager, I would have regular run-ins with homeless people. Most of them ended nicely. They would be kind and cordial and bid me a good night even if I did not give them anything. Other times, I would flick my elbow a certain way and drop the Maglite out of my sleeve. That would only happen if I got that "feeling" that they were going to be trouble. They would see empty hands, approach me with the rehearsed story about their girlfriend having seizures and needing medicine, or whatever. Then suddenly I would step back with this 4 D-cell Maglite in my hand. I did not yell at them or make any aggressive moves. I let the lamp make my point. And it did. They simply backed off and spread the word that the guy in the suit was not to be messed with. I actually developed a sort of working relationship with some of them. One guy even warned me about a potential mugging attempt.

The mugging attempt is actually a pretty good story.

CONVENIENCE STORE MUGGING ATTEMPT

I was in a convenience store in Downtown, USA. I was chatting for a moment with the store clerk who towered over me. I stand six feet tall, and he was nearly seven, and bigger at the shoulders than I am. Then I saw these two clowns come sauntering into the store. They did not look at beer, chips, magazines, or anything. They just stared at me the whole time. I was wearing a jacket and tie, so that meant I must be loaded, right? I must have money because I was wearing a suit. They would not take their eyes off me as they walked clear around the store and shopped for nothing. They just stared at me and my $30K credit card. Mmmm...boy! Well, when they left the store, they were not much smarter. They stood outside the entrance and just stared at me some more, like I was a T-bone steak on legs.

Almost on cue, this homeless guy came in and started stuttering. He was obviously suffering from some kind mental disability, but his heart was in the right place.

"H-hey man! Those out there w-w-wan-uh...w-w-w-wanna t-t-t-t-alk to you."

"Oh? About what?"

He would not say about what, but he did use his hand to mimic sort of a sock puppet jabbering in the air, while rotating his hand in circles. I, to this day, don't know what that was, but I do know that it must have been nothing good, so I thanked the man, and he left the store. I hoped that those two guys did not know that he had just tipped me off to what I already knew. Those two fellas were up to no good, and I was their target. Idiots! They gave themselves away. Well, I stood there for a moment, and the clerk asked me what I wanted to do. I was not going out there alone; that was obvious.

So the clerk said, "Well, let's go out there together. They are still on store property, and I want them to not hang out there."

We started toward the glass double doors, purposefully, and when they saw the two of us looking right at them, they knew the jig was up. They were not going to deal with me and my new friend. They skedaddled before we even reached the door. That was so funny, how these two did not realize they had given themselves away just by their conduct in the store. But they certainly took the hint when I and Tiny Storeclerk were approaching them! We paused at the door and laughed a minute, gave it some time, and then looked out the door. It seemed that I was out of danger, so I thanked Tiny and went on my way. On my way out, I did notice a thin young man, ninety-eight pounds, maybe, and about five feet tall. I figured him for some skinny opioid prince and did not feel particularly threatened, but I did keep my ears open and my eyes peeled, just in case.

Well, sure enough, I get up the sidewalk maybe thirty feet and hear the *thumpa-thumpa-thump* of feet running up behind me. No way was I going out like that! I spun around and jabbed my finger toward him and shouted, "STOP!" He did. I was leaning slightly forward with a really mean look.

My nostrils flared, my posture forward, and my mannerisms generally aggressive, I yelled, "Back up now! Three steps!"

He did. "Don't you ever run up on me!"

He stammered about how he would never do such a thing.

"Keep your hands where I can see them! Don't reach for your pockets or behind you!"

He stood there with his hands up, terrified.

"If you ever come at me again, I will bounce you off this sidewalk like a basketball! You got me, you miserable little punk?"

He quietly stuttered his "Yes, sir" / "No, sir" at me, and then I told him to get lost. He did.

Then I heard someone chuckling. I saw a construction worker leaning on his shovel shaking his head, laughing with a mile-wide grin. He told me that he did not know what that kid was thinking, he had tried to jump one of his guys earlier, in the same way, with about the same result. We agreed that if he was going to mug people for a living, he had to put on a few pounds and grow more because his tiny frame was just not up to the task. I've coughed up stuff from my lungs bigger than him! That was really a shame, how this young man wasted his mind and life. But that is how life on the street goes. One poor choice leads to others.

HISTORY AND REALITIES OF THE SECURITY PROFESSION

People assume that security simply branched off from the police and became sub-police officers, but that is not true. If it were the truth, then security officers would be much better trained and would likely have some kind of limited law enforcement powers from the cop's jurisdiction. It would be an arrangement sort of like the physician's assistant who works on a sponsoring doctor's license. The security field would generally be much better off. No, security did not branch off law enforcement. It did not branch off the military either. Security started all on its own.

There was once a man whose name was Allen Pinkerton. He was a private individual who ran a company of private detectives during the Civil War. They also claim to have foiled an assassination attempt against Abraham Lincoln. They were not a military agency; they were a private agency. They were private investigators or private detectives. This company used an iconic open eyeball to advertise in the local paper and used a slogan: "The Eye that Never Sleeps." From this was coined the term *private eye*.

The Pinkertons were used during and after the Civil War, and since there were not a lot of controls in place in the mid-1800s, they could pretty much do as they pleased. They were seen by some as heroes and by some as villains. The villainy or heroism was largely in the eye of the beholder. They continued through the years and were actually used against coal miners who were on strike. The unfair, unsafe working conditions and "company store" rackets that charged ridiculous prices for common goods which the isolated, mountain-dwelling miners needed but could purchase nowhere else caused frustration and rage. Pinkertons with ax handles would actually charge into the striking miners and beat them up. Some men were actually killed.

In this sense, private "detectives" and "security" details got a rough start in history. Things have since changed, and the role of the private security professional has changed and developed down a different path over the years. The current security professional can be used as a tool of enforcement, yes, but there are also softer roles for the security professional in corporate environments. Some security clients prefer to use a white shirt, jacket, and tie in their lobbies so that their own clients are greeted by a more professional and perhaps even friendly look. Other clients prefer a "hard," or more official-looking uniform that conveys a look closer to law enforcement; they may be armed or unarmed. But gone are the days where security teams are used to break strikes or perform acts of violence.

The security companies of today have strict rules they must follow, and these rules vary from state to state. Few are the federal requirements or restrictions on the security industry, other than those common to other businesses. Some states allow more leniency toward the look of security officers compared to law enforcement. Other states are very strict and will not allow any security personnel to don colors remotely similar to any police agency or functions, including the color of T-shirt they wear under their uniform. Training and educational opportunities for security professionals are limited largely to whatever the company offers, but most companies don't offer quality paid training or education opportunities. Licensing is generally left up to the individual states with some opting to license them thru their Departments of Public Safety, or to not require any licensing at all, instead leaving the security officer to be licensed in whatever city where they perform their duties, regardless of their residence.

Required training and education remain at nearly nothing, other than that which companies provide their people to fulfill state requirements. As little as a few hours of training in some states suffices to create a duly licensed security officer. There are usually different requirements for arming people—that is, to qualify them to carry firearms as part of their duties—but even these officers often lack training that is reasonably sufficient. Many times, these armed officers are given training enough for a security agency to "check the box" that their officer has been trained. Some companies provide psychological testing for their security officers; others do not. There are no federal standards for security officers, no standards for states to meet criteria to license security officers, armed unarmed.

While police officers are required to complete post training to even be considered as law enforcement material; security officers are not. This results in poorly trained, armed individuals who may look like authority figures, working posts and dealing with the general public. In this author's opinion, this is a dangerous practice and is plain inexcusable. I believe that there needs to be a federal standard for states to meet to have private security agencies in their state. These private agencies, as businesses that set an armed presence out in the public, need to meet training standards that are far stricter than current standards.

However, in their defense, being participants in a competitive and free market, security companies are challenged with the cost of training their people versus what clients are willing to pay. With clients who are willing to cancel a contract over pennies an hour per security professional, agencies are obligated to cut costs wherever they can to stay competitive. These cuts usually take place in training. What it comes down to is how much clients are willing to pay for safety and security.

Things did change for the industry after 9/11. Before that horrific terror attack on American soil, there were practically no opportunities for security professionals to become trained or educated much beyond what private companies offered. Now there are security management degrees available all over the country, and many of these programs are geared toward Homeland Security. I am a holder of one of these degrees. I worked very hard to get a master's degree in security management. But even after getting all of this training, I hit a glass ceiling quickly among private agencies.

The trouble I ran into was that companies did not understand the value of the education. In many of the current security monarchies, the founders of the private security agencies were not themselves educated. Some companies are run by people who had no more than high school diplomas themselves when they started their businesses. They did flourish, yes, and became giants. But these giants of industry lack the ability and capabilities that may be provided by educated leaders. The public hires these companies in full faith that they are getting their money's worth, that they are capturing a contract with the best security professionals the industry has to offer. But the fact is that there is a widening gap between perception and reality.

The officers they are placing in uniform may have hours of "training," yes, but who trained them? Did the trainers themselves know all they needed to know to pass on to the security officer? They probably did not because training is expensive and in order to train security professionals to the best training and education standards available, the security company needs to charge the client accordingly. Clients are not willing to pay that kind of money, so the security industry has to hire who applies. When the wages are in the toilet, only people who will accept low wages and are willing to work for such wages.

There are two major obstacles to getting security to the professional level where it needs to be, in order to truly produce a highly functional product. These obstacles exist at the highest levels of corporate thinking and are a huge stumbling block to the security industry. The first one is that security is not a money-producing institution. It is a money-consuming institution. The security team does not produce money for the corporation, it is not a profit-generating asset. The second one is that you cannot prove a *negative*. The security team, no matter how great they are at what they do, no matter how many accurate reports they file or how many hours they work, how many patrols they do…*security officers cannot prove what did not happen and how much money they saved the company just by being present.*

The illustration of this principle, the principle of the negative, is very simple. A hardware store decides to sell barbecue grills at a steep discount during the Labor Day weekend sale. They have all their grills parked outside of the store. They are linked together by a simple dog chain run through the legs of the grill stands and are padlocked to the building by an eye hook. Rather than spending the money on all the man hours and risking any heavy-lifting injuries to their employees, who would have haul heavy grills in and out of the store, they hire a security company to post a guard outside the store. All night long, the security professional sees cars start to drive into the parking lot after the drivers see the grills sitting there, ripe for the taking. They see the unarmed but uniformed security professional, alert and doing their job, watching the grills, and *boom*! The cars leave the property immediately.

The security professional can state in their report that they saw seven cars between 2300 and 0001 hours, nine cars between 0001–0100 hours, eight cars between 0100–0200 hours, and so forth—all pulled into the parking lot and then left the property when security appeared, but they could not prove how much property they saved because they did their job right and *prevented* anything from happening. This principle applies to every form of security out there. The high-rise corporate patrol cannot say that they prevented $2 million with of damage to the company today because a group getting ready to break in and steal the information decided it was too hard of a target with security personnel diligently watching the entrances and cameras.

Since it cannot be proven that security prevents things, since a hard, fast dollar amount cannot be assigned to the value having a security program, all the corporation sees are the beans they are counting. That is understandable, but it is a major issue that companies do not like to spend money on something where there is no hard, quantifiable value. They never have the money they need for their security program because they just don't understand the actual value. They understand the perceived value and nothing more. The same argument could be provided for the services police provide, but cities also get money for their coffers from police activities in the forms of fines and tickets. While fines and tickets may not offset entirely the cost of having a police force, it certainly helps, and the money is a hard, quantifiable asset that the city can count and put in the bank. They may not be able to prove everything the police prevent, but they can see the money they bring to the city budget. Plus, police actually arrest people and can prove that they prevented this or that damage to a business, or a citizen's home because they have the actual criminal in custody who was about to commit the crime. The police can prove their value to the world and can therefore justify the costs of training and decent wages to keep good officers on the force. Security does not have that value.

Think, too, of the housekeeping and custodial services in a building. When housekeeping is missing or is present but not doing their jobs, it becomes immediately visible. Trash overflows. Restrooms are filthy and stink. Floors are dirty or are simply not polished and look dull. The effects on the atmosphere and ambience of the lobby and halls is immediately noticed. The immediate environment of the building is brought into question when it is left unclean and generally unattended. This causes an immediate impression of disquiet and disease to an unclean, unkempt area. So you see, cleaning services can immediately prove what they prevent. But security cannot prove what they prevent, so in the eye of the beholder, who has more value? They who keep the place looking good and smelling nice? Or the uniform at the desk who says, "Good morning, may I see your badge displayed please?" and lets that potential criminal know he will be seen and checked for ID?

Again, can security prove that the eco-terrorist group was blocked from accessing the building when they sent their point man in to see how security would react? No, all they can say is that a really nice, random stranger made it is far as their desk and left the property when asked for their badge. They said, "Oh, this is not the right place, sorry," and walked out. They cannot prove that the animal lab downstairs was not robbed and burned because security was there. They cannot prove that the papers will not be plastered with images of the XYZ bio-firm losing millions of dollars a month until that unique equipment and technology can all be replaced. So again, the security team cannot show the client how valuable they truly are.

There is a living example of the attitude that people have toward security, one that is very graphic and proves my point succinctly. An Anytown mall would cut corners on training and equipment for their security team. They would constantly send their people into danger among gang members and thieves, but they would not pay for enough people to allow adequate coverage. I worked at this place, so I knew from the inside how things operated between management and security. Eventually, I left that place for a better job in corporate America. But one night, I found a sea of red and blue on the property where I used to work. *There was a mass shooting.* In the days that followed, there were security people at every entrance, constant mobile patrols, and every person who walked into that place knew they were being watched. All of a sudden, when lives were needlessly lost, when lawsuits were about to be filed, when media covered that property on a national basis, there was all kinds of need and demand for tighter security from the chiefs of industry. The bean counters suddenly understood that there was a different kind of bean involved. Then, when the smoke cleared, they went back to the same understaffed, underfunded way of operations. Why was there the sudden increase in security presence? Because the perception suddenly put the importance of absolute security in the spotlight! A real value was assigned to the need for securing the property.

Of course, by now, the horse had already escaped the barn. But boy, that barn door sure got locked behind! Yessiree! We have us a secure mall now! See that—actions news whatever show? We have people all over this place! Everyone being watched now! That shooting could not have happened because we were deficient! Look at the people we have and our willingness to protect our clients. What a tragedy! But we have proven now that we are ready for anything! Then as soon as the furor died down, the perceived value of security diminished, and they went back to business as usual. Even though people died, nothing really changed for the better. Not really. When things went back to normal, the dysfunctional security department returned to its normal sloppiness.

SAVING THE SHOW

One of the greatest things I ever did went unheralded. Most true heroics from every walk of life do go unheralded. And this is not a story of bravery and courage under fire. It is a story of sentiment, timing and inspiration. This was one of those moments when I went forward and did the very unlikely, something that most people would never think to do. As it started out, I did it for my kid, but it turned into a big favor for a lot more people than just him and our family.

I was working as a security officer / EMT at a corporate setting in Anytown. I had been on the post for a couple of years and my kid's birthday was coming up. I have sacrificed a lot of birthdays and other family events for this profession, which has repaid me so little. The returns have not met the sacrifices. On this particular birthday, my son was turning six, and it was on a Saturday, which normally was my day off. But the client wanted the whole security team on post for this big event that was coming up. It was a yearly thing they did, and they needed, understandably, all hands on deck.

The event was, this year, of all things, The Royal Hannefords' Circus. They were a smaller circus, a traveling show, and the client was promoting the heck out of this thing as sort of an employee's appreciation deal, and it was right on my kid's birthday. I asked for it off. No dice. I rolled again and asked if I could bring my kid to the circus for his birthday, and I crapped out. Luck was not a lady, and it was ticking me off. This client was not very understanding, and they did not even have the courtesy to explain to me why they were being such sticklers. My coworkers understood and they were not going to begrudge my kid being there. But the client was firm on the position that this show was not for "the help"; that was for client employees only.

GEORGE E. KELLOGG, MSSM

Well…heck. I was beaten, and I was holding a grudge. So true to my character, I was going to take this chicken poop and make chicken salad. I figured that if I could at least get some souvenir pictures of the performers or something, or collect some autographs, it would be at least some small compensation for what they were forcing me to do. Now the timing of this thing was absolutely amazing! On the night before the show, I was on duty, and I made an excuse to myself to "patrol" the circus area. And actually, it was a good idea in general just because this was a unique condition on the post. So really, I was within my rights and doing my job. It just happened to be at a circus setup, which, I must tell you, was really cool. I love circuses, fairs, carnivals, anyplace where folks gather to be happy.

So here I was on patrol and the perfect movie setting popped up right in front of me. I arrived at the exact moment when this older gentleman in a suit was shouting: "Whaddya mean ya got no spots? We need those! What the —— I pay you people for?"

The reply came from the road crew that the weather in Pennsylvania was too wet and cold; it would have wrecked the equipment trying to carry in the trucks. I did not know that about spotlights, personally; but whatever, the bottom line was that they had no spots.

I approached the fellow wearing the ringmaster gear, the uniform with the white pants flared at the hips, red jacket, boots, etc., and I asked him what was going on. He told me about the spotlights and how they could not carry the gear outside in Pennsylvania from where the show traveled, and now the show might be ruined. They could not have the tents set up and run the circus without lighting. Everyone would be sitting in the dark, watching the dark. Dark was not very entertaining and cell phone lamps would not help very much. He did not know what they were going to do now, because it was already about 9:00 PM, dark, and they were in a strange town about which they knew virtually nothing. They had no way to find or retrieve a spotlight.

This is one of those moments that separates the men from the real men. Any man would have said, "Stinks to be you. That's really a shame," and would have just moved on. That is any man with any common sense at all. But being a real man of uncommon sense, or perhaps no real good sense, I went for broke and told the ringmaster with easy confidence, "Let me see what I can do." I had no idea what I was about to do. To find a spotlight in a desert city where I only knew my way to work was "impossible." Well, I had made my share of "impossible" things happen, yes, so I went for broke and tried. After all, failure would not cost me anything. It literally would not hurt to try and maybe, just maybe, I could get that autographed picture of the circus cast! So I went back to the office with full confidence that while I had no idea what to do, I would do *something*. So I did. I did something.

I was not really familiar with the internet at that time, and we had yellow pages handy. I pulled out that thick yellow book and "let my fingers do the walking." I found a couple of numbers for lighting and entertainment. I had no hope at nine thirty of finding a spotlight but being a champion of hopeless causes and really wanting that chicken salad sandwich, I smiled and dialed. Then, after two or three tries, there were not that many more numbers to call than that, some guy actually picked up the phone! He said that I had timed the call perfectly, within about a five-minute window, because he was entering another show. He said he could talk to the circus about an hour, if I wanted to call him back. Well, sure, I just might find the time to do that!

I went back to the ringmaster and told him that I might have a spotlight for him, we would know in an hour. I had a company that would likely provide one, and I had to call them back because they were busy at another show. The ringmaster kept hope and told Mr. Hanneford (RIP) that he thought we solved the problem. Keep in mind that I acted like I did this sort of thing all the time, but in my mind, I knew this was some kind of miracle. I had no idea how I pulled it off, but I did. The five-minute window was what really blew me away. So I went back to work for the next hour, looking at stuff. All the stuff looked fine. Then the hour passed.

I called the young man back, and he said that he had a spotlight for us. Yay! So I kept him on the phone and put the ringmaster on with him. They talked and made a deal. Seventy bucks for a spotlight for the day. Two-hundred-foot throw. Watts, light, candlepower, etc., the situation was perfect. My heart sang with violin music. Then the sour note, that squeaky, nasty screech only a violin could make, and the music halted. The company did not deliver, and the ringmaster had no one to pick it up. Dang! What now? Then inspiration struck again. I asked for the phone and talked to the guy.

I went, "Uh-huh, okay, yeah, I will have somebody out there tomorrow." The ringmaster got frustrated, understandably, and emphatically stated, "I don't have anybody to go get it!" I said, "It's okay, I know right where this place is. I can pick it up for you before my shift."

The gratitude in that man was so sincere that he made all my trouble worthwhile, even if I did not get my autographed picture.

The next morning, I was in Anytown, and I went to the ring-master to complete the errand. He handed me a $100 bill, and off I went. I was two hours early for my shift, and I had my uniform in the car. I was not on "official" company business, so I wore my street clothes. I met the guy with the spotlight at the designated time, and we exchanged merchandise and money. I got change and took the light back to the circus. I met the ringmaster and the circus owner, Tommy Hanneford. He was very grateful. The ringmaster refused the change and said that I could keep "for my trouble." They asked me if there was anything they could do for me. Well, as a matter of fact... I outlined to them the problem I was having with my kid's birthday and the circus. The ringmaster said they would treat him as an "honored guest" and announce his birthday over the loudspeaker. They told me to bring my whole family. When I said that my boss would not allow it, Tommy said, "This is my circus, and I invite whoever the —— I want."

So I went to my account manager and reported the whole event. I told him about the crisis, the lack of the spotlight, the show not being able to proceed without it, how I drove miles out of my way to pick up the money and the spotlight, and so on. The account man-ager at that point should have walked over to our client with me, but instead he sent me alone. I thought that was a rather cowardly thing to do. So when I approached the client, the ones who were barring me from bringing my family to the circus on my kid's birthday, I did it in my manager's name, telling that he sent me to them. I was not going to look like a rogue security officer trying to score something I did not deserve by jumping the chain of command. We were to never approach the client about anything without management's consent, as it should be. When I outlined the story, they were full of questions about how I managed to find a spotlight. They were stunned at what I did.

Then the time came for the big favor. I told the client that the circus owner was very grateful, and if the client liked, he could talk to Tommy Hanneford himself. The client said that would not be necessary, but what did the owner's gratitude have to do with me? Well, I said that the owner invited my family to the circus, and I was supposed to go and pick them up, but it was a forty-five minute trip, one way. It would take almost two hours to bring them. The client just nodded very slowly the whole time I was telling him all about this thing.

And he said, to my surprise, "Okay. Go get them."

And I did. Then I spent the whole time inside the tent, watching a wonderful show with my family, listening to the ringmaster announce my son's birthday over the loudspeaker. That spotlight on the performers was there because I put it there. I did it against the odds, with the help of a conspiring universe, or if you want to know my belief, it was the power of God. Nobody gets as lucky as I did without some kind of a boost. Too many things had to fall into place all at once, with impeccable timing. Call it what you like, but I know what I know.

I have to say that of all the funny, weird, scary, and great things I saw as a security professional, this story is by far my favorite. My wife was so excited to tell the kids what just happened, and the kids had such a great time at the show…it was worth the grief I had to put up with to get the job. I do know that my family was not the only benefactor that day, that everyone there benefited from what I did, but doing that for my little boy on his birthday was its own reward. That was about the greatest thing I ever did on the job. And kudos to the client. That guy was normally the biggest jerk ever, or at least he acted like it every other time I dealt him, but on that day, even he knew when he was whipped. I earned the right to bring my family to the circus, and he knew it. He relented. That was probably the second greatest thing about this story... I did something that even the mean boss-man had to admire.

As a security professional, I have been given the opportunity to do things I would not have otherwise done. I have met celebrities, gotten very close to millions of dollars in diamonds I would never be able to approach otherwise. I've been backstage at NASCAR races, met the Denver Broncos cheerleaders, and on this night, after that circus was over and I was chatting with the ringmaster, family in tow, I stood in the center...the very center of the center ring of the Royal Hanneford's Circus. That may not seem like much to anyone reading this, but to me that was a *huge* moment. And it was a moment I will likely never have again in life. Even though the crowd was not there, the seats were all empty, I got to stand in the big top of a little circus and just imagine for a second that laughing, clapping, cheering crowd. And in that one second, they were all cheering for me...the unknown man who SAVED THE SHOW!

BULLIES WHO BROKE THE MALL WINDOW

One Friday evening at Anytown mall, there were some punks who wanted to play video games, but they did not have any money. You know the type. They don't have their own, so they will take yours. These loser punks decided it was time for them to play video games at the Anytown mall arcade. They surrounded this little old lady, about four of them, and demanded money. She gave it over to them and left. Security never saw them, but we did get a report from one of the mall tenants that these kids had scared this poor lady out of her money. I don't know how much they got from her, but I do know what they did. They left after we got their description and found them in the arcade. We forced them out.

This was not a big dramatic story, no, but it did my heart good to hear about them getting run out of the place. I was not part of the call, but I did get a report to write afterward. The report was not about money or trespassing or any of that. The report ended up being a damage report. The thugs returned later that evening and threw a big rock through our window. That was all there was to it. We heard the glass break, and the rock skitter across the floor. We picked up the rock, housekeeping cleaned up the broken glass, I filed a report and…done!

What did they prove by breaking our window? Nothing. What was gained? Nothing! What was lost? A sheet of tempered glass and some of our time cleaning the place up. A report was filed. No big deal. I guess the punks felt vindicated…but…well, who cares really? I did not care. The mall did not care. Breaking our window was nothing to us really. It was the act of cowards, like many such acts I witnessed as a security professional. People are funny, indeed, when do petty things and feel so big for doing them. Boy, yeah, they really showed us! Honestly, we just did not even care.

THE EVIDENCE FELL

We had a case of suspected shoplifting. A store manager reported that three young men were in her store and that she saw one pocket something. The boys, all three of them teenagers, swore that nothing was wrong. All we security pros had to go on was the insistent word of the store manager. There were no cameras in that store, which specialized in selling candies. I was not on the scene for the initial accusation.

The kids were brought back to the security office, per our protocol. We had two of them there, brothers, and a third kid was their mutual friend. So we have these three kids with us and they were telling us that there was nothing wrong. None of them stole anything, and they were not moving off their story. We really had nothing at all, and they volunteered to come to our office. Had they not, there would have been no case at all.

We were questioning the kids about this situation, and we were about turn them loose when one of them who had removed his jacket shifted in the chair and plop! Out popped a roll of some kind of candy. My boss did not see it. I bent over and picked it up. I showed it to my supervisor who was an ex-cop. She asked permission to look through the rest of his jacket pockets, as the candy was brand-new and had the store's sticker on it. The kid consented. and she cleaned out his pockets of several kinds of candy. All brand-new.

Then we asked the rest of the gentlemen to please empty their pockets onto the desk, and they did. The only one who had nothing on him, that we found anyway, was the brothers' friend who kept insisting that nothing was wrong and that we were "being stupid" and so on. We called the police and the officer who responded was one of the really nice guys. He was a big man, wore body armor, and carried a .40 cal. He once referred to 9 mm as "weenie bullets." It was not relevant to the story, but it gave me insight into his character. He was that big, gentle guy whom you probably would not wish to cross.

Well, on this day, he worked the shoplift with us in his usual calming and kind way. He was almost mechanical about it, not like the "Officer Warpath" I speak of in these stories. Now, when he finished with the reciting of rights, explaining them carefully and clearly to the kids as per the prewritten form that he must have nearly memorized by repetition, he wrote the tickets. Then the third young man who thought that the whole thing was just, oh, so amusing, was asked by Officer Friendly to come into the manager's office and to shut the door behind him. Now, we don't know what was said behind those doors. But we do know that Officer Friendly came out with a deadpan look on his face, and that kid, who was lying to the police to cover for his thieving friends, was no longer smiling.

Having finished our business with this bunch, we turned them loose and let them go about their day. They were, per protocol, all three trespassed from the mall for one year. I don't know what the cop said to that kid, but I think it changed the kid's life. I think he was well educated on why one should not lie to the cops when they were being questioned. I hope the kid learned his lesson and that was the last brush with the law he ever experienced. If he was smart, it probably was.

YEAH... HEY, IT'S GARY

I'm including a story here with my brother's permission. He and I have a lot in common, being in the security profession and then both leaving for jobs in the medical field. He is a respiratory therapist now, b this story was just too amusing to leave out of the book.

A man had been brought into to the Anytown mall security office. This was one of the same Anytown's I worked at. I don't know the original reason why the guy was popped by security, but the cops were now involved. The question now though was not even the issue that brought him in. The question was about his identification. He had surrendered his ID to the police for checking, and the background came back clean. The problem was that the cops did not believe that the picture matched the suspect.

Of the two charges of, say, shoplifting and presenting false identification to the police, I think that presenting false ID would be the worst of the two. It is not something that I would try anyway. But people being what they are and believing they can fool all of the people all of the time, some of them simply *must* try to get one over on the police. Do they succeed? Certainly! But this case may just play out a little bit differently than intended by the perpetrator.

John Doe from Anytown insisted that this was his identity as presented on the Anystate driver's license. He insisted that, yes, he was indeed John Doe. The cops were not convinced. Now, I don't know about anyone else, but personally, once the police are involved, the "jig," as they say, "is up." What a jig is exactly, other than a fishing lure, I am not really sure. But whatever it is, the jig is up when the badges close in and start asking questions. At the very least, you will stop what you are doing and go home, maybe with a ticket or maybe not. At worst, you don't get to go home at for a long time. In fact, they give you a different kind of home. Perhaps John did not care in this case. The police kept hitting him up with questions about his ID. He was pretty good about insisting that was his driver's license, but the cops were just not buying it.

The trouble is that in some of these cases, the bad guy can get away with his story because the police have no other reason to hold him. If the crime was not serious enough, the PD probably would not go to the trouble of running down his identity, even if they think he's lying. Not without some other compelling reason. So yes, once in a while a liar will get away from the police. I have seen it happen in shoplifts where you know that person took something, but no one saw it, and there is not any evidence, such as video to allow for a search. It is frustrating, but it does happen. And I suspect that this was one of those cases where the police would be fairly helpless if the guy just stuck to his guns and swore that this was his ID.

In any case, there they were, and the cops were leaning on John pretty hard. Yes, John insisted, that was his picture. He could not help if the DMV did not get a good likeness. It was not his problem the picture did not match his current looks, and so on. Then John checks the time and asks if he can use the security office phone. My brother granted him permission as long as the cops did not mind… so John picked up the phone and made his call. My brother was just casually sitting there, feigning disinterest. After all, his role was done, and the suspect was in the hands of the police, right? And John was not paying attention to my brother because the dumb security guard was not a concern; it was those pesky, persistent police!

So here my brother is actually far more intent than he was pretending to be. We were raised by the same people. He knows what I know about surveillance, psychology, eavesdropping, and so on. He was quietly and calmly listening on the phone call to see if he could capture a clue on Mr. Doe. Then, magically, it happened. The cops were not really paying attention, probably trying to get something on this guy, but fortunately, my brother heard, "Yeah, hey… This is Gary… I'm gonna be late."

BINGO! Well, Mr. Doe had no clue that he had just been made. He finished his call and turned back to the cops. They started in again, and at precisely the correct moment, the security pro said, "Hey, Gary?"

And Mr. Doe looked up and said, "What? Oh maan!"

The cop smiled then and said, "Okay… Gary…shall we start over? You want to talk to us for real now… Gary?"

And Gary did start over with the whole story. I still don't know what he was busted for initially, but he made it much worse by lying about his ID. The thing was that now he was going to answer for why he was using his brother's driver's license. And maybe his brother would have a question or two to answer as well. What I did learn was that Gary had his own license suspended, and that was why he begged, borrowed, or stole his brother's driver license. It was just classic how my brother got one up on the guy by catching him off guard, so he answered to his own name. Funny stuff, that was.

HUMAN NOISES AND NOISES OF THE NIGHT

There are different kinds of noise, you see. I know that sounds sort of odd, but it is very true. There are different qualities to sounds. There is the natural sound of some object falling to the ground or banging against another object. Then there is the sound of a human being trying to cover up the sounds they are making. I don't really know how to describe the difference between noises, except to say that a human noise has a certain "clear" quality about it. Whereas a natural sound of something falling has kind of dull quality. I don't know how else to describe it, but that is just the way it is.

Being able to discern the types of noises is very important when your life could be at stake. When you are on guard duty, you never know what can come at you out of the darkness. This is especially true in a close community like an apartment or condominium complex. I was on patrol, and it was just after midnight. I was walking past one of the properties and *clink!* I heard this particular sound that just rang out in the night as being a definite and distinct human sound. I could discern by the abrupt ending to the sound that it was not only a human making that noise, but this human was trying to conceal that noise. They did not want to get caught.

A number of questions flow through my mind in situations like these. I have to weigh out the risk of what I am about to confront. All I knew at this point was that I was alone, unarmed, and without any immediate means of getting backup. I had my flashlight, and that was about my only asset. Now, since this person was hiding, that meant that they were afraid of being discovered. This begs the question of whether or not their fear of discovery would cause them to respect me enough to be compliant if I made some kind of demand. I could also be fairly certain that there was only one person involved here because of the stealth, or attempt at stealth. I have found out through hard experience that two or more people are far more likely to challenge security than a lone person. So…a lone person hovering behind a property in the wee hours could be a burglar. So…are they armed? That is the next question. No way to tell. That alone gives one pause for thought: Am I at risk right now for being shot? All these things and more soared through my mind at the literal speed of thought. And that is pretty darn fast!

So after the few seconds it took to mull this over, I made the decision. This was worth the risk of making a confrontation.

"Hey! You! Whoever is back there, you come out *now* with both your hands where I can see them. Then I saw movement, and in that same instant, I smelled the reason for the stealth. The familiar scent of burning *cannabis sativa* wafted through the air, to my nostrils. Agh, what an offensive odor! I still couldn't believe that people take that stuff into their mouths on purpose! So anyway, this heavyset, long-haired, and scared-looking guy of about twenty-five years came out into the open. His hands were up, and he was really nervous.

"Hey! Hey, man… It's um…it's just me, man. I live here."

I told him that was fine, but asked why he was sneaking around.

He proceeded to hand me some line of baloney about how he was having a hard time sleeping and just wanted to come out and look at the stars. Yeah, I bet he was seeing stars and probably a few psychedelic planets too! I told him, "Look, don't lie to me. I smell what you are doing out here, okay?"

His eyes got wide, and I told him that if he wanted to smoke a bowl in the middle of the night behind his own place where his old lady would not catch him, that was his business. I did not really care. And I honestly did not care because the cops did not care and would just bust my chops for wasting their time if I called them out for some lazy hippie smoking a bowl at his own house. But when he found out that I did not care, and that was I not a cop trying to arrest him, he was quite happy!

I did not apologize for disturbing him, but I did make it clear that I was not there to make a drug bust. I heard a noise, and I responded to it to see if someone was busting into his place. He said he was grateful for that, and he probably really was. But he was more grateful for not going to jail! I just left the scene and let him get back to toking his bowl.

Looking back on this reminds me of another funny story, and this time the noise scared me more than Sonny Jim the Midnight Toker. I was on a construction site, for insurance reasons. I showed up, did not relieve anyone, just called it in, and started walking around. I was supposed to be all alone, so any human noise was going to be really bad news. Theft of construction supplies like bundles of lumber, pallets of piping and copper of any kind was a big deal. So there I was in the dark preventing theft. Suddenly, from out of nowhere, came the hammering. Hammering! Who the heck would be out here hammering at this hour of the night? And working without lights? That could not be good at all. I carefully began to work my way toward the sound. It was a surreal experience, not because I thought someone was working at night, but because whoever this was did not use any lights. I saw no signs of human presence on the site. That was the strange part. I freely admit that this made the small hairs stand up on the back of my neck and caused cold sweat. I was not afraid of a construction worker getting in some hammering at that hour; I was afraid of the strangeness of the situation and how out of place all this seemed. Then… the hammering suddenly stopped, so I stopped, surveying the desert landscape. Still no lights. No human sounds. No car engine starting for people to leave the scene. I had nothing.

Then the hammering started again. *Bam! Bam! Bam!* But now I started to realize that there was a certain cadence to it. The banging was steady, too steady to be from a human hand. The noise would start, then stop, then start again. Always from the same location, per the sound. That did not make a lot of sense to me, the thought of someone working, always in the same place and always with the same rhythm of hammering. The same sound, exactly the same sound, came from that very same direction. I stopped feeling quite so nervous, because I believed now that I was alone and this sound was not caused by a human. It would start and stop, start and stop. I reasoned out for myself that there was something changing in the environment and it would cause the banging sound intermittently, so I started to pay attention, close attention, to the property, the smells, the desert dust, any odd noises, temperature, all of it…in the air. *The air!* That was the key!

I realized at that moment that the air was changing. Not in any bad way, but with the breeze…whenever the breeze would blow, that banging sound would start. Now I had something to go on. I was not dealing with some pranksters trying to lure me into a trap; I was not dealing with some honest man trying to make some hay by pulling OT in complete darkness, with no lantern. No, what I was dealing with now was Mother Nature. So every time the breeze would start, I would trace the sound. When the breeze stopped, I quit moving but would not leave the place where the wind stopped so that I would keep my sense of direction. Finally, by tracing the noise as the breeze blew, in about ten minutes, I was able to trace the sound to its origin. The answer was very simple: there was a piece of tar paper attached to a one-by-two stick of wood. The stick had broken off of a wall that was being assembled at one of the home sites. That stick would hang by its tar paper flap quietly until the breeze started and *bam, bam, bam!* The "hammering" would start again. Needless to say, that piece of wood found its way to the ground where it would not jump up again and cause me any concerns for the rest of the night.

This is just one example of how spooked a person on guard duty can get in the middle of the night over a big bunch of nothing. It is an example of a security professional doing his job even when circumstances are somewhat uncertain. Noises in the night are a bit unnerving, when one is responsible for a particular property.

LEAKING PIPES, FIRE SPRINKLERS, ETC.

When a security team is contracted to protect a property, they are not just looking for bad guys who may come from the outside. They are not just looking for criminals who might be doing an inside job. Security, though difficult to define even for experts, is at least partly a condition of property and people that should instill a reasonable sense that things "will be all right" because security devices and security personnel are in the building to make sure things and people stay safe and unharmed. Part of security teams' duties include watching the property for damage that may be caused both by criminals and by internal conditions. By "internal conditions"—I mean events, occurrences, or conditions which are within the structure that the security team is protecting. There is a story that took place over a weekend, which involved several people losing their jobs.

There was a high-rise building in Anytown, USA, where a security team was on patrol over the weekend. The hourly logs were kept faithfully, just like clockwork. People came on duty and were relieved from duty all weekend long. Logs of visitors and vendors were kept faithfully, and there were no unusual events or incidents reported. Certainly, being in Downtown Anytown, there were going to be certain miscreants and errant drunks or beggars working the block, but these were the norm, and they were always handled with courtesy and professionalism. All in all, it was a quiet weekend. But come Monday morning, the story changed just a little bit.

When the Monday morning crew took over, someone noticed something quite out of place for the building. There was a *large wet spot on the carpet at the seventh floor beneath a drinking fountain*. Now, if there was housekeeping or a carpet service in the building over the weekend, maybe…just maybe…it could be forgiven if security was to overlook such a condition. Even then, a large water spot should have been immediately brought into question, or at least logged into someone's daily activity report. But this anomaly, even though it was completely out in the open and not hidden in a closet or office space somewhere, was not so much as even *mentioned* in anyone's activity log. Nowhere did anyone mention that they saw a big water spot on the floor of the seventh level near the water fountain.

So when the Monday AM patrols found the stain and immediately reported it to the supervisor, it was acted upon instantly. The day supervisor knew that this was unusual, and it needed to be sent up the pipe to higher-ups right away! This one move, this single decision, saved the entire contract, if not half a dozen jobs which were immediately lost that Monday morning. Those job losses would have never occurred if someone had made a simple phone call over the weekend, or at least noted in their report there was a water spot on the carpet. The supervisor who saved the contract heard his people, listened to them intently, and then went and checked the area himself before calling it in to the building engineers. That way, the supervisor saw with his own eyes, surveyed the area personally, and was able to give an accurate report to the client.

You see, this was no ordinary water spot. This was water, yes, and there was nothing unusual about it; there were no poisons or corrosives in the water...other than the water itself. Any good chemist will tell you that waster is a universal solvent, which means that anything water connects with will eventually be dissolved. And that is what caused the problem. In this case, that water stain on the carpet that went overlooked was caused by a leaking pipe that descended from that water fountain to the lobby of the building, and that water had been leaking for more than a weekend.

Water, like most things in nature, seeks the shortest distance to travel between two given points. That water wanted to run straight downhill, so it did. But a few drops every so often would get caught at the base of that fountain and would run down the pipe. The drops would stick there and were wicked away from the pipe by the natural action of the carpet fibers. This is a perfectly normal and natural way for water to behave. It was not spurting or flooding, which would have surely been reported, but it was slow, gradual, and moved so slowly that no one really thought much of it until it was too late. Fresh eyes from the morning shift found the water and immediately recognized that it was an unusual condition that needed to be reported and dealt with immediately, so it was.

One may be tempted to think that a piece of carpeting was not worth the price of six jobs. One may even be right in that case, depending on all the circumstances. But in this case, it was not just an odd piece of carpet that had been affected. *It was an entire seven floors of the high rise that had suffered the effects of a slow leak over a long period of time!* As things turned out, this water leak that might have appeared so simple had far reaching consequences for the building. The wet carpet was not the big deal. The big deal was all of the drywall, wood, and internal wall structures which had been damaged over a period of many months. The water on the carpet was a very late sign of serious internal damage to the walls of seven floors of skyscraper. The water damage, the mold and mildew, and all the inherent problems that came with this situation tallied up into quite a bill.

In this case, security was being held responsible because the weekend shift did not report it. The client realized that the whole of the damage was not in any way caused by security, but they were upset that the mess was not reported when security first spotted it. The contention was that security officers should have been savvy enough to report anything unusual that they found on their rounds. And that was the truth…and it was the reason why the weekenders were the only ones who lost their jobs, including the supervisor. The client did not hold the security company itself completely responsible because this was obviously an invisible and long-term problem that started with a bad soldering job done on a pipe behind a wall by a water fountain. But why no one reported the water spot on the carpet, proven by camera to have started late Friday night, could not be answered sufficiently to leave the weekend shift on the payroll. Had even one person spoke up with a two-minute phone call, the weekend shift would have never been brought into question, would have never been called on the carpet and would never have been fired. In fact, this particular client was very fair and would have celebrated that shift with accolades of some kind. This was a hard lesson to learn for that team. But learn it they did.

A/C REPAIR AND SUCTION LINES

This experience came about on a post that was unique in that I worked for Anycompany in Anytown, USA, as a patrol officer. The company I worked for was a mom-and-pop company, whose owner had very little control over what his team did. They were generally a bunch of kids who really thought they were some kind of cops. One team member was a police academy washout from a different state; another team member was alleged to have been barred from ever joining the police by some legal action taken by his father, a career police officer. The court action in that case barred the young man from becoming a police officer, and the case was actually sealed by the judge so that the son could never see what his father said to bar him from becoming a cop. After I got to know that young man a little bit and saw how he behaved, I suspected some mental health issues in his case.

The man who ran this company set out with the idea that he wanted to make his company operate as close to the Anytown Police Department as he possibly could. This eventually led to statewide repercussions for the security profession in all of Anystate. It may be hard to believe, but it is true. These guys were really getting out of control, and because of their conduct, something needed to be done. They actually had to enact new laws to stop untrained and uneducated people from assuming far-reaching roles as security professionals. They were actually starting to branch out into actual law enforcement. They formed their own little club of security groupies who thought they were becoming police officers, but without legal authority. One of them actually performed a traffic stop, accusing someone of speeding. The police got involved in that one, and it did not go well for the security team member. This was why they passed laws that affected the whole state; the conduct of the few and proud that crossed the line was becoming a real problem, and they could not single Anycompany out for selective enforcement. They had to make laws that applied to everybody or nobody.

You see, this little security company had probably a dozen employees, but their way of doing business was truly unprofessional. They owner of the company did not have any real idea of what his people were doing. He did not know how they were dressing. He had no control over their conduct. He did have them driving around in decommissioned police cars with the light bars still intact and his company logo painted over the old Anytown PD logo. This was how his guys were doing traffic stops on city streets. They had light bars with reds and blues like true police cars. People often thought a security officer from that company was an actual cop, particularly when the security officer got out of the car, dressed in police colors! These guys were actually wearing uniforms that looked just like police officers, but with different patches.

Eventually, statewide laws were passed that prevented security personnel from so much as wearing a T-shirt that matched police colors, even if was beneath their uniform. Those laws were related directly to this one security company and its general policies. It was pretty obvious to anyone who was paying any attention at all that the security professionals working for that company were trying to be as close to cops as they could get without all that silly training and oversight!

To illustrate how far these guys took their police act, I will now share a story from someone I knew very well. This person had a run-in with one of these security people, and it did not go very well at all.

A pizza delivery man, who will remain nameless for the moment, was on the job, delivering pizza pies for his employer. When he entered an Anytown retirement living resort, which was really like its own little town complete with grocery stores, pharmacy, barber, and hair salon, etc., he saw red-and-blue lights in his rearview mirror. He believed that he was being flagged down by the police, which was nothing unusual because this particular pizza guy was known by the police as a reliable witness. He had helped police several times before by telling them when he saw a certain person of interest, a vehicle they were looking for, or something out of the ordinary. They knew they could count on him to give them accurate information. He had actually helped them with cases in this manner, so it was nothing unusual for the cops to want to talk to him.

When he pulled over, he patiently waited for the cop to approach the car, and when the occupant of the car with the light bar approached him, the pizza guy got *mad!* It was not a police officer, but one of the security people from the above company. The pizza guy saw who it was, and this exchange was made:

"Who the —— are you? And why did you just pull me over on a public street?"

"Going a little fast, weren' cha?" he responded smugly. (Mistake!)

"What business is that of yours? You're not the police, and you can't pull me over!"

"Well, I just did, and you were going too fast."

"Get back away from car door!" Pizza guy got *out* of the car.

"What are going to do about me 'going a little fast'? You *can't* do *anything* to me!"

"Uh…well… I got a gun!"

"And what? You pull that thing on me and I'll shove it up your —— and pull the —— trigger!"

"Um…uh…um…well…don't speed in here anymore."

"And if I do? Oh, you're walking back to your patrol car…yeah, smart moving."

This was a flagrant attempt a being a cop. Now, a lot of people probably would not have known the difference between this security patrol and a real police officer because most people don't think to check for patches. Could this have been a case of impersonation? I don't know. I really don't know, because while the pizza dude was under the *impression* that this was a police officer, the security professional never actually presented a counterfeit police officer badge, and he never identified himself as a policeman. But his car certainly looked like a police officer's, and his uniform matched to the untrained eye. So I don't know if that was actual impersonation, but I do know for sure that the traffic stop was clearly in violation of the law. A private citizen with private policy enforcement authority on private property interfering with a citizen just going about his daily job on a private street, whether he was speeding or not, was clearly stepping out of his own role and was attempting to enforce law on a public street. And he likely had been getting away with it for a while. I would suggest at this point that he could have at least been cited if not arrested, depending on what a real police officer would have wanted to do about his bold and dangerous move in pulling over an unknown citizen's vehicle. I think that a lot of people complied with this guy because they did not know their rights or the security team's boundaries in this situation.

But the pizza guy did know his rights, and he knew this was not a police officer, but was instead a private citizen who just overstepped his boundaries. Now, I may not agree with him in yelling at the security team member and threatening him, but I do agree with the pizza guy standing up for his rights as a private citizen and for calling this guy on his nonsense. That security pro was wrong. Dead wrong. And that was not the first time he pulled someone over, I'll wager, simply because he seemed to be used to doing it, per his demeanor as described by the pizza delivery guy who respected police officers and was glad to help, whenever he could. I was told that the security pro walked with a swagger and approached the car without hesitation. The security pro did not understand the law. The property was a living resort for seniors, yes, but the streets were still public streets and security officers do have a certain type of authority granted them on private property only. Their authority ends the moment they cross the boundary line into a public domain. So if the pizza guy had driven across someone's lawn and was still on that person's property when security approached, then security could enforce policy with that pizza guy, within the bounds of law. But in this case, the security officer could have been in serious trouble if the pizza guy had decided to call the police to report the incident. But the pizza guy let the security guy go and nothing ever came of it.

Now, I am going to tell you a story of something actually heroic that some members of this security company did perform legally, within the bounds of their job. A call had kicked out over the radio of shots fired on a property patrolled by this company. Security officers responded and arrived first on the crime scene. They encountered a body lying in the street, with a puddle of blood oozing from its head. The body was that of an adult male, and there was a man standing on the property they were protecting, brandishing an AK-47. He did not like security showing up to interfere. Two of the security team members rightfully and legally ordered the man to drop his weapon, and when he refused and started to bring the gun up to aim it at the security team, they pulled their handguns. The man telling me this story, a credible person with whom I had personal history, said that when he saw that barrel come up, he started to squeeze the trigger on his revolver and just as the hammer was drawing back to release and fire the shot, the AK brandisher changed his mind, dropped his weapon, and surrendered. The police arrived and took matters into hand, arresting the suspect.

As it turned out, that man who everyone knew just *had* to be dead...groaned. And since dead guys don't generally groan, the security, police, and fire team members surrounded him and discovered that the bullet which had been fired at point-blank range did not kill the man after it hit him in the head. No...instead of creating a vital wound, the shooter squeezed the trigger at the instant the victim flinched and turned his head! The rifle went off, the muzzle flash issued forth, and instead of the bullet piercing the man's skull, muzzle flash just burned out his eyeball and the bullet, due to the angle of the man's head, had merely penetrated the skin and followed the scalp around the temporal bone, only skimming the surface of the skull, and then it popped out of his scalp at the back of his head! That was why he was lying there in so much blood. The scalp had been torn loose, along with all those blood vessels, and when the bullet left the back of his scalp, it made a hole for all of that blood to come rushing out. The cops and firefighters were amazed at this man's survival.

This story is a case where a security team did all the right things in the right way, even if they were part of a terrible security company, even if a lot of their coworkers were contributing to the stereotyping of the security field. We learn from this story that nobody is wrong all the time and that there are a lot of good people out there doing good things. We also see here some of the real dangers that security professionals often face. In this case, they could have even shot and killed a man with a gun who was trying to kill them, but fortunately, they did not have to pull the trigger. This was one of those cases where security team members were exposed to dangers that were on the far end of extreme, and they behaved admirably. One or both of them could have been killed, but they performed their duty and did it right. This is one of those instances in which they went unsung for doing something truly heroic. Had one of them been killed, there would have been blurb in the paper, if that, and they would have been buried without fanfare by their grieving loved ones, without so much as an American flag adorning their coffin.

PIPE BOMB OR PY-THON?

This was a snafu that actually ended up in the newspaper. This was an event that happened to me personally, and it could not have gone worse. I was in the security dispatch center of Anytown mall. It was a typical day, but this mall was also in a rough part of town, so pick your definition of "typical." On this day though, things suddenly got out of hand really quick with a single phone call. I was dealing with a contractor when the dispatch phone rang.

"Anytown Security…may I help you?"

"Please, sir, dere is a 'pibom' in my bathroom."

This man had a very thick accent, and it was very hard to actually understand what he was saying.

"Wait…did you say, *pipe BOMB?*"

"Jes…pleez! Dere iz a pibom in my bathroom, in the toilet!"

"Okay…there is a pipe bomb in the toilet?"

"JES! JES! Send helb pleez!"

"Okay, don't panic. You say it is a pipe bomb, right?"

"JES! Send helb pleez!"

I got the name of the store from him. It was very similar to the name of a different store. It was very easy to mix the two places up, if you were not careful. It could have been very easy to go to the wrong store, and that had happened before. Now it was time to make a decision. How do I handle this without proper guidance from any policies or guiding documents? Well, since I was the dispatcher, there was no way that I was going to call that out loud over the radio, in that neighborhood where people could listen in. I looked around for our bomb threat checklist, but there was none, as there certainly should have been! So I was on my own with my mind racing through what I should do next. I called my supervisor on her cell phone and told her that the Anystore had an issue.

She asked me if I was kidding just now. I told her that I was not kidding and that I would not kid about a bomb in the mall. She took me very seriously, as she should have, because I was serious. I did not have the caller on the phone anymore, so she reported the matter to the security director, and that was when pandemonium broke loose. That security director who constantly told security team members to keep their heads and to not panic lost his cool and, being a man of some size, went thundering down the mall. That drew attention. Then he ran into the wrong store with the similar name and asked out loud in front of people if they had a "pipe bomb in their restroom." Well, that did it. It started a chain reaction of panic in the mall patrons and then when he discovered that he had the wrong store, he did the same stupid thing in a second store. That was just what that ball needed to keep on rolling.

When he asked the same question in the second store, the correct one this time, he was led to their restroom. And there, in the bathroom, or more correctly stated, in the commode was a tiny and harmless snake that had escaped from the pet store upstairs and somehow got into their toilet. The panicked individual was apparently an "ophidiophobe" or a person who was extremely afraid of snakes! And with his thick accent, clearly not his fault, he was saying "python," but it came out "pibom." Or on the phone, I heard "pipe bomb." So the boss somehow fished the "pibom" out of the toilet and put it in a cardboard box for delivery to the pet store. By now, a crowd had formed, and some bozo wanted to take a picture of the little snake that had caused such a huge panic at the mall.

Naturally, I had gotten called onto the carpet, and I was face-to-face with the security director who had a lot of faith in me, but who was now in a pickle. He was in a pickle because he had to either own up to the fact that we did not have much training in bomb response; we did not have a written protocol for bomb threats; and we did not even have a bomb threat checklist of questions to ask a caller who was threatening or reporting a bomb threat. On top of that, he had to account for why he said the words *pipe bomb* out loud in a mall setting among a crowd of people, and in the wrong store to boot. Sooo…he did the best thing he could: That fatherless son of a pirate ship's cannon blamed me for "having him run down the mall and attract attention to a false alarm that I put out."

Forget the fact that I was alone in a dispatch center that did not have the proper document for responding to such a threat. Forget that he said the words *pipe bomb* out loud when there was only a need to pull the store manager aside and quietly explain what was happening. Forget that he was at the wrong store. Forget all of that. Forget it because I was the one who took the call. I did the responsible thing… I kept it quiet. *He* blew the thing out into the public eye. The story did appear in the newspaper, but fortunately, that was where it all stopped.

The worst part of it was that I accepted the blame and was terribly ashamed. I did so because I did not know any better at the time. Only years later, after getting an education and realizing that I was not at fault did I understand that he was covering his own tail feathers. He was covering himself because he knew he blew it, and he was not about to let that get dumped on him. He was not about to accept responsibility for this whole fiasco that he caused. All I did was observe a situation, in this case through a phone call, and report it. He supplied the juice to put the whole thing into the public eye. And from the public into the newspaper. Our best guess was that someone in that crowd, probably that onlooker who wanted to take a picture of the little snake, called the newspapers and got the small story printed in the paper.

All the fuss and bother would have been avoided and no one would have ever known about the "pipe bomb at the Anytown mall" if one of two things had happened. The first thing that could have happened to quell this whole fiasco into the silent response it deserved would have been for a proper bomb threat protocol with proper questions to have been posted at the dispatch office. It is simply ridiculous that a mall security dispatch center would not have a bomb threat checklist that is so very common to offices and businesses around the country. Particularly in a mall which served such a rough neighborhood, with a reputation already under its belt for

GEORGE E. KELLOGG, MSSM

having at least one teenager murdered there. A bomb threat protocol should have been one of the first things established there. I am so adamant about this because if a checklist would have been available, I would have started asking questions such as the following:

1. Where is the bomb located?
2. When will it explode?

By the time I reached the second question, I am sure that the caller would have clarified that we were not dealing with a bomb at all. That would have diffused the whole situation. A second way for the situation to have been quietly dismissed into the night without a news story would have been for the boss to go into the correct store, pull the manager aside and find out just what was actually going on. He did not need to involve the public and cause the panic, then blame me for doing my job. My only mistake was to not keep the caller on the phone like I should have, but that would have naturally happened in the flow of events if the checklist with the proper questions on it was present.

Fortunately, nothing really came of it, and there was no fallout or additional events because of the news story. We were concerned about copycats trying to set a bomb, but no one did. This situation could have led to other problems, but it never did. Thank heavens!

I WILL PICK UP THE CASING IN A GLOVED HAND

I was working with a team of security professionals who had a couple of bad apples in their barrel, but this one guy in particular was causing problems for the community and the police. He worked at Anytown hotel, a rather nice post, really, and one that could have been very cushy except that he kept stirring up problems. He was not a very smart person and was really into the "quasi cop" thing; he really thought that he was doing the police a service. The truth was that he was causing problems by jumping down people's throats like they were felons or something, just because they happened to

300

be homeless. His behavior caused a reputation to spread concerning that property, but instead of solving a problem by causing homeless people to stay away, people would show up there to mess with this guy. They did it because they were bored and looking for trouble. They would find it with him, but in a way that he could not touch them. They would stand at the edge of the property and bug him. He saw himself as a heroic character "helping the police" when the truth was that he was a clownish figure causing trouble for an already overburdened police force.

Well, one night when I was supervising, he called me to the hotel. There was a report of shots fired. I knew he was not an armed security patrol, but since when did that stop someone from bringing an illegal gun to a post? Fortunately, that was not the case. It turned out that someone had come through the parking lot and fired off a couple of shots. We never did find out why, but what I did find out was that this security pro had injected himself into the middle of the investigation, needlessly. Not only that, but he had followed the police off the property where he was authorized to work and was standing around chatting with them, like he was himself a police officer. Something eventually came up about casings on the scene, and they sent him back to the hotel to find a casing from the shooter.

I came onto the scene and found him combing the parking lot. I asked him what he was doing, and he said that the police sent him to look for evidence. He told me that he was there to look for casings from the shooter's gun. I was curious about what he might do if he found a casing, and he said that he would pick up the casing in a gloved hand and carry it across the street to the police. That hotshot had the wrong answer, and I told him so. I gave him a directive to *not touch the casing*. I told him to leave it exactly where he found it and to call the police immediately, preferably by a non-emergency line if at all possible. His touching that casing in any way, moving it, kicking it, stepping on it, or picking it up or removing it from the scene of the crime would contaminate the evidence. I told him that he was *never* to touch any evidence on any crime scene, ever, and that when the police were busy discussing things, that he was not to join the party. I am happy to say that at the time of this writing, that that person is no longer employed in the security profession. Any person who does not have enough presence of mind or job knowledge to realize that he is a citizen and not a police authority who is authorized to handle crime scene evidence, does not need to be in this profession. It is hard to say how many crime scenes have been wrecked by well-meaning citizens from all walks of life.

Sometimes the loss of evidence happens when a paramedic is unable to preserve bullet holes in the clothing of a shooting victim because clothing has to be cut away from a wound. Evidence may be destroyed when a homeowner actually enters his burgled home to determine what might be missing before the police can arrive the secure the scene. How many security professionals with a lack of training go into a crime scene and add extra footprints or fingerprints because they are "looking things over" before police arrive? There are a lot of ways to destroy evidence, and the most common way is to be where one is not supposed be, touching things, or stepping where one should not step.

As for the security pro in this event at the hotel, it was pretty evident to me that he was told to go and look for a bullet casing because the cops had already been over that area during their own search and found nothing. Sending him back to the property to find something that did not exist was a good way to get rid of him. He had no business standing in that circle of police officers, uninvited, particularly when they were off the property he was watching. Security people need to be very careful to do just their job and only their job. But before they can do that, they need to fully understand what the job is and what it is not! For some guys, knowing what *not* to do is more important than what *to* do because they get caught up in their role and start to expand that role in all sorts of imaginary ways, which can lead to big trouble.

PRIVATE COMPANY, PUBLIC WORK

It is very easy for security personnel to lose sight of their actual duties and it is easy for lines to become blurred because they are doing public work for a private company. This is especially true for security professionals who work for public transportation lines or who have a lot of public contact such as in a high-rise building that is open to the public. Security needs to understand the rules around the property where they are patrolling. This would include surrounding public sidewalks commonly found at larger properties like the aforementioned high rise or a shopping mall. These types of posts are private property in place for public use and things can get a little confusing. The nature of the security professionals can seem to be more like police work when they are on buses or trains as part of a public transportation system, or in shopping malls, in particular.

I don't have a lot of experience with the public transit security duties, but I do know that the trains and buses are owned by some municipality in most instances and that they authorize their security personnel to do certain things within certain strict boundaries. I have a lot of mall security experience though. Because of what I have seen in mall security, I would be compelled to say that being a "mall cop" is about the closest thing to being a "real cop" in the security field. There are some who may disagree with that assessment, and have good reasons for doing so, and my response would be, "Yeah, you might be right." But the reason I say that mall security is about the closest thing I have done to police work is that there are a lot of elements that mall security and police officers share in the performing of their duties.

Mall security teams are often required to approach people who have committed crimes before the police are called. They often will take suspects into custody and may even handcuff them. Mall security teams encounter potentially violent people, at times while they are committing violent crimes. Mall security is in constant contact with a very unpleasant public at times when they would rather not be there, such as around holidays, just like police officers. Mall security is expected to coordinate as a team and protect one another. They also, in some circumstances, will be called in to assist the police. Other times, mall security can enter places on the property and have a look around when the police cannot enter without a warrant or permission by the store lessee. With certain restrictions, the security teams of the mall may enter the retail establishment and ask questions that police cannot. So really, the cops and the mall security personnel do often work together, and this is where lines between what should and should not be done can blur.

For instance, when a police officer who is chasing a running shoplifter on foot catches a ride in a security vehicle with a security officer driving it, and orders that security officer to drive off site for one reason or another during the course of the chase; has he or she just deputized that security officer and expanded their legal protections beyond the property boundaries? Who is liable if the security officer is hurt during the course of such a chase? What are the legal liabilities for the municipality which the cop represents, the security pro themselves, and the mall? What are the liabilities to the security company? Has that security pro been given expanded powers of arrest under the order of the cop? These questions may or may not have easy answers; I really cannot attempt to answer them here because I have not really studied the laws governing the police and if they may deputize security professionals.

I suppose the laws would be the same for any other citizen getting pressed into service by order of a police officer, but what are those laws and rules? Does the security uniform add any element to the situation because of the impressions perceived by the public? Again, these are some gray areas that security personnel can find themselves dealing with in mall security, and this is why I believe that security personnel should be better-trained and fully informed in the laws of the federal, state, and their local municipalities before being permitted to provide security services. They should also have in their benefit packages accessibility to some kind of legal services provided by actual attorneys and not just paralegals willing to type out a couple of documents and call it a "legal defense." All this, plus full disclosures of the risks inherent to their position. After all, if they are going to do some of the things that cops do, shouldn't they have some of the same benefits? Not only that, but with better training, they should receive better wages and more respect from their respective communities.

UNCLE DOE DIED OF A HEART ATTACK

One New Year's Eve at an Anytown hotel, I was called to meet with one of my officers. There was a situation that needed our immediate attention. A family was having a New Year's Eve function, and they had several rooms at the hotel. They had gone out to dinner but left one member behind because he was a little tired and did not generally feel well. It was December 31 and a time of celebration. The family had come back from dinner in an appropriately jovial mood. They were a little loud, as families often are, while rejoicing in one another's company. There was nothing inappropriate in their behavior, everything looked on the surface like everyone was going to have a great time.

Then, after returning to their rooms, something went wrong. I was not there for it, but I could easily imagine the family member entering the room to get their Uncle Doe out of bed because it was time to have a party. One family member went in to get him while others were standing about joking good-naturedly about "lazy Uncle Doe." Then it took too long to wake him up. A family member called out first from the doorway. Then they approached the bed. Uncle Doe was deeply asleep, but something did not seem quite right. They approached with their instincts, telling them that the impossible has happened and they are the first find him. But that can't be, can it? It was just dinner! They approach the bed and finally try to shake Uncle Doe. He does not respond, and they realize that their worst fear, their primal instincts and fears welling up in their gut with all that bile were telling them the truth.

But it couldn't be! He was only alone for a couple of hours! He was fine! He had to be fine! They shook him again and cried out for help! Somebody call 911!

"I can't wake up Uncle Doe! Get in here and help me! I don't think he's breathing!"

The family crowded in, several people tried shaking him, and his wife, now a widow, pushed through the well-meaning but panicky crowd! Doe! Wake up! Come on, baby! Wake up! Oh, God! Please no! Then somebody called 911, and somebody alerted the front desk.

The front desk called security, and security called me, per protocol, for some backup. He was losing control of the scene, and nobody was paying attention to his instructions. When I got the call, I was already familiar with the type of scene, having been a 911 dedicated EMT in the Phoenix Metro area years before.

I arrived on the scene to help my security officer after the firefighters and paramedics were there. They were heading up to the room. We were behind them, but trying to clear the crowd out of the way at the same time. At one point, we were in the lead. We got the medical team to the room, and they had us help with crowd control. We managed to get the twenty or so family members down into the lobby. They were just beyond reason and out of their minds with grief and panic, trying to get their heads around what had just happened. The poor man was dead, certainly, probably had been lying in that bed for a while before they found him. We had to encourage the family members to clear the room and allow the paramedics to work; we managed to help coax them downstairs into the lobby.

While in the lobby we had this one young lady who was obviously beside herself with grief, insisting that we "Go back up there and do some CPR or something," which of course we could not do. It is not possible to be rational with someone who is not rational. We could not interfere with the paramedics because not only was that illegal, but they were certainly doing more than we could ever do for their family member. We tried to console them, but what could we really say? One of the cousins just walked by a plant and *wham!* He knocked it to the floor. There was no damage done, really, and I told the young man that he could not tear up the plants like that, no matter how much he was grieving. He did not do it in anger, he just did it. Frustration, a need to lash out, give it a name. Whatever he was feeling, I was glad that he did not take it out on a person.

There was a police investigation that took place, strictly procedural, and not because there was any thought of foul play. That was a tough New Year's for that family, and I had nothing but empathy for them. That was a very sad scene, and one in which security was completely helpless. All we could do was to try and keep order and give the people a place to sit or stand while their dead family member was lying there, being attended to by the medical team. I hope to never face a scene like that again because there is just nothing that can be done. We were helpless to do anything but keep order. I don't like feeling that way.

SBARRO'S ROBBERY ANYTOWN MALL

In the Anytown mall, they often had a single security officer covering the inside of the mall while a second team member was on the outside. It was a common thing to hear contractors working at night, because the mall was new and there were tenant shops that still required some work. The builders would be pretty noisy because they were doing work that the mall could not allow during the day. Drilling, hammering, grinding, and so on could not reasonably happen during the day with all the shoppers around. It would be just bad for business, and it would give people a poor first impression. That is why our guy suspected nothing.

We had our interior patrolman, one who worked pretty hard at his job, making the interior rounds. We did not have a set course for patrol because that would create a predictable routine. The one thing security should never be is predictable. So yes, were doing things properly and by the book. Our patrol did what he was trained to do: He left workers alone when they were busy inside a client's space. When he heard the beating and pounding inside the Sbarro's Pizza, he thought nothing of it. He patrolled, he did his thing, he was doing fine. But the stuff really hit the fan the next morning when the manager arrived.

Sbarro's Pizza, which sat right on the food court corner of the main mall, in plain sight, was burglarized during the night. The manager went inside of his store and found that not only had the place been broken into, but the wall safe in his office had literally been torn apart! The manager was incensed! He asked the security manager, a retired police lieutenant, what kind of a joke outfit was he running? This was a hard thing to answer because, really, what excuse do you offer somebody who just had his safe ripped out of the wall of his store which your security patrol passed by several times? There really is no true excuse for any of that. You can say whatever you like, how our guys hear these noises all the time, how there is construction constantly happening and so on, but does that really pacify the party who has been wronged? Nope.

I fully understand that too, because each tenant had to pay a certain amount every month to have security protection provided by the mall. The tenants who did not pay, simply did not have the mall security team watching out for their property. They assumed responsibility for their own problems, and the only way that a burglary would become mall security's issue would be if the burglars did some damage to the mall itself or if they used mall hallways as an escape, or somehow broke that imaginary, but very important line that separated the tenant's private space and the mall space.

In this case, that breach may have occurred, and the mall property may have been trespassed, but we had no way of knowing if it was. There was nothing to really report other than the hearing of normal "construction noise" and a store manager reporting a burglary. No cameras were set up in that store, and this mall did not have cameras either. Looking back on it, I don't understand how we ever really did our jobs without cameras. I guess I was just a pretty naive kid at the time and it never really crossed my mind. But I will tell you one thing, it sure crossed our manager's mind! That Sbarro's manager made sure that the thought crossed the mind of our boss over and over again...

Knowing how things like this flow—downhill—who ended up taking the brunt of it all? Yep. The guy who did his job the way that he was trained. This chewing out was not warranted because he was there doing his work. He was on patrol. He heard the noise. He knew there was activity inside that store, but he also knew there was a lot of construction work going on and this noise was nothing unusual. There was no protocol that required the security team to question workers who were doing their job in the mall at night. There was no policy requiring managers or owners to call security and tell them that they were having overnight work done in the mall. The security team member did what he was told to do, he did it correctly, and still he was getting chewed out.

This is one of the biggest gripes I have about the security field; poor training! That, and security professionals like this guy taking the blame for a lack of policy or written procedures for the post. This is just plain unfair and all too common!

HOMELESS PREDATOR / THIRTY-TWO TROPHIES

In Downtown Anytown, anything can happen. Every city that I have lived in has basically the same gripes: homeless people, drugs, crime, murders, and so on. Every town is much like any other; there is always that element of people who must prey on others to feel, I don't know...satisfied? Vindicated? Some folks just want to cause misery for whatever their reasons are. You can make all kinds of arguments about whether or not people can be born without a conscience and what motivates the criminal mind to become sub-humanly brutal. When I was a younger and more idealistic man, I used to just cringe when people would talk about how this man or that woman was an "inhuman predator." My view was naive, and I thought that we should "try to help them." That was before I started to face the grim reality on the street and out in the world that some people just do not have empathy. They have no concern about how badly they hurt someone.

Granted, the hurts can be different; they may hurt their lover emotionally and laugh. They my knock their kids around without remorse, but look "perfectly fine" to the world around them. They may make people think they are crazy by doing things and then denying they ever did it. There are many forms of abuse that non-empathic people may inflict on others. But for this story, we need to only be concerned with the violent criminal. This is the kind of person who makes the headlines. The cold-blooded one. That guy or girl who can just wrest the material goods from the grip on another and not even think twice, the one who will even kill you for what you have simply because they want it. They don't need it, they may not even particularly like the item they have their eye on, but they still want it…and they want it because it is yours and they don't think that it should be. It should be theirs, even if they throw it away later. They want it because they want it, and they will hurt you to get it.

Some such predatory criminals love what they do. They may be wealthy executives, they may be down and out on the street, or any degree in between those extremes. Wealth is not usually their goal, though they may attain it; their goal is to hurt you any way they can. That is the real goal, and if they profit from it, even if the benefit they get from hurting you is imaginary, so much the better. Such people don't always end up in prison, but I do know of one who did. I don't know who he is, don't really care either; I just know that our local police were able to stop him with the help our security team and the building management.

Our security team knew very well where the crimes were being committed. We had made many written reports of activity in the area of the high rise we were protecting. Every night we would run people off the property who did not belong, and several times a week, one of our people would receive a threat from somebody who did not "like being told what to do." We had made enough reports that the police started to take us seriously. They knew where most of the trouble was and they knew our building would give them a great vantage point from which to observe "Anytown Park." The park in this case was just a small patch of grass with some public pay toilets on it. I doubt that it was even a quarter acre. There was nothing attractive about the place. There were no amenities except the public pay poopers.

All day long, day in and day out. Day in and day out…it was always the same. The same people loitering and lounging. Just sitting around, watching the world go by while time passed them by, and they were just content to sit there and waste their lives. A lot of drugs and money changed hands there, as is very common among homeless. There were never any really big buys, naturally, but there was a steady flow of $5 and $10 bills being passed about, and that was just enough trade to interest the police. Out of necessity of law, they could not share with us too many details of what or who they were specifically looking for. Ultimately, we just did not care. We were interested in cleaning up that park so criminal activity would stop seeping out onto our property in the form of stoned people making problems for us at night.

The police detectives worked up some of kind of deal with the building management, and we were on hand if they needed anything from us. The police set up an observation post just like the kind you see in the movies. They had plainclothes detectives, binoculars, video cameras, and they could see exactly everything they needed to see. They were set up in our lobby, and the people in the park were none the wiser. They were not paying any attention to what was going on in our building because, well, why would they? There was no reason why they would ever suspect they were being surveyed. As for our team, we just kept quiet about the whole thing, and we stayed out of the way. Operations for us were completely normal. Finally though, after about two weeks, the big day came!

I was not an eyewitness to the bust, but I did hear about it. Our guys did not even know that the big day had come until they saw all the activity at the park! I could easily see in my mind's eye how it went. One minute, things were completely normal. People were just lying about, some were smoking weed, some were dealing "stuff," others were just chit-chatting or sleeping, and a few were drinking out of paper bags. Then suddenly, all at once, there was this explosion of activity! *WHAM!* From dead quiet to completely insane in an instant!

Cop cars, uniforms plainclothes, hoboes, everybody was just running all over the place. People were yelling and hollering, getting tackled, pinned, cuffed, and so and so forth. It was quite the sight, I am sure. When it was all said and done, we were told, they arrested over thirty people and many more than that were cited and released. The police shared what they could with us, which was not much, but there was one bust that seemed to stand head and shoulders over all the others. This one stood out not because of the stature of the individual, though he was a pretty big guy, but the heinousness of his acts set him apart.

The man was mugging people for his living. He took their money by force. Then, on top of that, he took their driver's licenses or other forms of ID. Certainly, this does not come as a surprise in the day where so many people make good money stealing people's identities. This guy, though, was not stealing identities for profit or to procure goods in other people's names. This guy was collecting *trophies*! He had over thirty IDs that he kept on his person because he was keeping track of who he mugged. He liked looking at the pictures and/or names of the people he took power over. He loved being a violent criminal. This is the kind of guy that should never see the light of day again…and I hope he does not.

EVEN THE STRONGEST (DHS OFFICER SUICIDE)

I once was about to travel with one of the regional managers of the Anyplace Security Company. He wanted me to drive him and some other company officers around Anytown and show them some of the accounts. That seemed like a great thing to do, sort of a good time at work. I was looking forward to it. But as things often do in the security business, everything changed all at once and the plans came crashing down around us. I was suddenly forced from the role of driver to the role of…well, I don't even know what to call the role, really. I guess you could say that I was thrust into sort of a support role for our security officer who just called in to report that a man was dead.

This man was not one of our officers; he was not a private security professional. He was actually a federal officer for the Department of Homeland Security. This officer worked at the building and was in charge of controlling access and securing the lobby. He was an older man, and up to the point we heard about his death, there were no reports of his behaving oddly or any such thing. The call was sudden, and our security pro was in shock because she worked with this guy and knew him. Or she at least thought that she knew him. Everything was normal that night, per her report. She saw his DHS vehicle; she identified by the video monitor and spoke with him. Everything seemed normal. He pulled right up to his reserved parking spot like he always did, and nothing was unusual. At least not until he failed to emerge from his vehicle. That was the unusual part. At first, everyone present thought that it was just him taking his time. No one thought anything of it. The security officer at the desk never heard the shot.

But someone did, or at least something attracted the reporting party to the scene. Then you can only imagine the chaos. The broken glass of the vehicle window where the bullet passed through. Shattered safety glass all over the ground. The shock of seeing a figure slumped over in the driver's seat. The expression on the dead driver's face, whatever that might have been. Maybe his eyes were open in shock. Maybe his eyes were closed, and his mouth was hanging open. Maybe both were closed in the sweet repose of misery finding its own end. Maybe he looked pained or angry. I don't know; I never found out. My role was not one of an investigator. My role was one of trying to keep my fellow security professional from falling apart.

I must give credit where it is due, in this case. She did not fall apart. She knew the man; she knew that this friendly coworker was dead. She would never see him again. But she still did her job. I sat there the rest of the night, with her, keeping my eyes on her. I was seated comfortably in the lobby with my laptop and papers to shuffle. I did not know this guy, true. But he was known to her, and to me that made him one of "us." He was a member of our team because he was important to her, one of my people for whom I was responsible. All night long I sat there, helpless, but still there to help. That seemed like an odd thing to say, a helpless man being on hand to help, but that was the case. I could not turn back time, I could not heal her pain, I could not fix what he did or try to talk him out of it. I was simply there, all night long, making small talk and watching her deal with her grief. It was a terrible thing.

Later, I was discussing this situation with one of my management peers, and he said that in his opinion, people in federal positions, as was his sister, so he knew this firsthand, often feel that they must be "strong." They have to appear invincible. That belief and feeling comes with the job. One does not dare admit weakness, lest his or her peers lose trust in them. This fear of losing trust or feeling "weak" means that the people in these federal officer roles do not reach out for help and do not admit to weakness. That leads to them becoming emotionally ill, and this can lead to mental illness. Maybe this federal officer who died by his own hand felt that he was doing the right thing; this was the easier way out than prolonging his situation. Maybe he felt that this was the only to end this whole thing honorably…perhaps he wanted to die "with his boots on," on duty, in uniform. I would never know because this was something that I just dealt with for a few hours. And yet it has been impactful still, these many years later.

In telling this story, I am led to think of a conversation I once had with a medical doctor. I don't even really remember how I happened to talk to him, or how this conversation took the path that it did, but somehow, this doctor and I started talking about war veterans and how they are treated when they get home. In the United States, we have military men and women who enter combat and then, God-willing, come home. They are simply thrust back into civilian life. Civilian life is certainly different than military life. In the military you are given your clothes, your food, your quarters. You are given a regimen of what to do, when, where, and how to do it…even if you don't know why. And military life on the base is certainly different than the life you have in combat; you are still given food and clothing and orders. You may almost never know why. But you do it.

The doing is different when you are on the front lines. Things are brutal, harsh, painful, cruel, inhumane, and yet there are hilarious times. There are times of great sentiment, camaraderie, and yes…boredom. But all that can be interrupted in a fiery cataclysm of blood and terror. One second a soldier or airman, marine, or sailor is talking to their buddy about their family or even their fiancée, maybe they are video-chatting with their spouse and child over the internet… *BLAM! BLAM! Ka-BOOM!* They are interrupted by intense fire! Their friends and fellow Americans are being fired upon by citizens who believe these brave Americans to be the Great Satan. These people are often the ones American forces have deployed to liberate…and now they are killing the very people who were sent to help. Seconds turn into minutes, minutes become hours. That buddy they were just talking to now lies in a heap of his own gore, the picture of their girl soaked in blood. Madness explodes loud and furious around them. There is the staccato of machine gunfire, the thunderous explosions, the hissing roar of shoulder-launched missiles, the screaming of orders and sudden interruption of speech, men and women dying suddenly, violently, and horribly in midsentence.

Then all's quiet.

It's all over. The dying cry out, the wounded call for help through the smoke, the smell, the burning, and the destruction. The able-bodied clean up, they ship out their dead and wounded, they attend to things the best they can, and they are quiet again, going about their routine, eating their meals, gathering the belongings of the dead to send home.

This horrific ritual is repeated over and over again.

Then one day, a greatly anticipated and welcomed day in practically all cases, the combat veteran is put on a plane and sent home. No debriefing, no bringing down from the intensity of the training and combat. They are suddenly dropped from a peace-hell-peace situation into a peace-peace-peace situation, but one where they are constantly expecting hell again. They are waiting for it. They are not used to peace, quiet, and comfort. Such things are always dangerously close to hell. Get too comfortable, that's when they sneak up on you. Get too peaceful, that's when your best friend dies. When it gets too quiet, it's because the enemy is out there ready to rip you apart.

The combat veteran never really settles into home life like he or she should. They are perpetually at war, waiting for the next explosion, the next attack. And when something at home does go awry, they overrespond as though that minor crisis, that missed newspaper, the broken dishwasher, or that unruly moment a child is having *is combat*...not because it is actually combat, but because the veteran's mind, nerves, and muscle-memory are still at war and have never really settled down.

I believe it is because of our handling of our veterans that we have some serious problems with divorce, suicide, and drug/alcohol addiction among our vets.

It is the same basic mechanism that works in the minds, nerves, and muscles of our first responders; firefighters, cops...security professionals. They never really relax or let down when they have high-intensity occupations, and it is true that many security professionals don't have tough jobs, but many do. These folks need understanding, and they don't always find it. That is why we have some of the difficulties that we have.

And here's the thing...a lot of our vets who have never really been calmed down from the combat-high end up in the security profession. So now we have people who will respond very well, yes, but who will also have serious emotional difficulties with not being able to respond with the appropriate level of intensity and only the appropriate level...it is hard for these folks to not go overboard or to not feel things so intensely. This likely is what led to the DHS officer killing himself after arriving for his shift. He was responding in an overly intense manner to things all the time, and that just became too much for him to bear.

Getting back to the doctor and our conversation, he led up to telling me what Israel does for their combat veterans. When their people get back

in from the field, before they send them home, they take time to "debrief" them. I don't mean using any kind of weird mental techniques or *Bourne Identity* stuff. Their debriefing takes place after they leave combat and have a formal debriefing with their superiors. Once they are done with all that "combat veteran stuff," they take them to specialized military compound. They have them there for six months. This is time for them to take a break and get to know themselves and civilian life again. They teach them that their "warrior" self will always be present, should they need it, but that they can turn it off now. They don't need the warrior self every day anymore. They are not in continual danger anymore. Lives are not spared or lost by their actions anymore. They give them six months in this special compound to come down off all the chemicals that their brains and bodies have used to keep them and their buddies alive.

During this debriefing, they are given time with their war buddies, the men and women they have trained with, fought beside and trusted with their lives to do the right thing, the brave thing, the important thing. They get to debrief together so that they are not suddenly pulled apart from their trusted surrogate family. They experience quiet time together. They have regular chores and some very loosely disciplined activities. They have horses and dogs for them to groom and play with. The animal therapy is particularly useful because they have something to take care of and watch out for. Dogs and horses are great friends to people, and they are very useful in helping the returning combat vets to "feel" again like their old selves.

They learn all over again how to be "just plain people". They learn to settle down, how to calm themselves, how to get over the combat fatigue everyone generally has after being in combat for any period of time. They do get some time with their families, but only brief visits because they want the veteran to become more like their old selves before they have a lot of exposure to the families.

Now, my purpose in sharing this is not to give an exhaustive study on Israeli debriefing techniques, but I am stating here that even if my doctor friend was incorrect, he at least gave me some very good ideas about how we should treat people with PTSD-inducing experiences such as prolonged combat. Whatever the case may be with the doctor's story, I can say that I know we don't handle things like that very well in the United States. Our men and women come home, separated suddenly from their unit and from everything they have depended upon to survive. They are taken from one venue of constant life-and-death struggle into "normal" life. They are suddenly plopped down into a civilian existence while they are still trained and conditioned for war. This is not good.

When I worked with veterans, I found that I could get along with them very well because I understand the soldier mentality. I was raised by a soldier, and I understand the challenges. When they come home, some become cops, some become insurance salesmen, carpenters, whatever. Others still feel the need to look over someone else and protect them. These guys and gals go into EMS, law enforcement, and security work because they know they can respond to whatever is thrown at them and deliver the protection that people who cannot protect themselves need. There is a great quote that goes something like this: "Good people may rest easy because rough men stand ready to do violence on their behalf."

GOD BLESS THE ROUGH MEN AND WOMEN PREPARED TO DO VIO-LENCE ON BEHALF OF GOOD PEOPLE.

DAVE AND THE BEER

This humorous anecdote is a story told to me by a former sheriff's deputy in Anytown, Anystate… It took place in a small mountain town where everybody knew everybody and the kids in the town did not have near the number of secrets they believed they did. The adults generally picked their battles and let the kids have some "fun," but not too much "fun." But in this particular case, the sheriff's office intervened because they recognized the risk that these pre-high school kids were taking by throwing a kegger at John Doe's house. It seems that John Doe's parents, Mr. and Mrs. Doe, were out of town for the weekend and trusted little Johnny to watch after the place. But if what I think is true, then Mom and Dad did *not* trust little Johnny, but they *did* trust the "village" where they were raising their kid. In this case the village did not let them down. Deputy Doe told the story something like this:

Word got back to the sheriff that there was going to be an under-age kegger happening at the Doe's place, little Johnny Doe playing the host. The deputies were well informed enough that they knew not only who and what and where, but they knew how as well. The why was obvious. Kids wanted to get drunk. So the deputies took all the information they had been fed, likely by the party who was sell-ing the booze to the kids, because he wanted to get the beer keg back after the cops busted them. You see, while selling beer to the kids was actually a crime, in a small town, things can work a little differently. The liquor provider likely knew the boys, what they were up to, and he was savvy enough to know that if he told them no, they would just go and get the booze somewhere else. So very likely, he helped the deputies set up sting "to teach that Doe kid a lesson." That way, they knew where the beer was from, they knew who sold it to the kids, they knew where to return the merchandise, and everyone would know that kids got "busted" and this story would be all over town, more particularly in "kid-dom," where the kids did not have near the secrets they thought they had and the adults picked their battles. On this night, the Sheriff's Office of Anycounty fought the battle.

So night settles in over the Doe residence. It is a countrified summer evening, nice and warm. Crickets and fireflies, babbling brooks, and…sheriff's deputies hiding in the bushes. The cops were there before the kids got back with their haul. They were posted and well hidden, chatting it up quietly about this and that, who got the best busts and the hot women. Then the car pulled up. One of the kids drove, likely a high schooler, and that was to be expected. He would hang out with the "squirts" if he knew beer was on the menu. So the car pulls up and kills the lights. The deputies got quiet, and now they were just watching. The kids, three or four of them, got out of the car and opened the trunk. They pulled a silver barrel out of the trunk, all tapped, hose attached, and ready to rumble! They started carrying the beer up to the house. The deputies preferred the beer to actually get inside because that proved possession without a single doubt, and with the kids indoors, they were contained and could easily be dealt with. No one can scramble away over the fence and get "clean away" with not nearly as many secrets as he thinks he has.

The kids had the keg, and they were hustling it into the house, in giddy anticipation of what they were about to do. It was gonna be "fun"! They were the hosts of a kegger party, and it would be the talk of the town! Indeed, they were right about that; it would be the talk of the town, but not for the reasons they thought. They got the beer about halfway up to the house when…a noise was made by one of the deputies. Somebody fell onto one knee or his foot hit the wrong twig…who knows. The kids, already afraid of getting caught when they were already caught but did not know it, keenly sensed it. One of them stopped dead in his tracks. He heard something, but not just something, he heard somebody…and he told his friends to stop. The deputies froze because if those kids had any brains, they would just ditch the keg and scatter for parts unknown and forget all about Johnny Doe's kegger…but being kids, they were short on brains.

So one them said, "Hey! Who's over there? By the bushes?"

Well, the deputies know that the jig was up, but one fella went for all the marbles.

He answered, "It's just me, Dave, man!"

Then the kids looked at each other, and one said, "Oh, it's just Dave…," and they kept moving toward the house with their prized silver barrel, Until one of them stopped suddenly, turned around quickly, and said, "Um, guys…we don't know any Dave!"

So they all immediately panicked, and instead of taking the secrets, they did not really have to parts unknown, and ruining the bust for the deputies, they all ran into the house, where they were now nicely contained. The deputies could hardly suppress their laughter, but they did. They were waiting with breaths abated, to see what would now happen with the shiny barrel of beer, sparkling in the light of a full moon. They waited, and the kids waited. They all, cops and kids, watched the keg, waiting to see who would finally flinch. Well, the kids could not resist, and since "Dave" probably ran off scared, they went out to retrieve the whole reason they all were together on this fine summer night.

The boys went outside, hastily glanced about, and then they retrieved their silver prize and hustled it into the house. Now the deputies had something. No excuses about how they were bringing it into the yard for their dad to retrieve at a later time, no blurry recollections of a bunch scared rabbits that looked like kids running off into the fields…now, this moment, the boys were all safely contained, in full possession, inside the residence, and they were likely tapping into it this very moment. The deputies left their hiding place, rushed onto the porch, knocked on the door, and the kids who did not expect a cop on the porch, much less five or six cops, were more than a shade disappointed that uniforms, smiling uniforms, were now present. Sheriff's badges look a lot bigger when you are the one in trouble! So…the boys knew they were busted, caught red-handed. Johnny Doe was especially frightened because he knew that the deputies were going to tell his folks for sure, and Mom would cry as Dad would holler at him for the disappointment of it all. Yep, Johnny Doe was a Dead Doe, and he knew it.

"Now, boys," one of the deputies started, "what we have here is a 'sitchyashun.' And I think you know that."

They nodded in agreement.

"Seems to me that we have a choice to make. Now you know that underage drinking is taken very seriously in Anytown. And you know that your parents take this kind of thing particularly serious. Don' cha?"

They nodded again in agreement. Johnny was in tears, knowing that he was Dead Doe where he stood. The deputies just glanced around and nudged each other as they barely kept from laughing.

"So," the deputy continued, "we have the right and possibly even the duty to haul all your little butts to jail tonight!"

That did it for the boys. They were all starting to break down, even the older one. The deputy let those words just kind of sink in for a minute. Yep, it looked like they learned their lesson.

"Now tell us, boys," started another deputy. "Did you learn your lesson tonight?"

Uh-huh, yep, they did, and a couple of them wiped their noses on their hands.

"Well...waddya guys think?" he asked the other deputies. "Think they learned?"

Everybody was in agreement. These boys learned their lesson. "So...okay...what do you boys say we just take this keg out of here, and we won't tell your folks...this time. Sound good?"

The boys were more than glad to get rid of that keg! It was the holy grail only moments ago; now it was just a stupid, old, shiny metal can! The deputies took that keg away, into to the night, into that town where the kids didn't have near the secrets they thought they had, and nobody went to jail.

STOLEN VALOR AMONG SECURITY TEAMS

Search the internet, and you will find all kinds of videos about people who pretend to be something they never were. You will see people who pose as military personnel who never were. You will see military personnel who became security professionals but who also are pretenders. They will sometimes claim too much experience on the battlefield where they never were, or they will pretend to be special forces or elite commandos when they never did anything like that. These people are especially irritating to me because my father was a Green Beret, and I have the picture to prove it, but the military has never owned up to that. And they probably never will because they can't for this or that reason. I get it, even as I kick and holler about the unfairness of it all. So you can see why I might bristle at the idea of someone claiming a uniform they never had the right to wear, when I was raised by one who wore it but could never prove it because they deny knowing him.

We had this one clown who was in the Navy, for about twenty minutes. He was drummed out, probably for being a doofus. He would rave on and on about how he knew this, that and the other thing. However, there was one glaring problem. He did not have "the look."

Combat veterans have "the look." "The look" is something that you cannot really define, but it is there. The shape of the arms, the bearing, and that faraway sort of dreamy but intensely alert removal from the present; some part of them stays lost in the past and you can see it in their eyes. Like they are never going to tell you why they are the way they are, and you better hope to high heaven you never give them a reason to prove they are the way they are. The look is something that is earned by trial of blood and fire. It is a combination of compassion, love, honor, duty, respect, discipline, horror, and death. Anyone who has had extensive dealings with war veterans knows exactly what I am talking about, and we children of veterans, particularly from the Vietnam Era, know the real thing when we see it. We know it because we were raised by "the look." When we see someone trying to claim it who never earned it, this is very upsetting to us, because we know what "the look" is. We hear the stories, and not even the worst of their experiences, and they keep us up at night. We have seen the trauma, the fits of unreasonable anger, the military discipline in the home, substance and alcohol abuse, mental anguish…we the children pay the price, and we know the price that other children pay for having a veteran parent. It may not be the same for everyone, some not as "bad" (if we can say it's bad) as others, but "the look" is still there.

When I would talk to "the doofus," he was always bragging about this or that, despite not having the maturity or discipline that even basic training gives a person, much less "the look." It is very hard to see people trying to claim valor they don't have. To me, that makes them an unstable person and one that I don't want to be around. Guys and women like that, though I've never met a woman who stole valor, but whatever gender they are, in my mind are unstable and dangerous. I have discovered by hard experience that such people are always out to prove something. They are always trying to be what they wish they could be, but know they can never be. They want to find trouble. They want to get into a scrape with somebody. Some of them even crave the idea of shooting somebody. Doofus is one of these types, and he always has these madcap adventures, exaggerated tales of how he did this or that in the field. These are the guys that give security people a bad reputation.

These guys have no idea what it means to actually shoot somebody. They don't know what that does to a normal person. They don't understand what it does to a cop. They don't understand that while these military veterans may have laughs telling their stories, there are a thousand tears and gallons of blood they are *not* telling you about. The people who steal valor are the ones who always end up in trouble with their company or who make a lot of trouble for the police, all the while they think they are "cleaning up the streets," something that good cops understand is just not possible. Police officers and deputies know there is no saving Gotham and that anyone who says otherwise is trying to get elected or sell something. Maybe both.

There was this one guy I worked with who had accomplished much. He was actually a black belt in his chosen martial art. He was an instructor. He was very good at what he did, but even with all of his great accomplishments, he just did not have enough. He did a stint in the military, I forget which branch, but he kept saying he was

323

a Green Beret. He would read all of these stories, on the internet or in some magazines, and he would claim these experiences as his own. And yeah, he was very narcissistic and unstable.

I bring this up because guys like this cause part of the reputation that plagues the security profession. They are very excited about their work, yes, and they may even excel at it in some ways. But in the end, they cannot control their personalities and they will inevitably stir up trouble for their team, their boss and their entire company. It isn't good to work with such people because they are willing to do anything to save their own reputation, even if that means ruining yours. They crave power, to live up to this false self they have created. They become very angry whenever someone challenges their false persona, dares question them on any point of what they did in the military, why they did this or that on the job, etc.

Some of these people are trying to live up to some image their family gave them to live up to, but they don't have the ability, so they settled for security work. This is the police academy washout that you hear about. Not every security pro is one, but many do come from military families and were raised with a very strong instinct to protect people and property. That was probably what drove me into the security field. I really like protecting people and property, but I am not trying to steal valor or be something I am not. I have chosen the health, security and safety field. I became educated in it. I am immersed in the culture, but in a way that causes me to do well as a professional. I now make a decent living at my natural inclination. Not many people can say that they do what they really like for their actual living. I am blessed to be one.

One other person I worked with swore up and down he had a family member in the CIA. He could not and would not shut up about it. And true to form, the guy was rather dishonest, disloyal to his coworkers and thought that not only was he the best they had, but he deserved to be in charge. He did end up in charge but got fired for practicing his ninja arts on his coworkers. He was studying under some master of the art at a martial arts school. I respect martial arts instructors generally, but I have to question the wisdom they display by keeping certain students in their classes. Some people are just going to be dangerous and this guy was one them. His desire to control his coworkers and show everybody how great he was, lost him the job and position he craved so badly.

I am going to end right here with this part of the story because there are other things to tell, other laughs to have. It is just unfortunate that these people exist in the field and make it so hard for everyone else because these types are the ones that the public remembers. A small percentage of bad apples ruin the image of an entire profession! And at the time of this writing, the police forces across the United States are experiencing the same kind of thing. They have a few bad cops roaming about, doing terrible things and the good cops would love to stop them as much as the American people want bad policing to stop. Just because you wear the blue does not mean that you are bad person, and just because you have a "rent a cop" uniform you wear to work does not make you a person who is a "wannabe cop"; it does not mean you are gawky or have the idea that you failed to excel in life so you are wearing some kind of uniform to pretend you are somebody. Good security people want to stop bad security people from damaging the profession just like good cops don't want bad cops ruining their profession. Two different career paths, but they want similar things. Both cops and security want people to understand that all they really want is to help maintain order and protect something or someone from bad people and other hazards.

HE STOLE A POSTER AND TRIED TO ESCAPE HIS CUFFS

There was once this one young man who was not very bright. Yes, I know, this theme is getting old and this book is full of people who are not so bright. But let's face it…if everyone was smart, we would not need all the first responders and law enforcement, would we? So let's get back to the not-so-bright young man. I don't know what this guy was thinking. He tried to steal a poster out of a barrel in front of a novelty store in the Anytown mall. The Anynoveltystore in the Anytown mall was always on the lookout for the type of people who would try to grab a poster and walk off with it. So what happened? You guessed it. Mr. Doe got caught. And the Anynoveltystore retail clerk called the security team.

I responded to the call, and there he was. Mr. Doe was smiling…which was rather peculiar…because most people, when they get busted and realize that they are in some legal trouble, are NOT smiling. They will usually try the "poor me" thing, how they are a victim, attempting to make you feel sorry for them so you will let them go. Or they tell some story about how they just wanted a gift for their loved one, or whatever. But whatever they had on their mind, it did not usually involve smiling because their situation was not funny, whatever it may be. This guy though…he was smiling like something was funny. I asked the store clerk what was going on, and he said that this guy just tried to steal a poster from the store. I had to ask the obvious question of whether or not they were pressing charges, and of course the store was going to press shoplifting charges.

Now, you may think that this thing was ridiculous, that they should not press charges over a few dollars in merchandise. If I was not in the know, I would agree with you, but since I am in the know, I will take a moment of your time and educate you. Most mall stores pay a lot of money per square foot for their space, and the malls have really strict rules about the appearance and cleanliness of the store, the types of signs they can put out and so on. All this also costs money. They must keep the store staffed and looked after, another cost. The electricity, the climate control, all that stuff is figured into the costs of business. By the time all of this is paid in full at the end of the month, they have a very thin profit margin. I know it is surprising, but it is the truth.

The thin profit margin is their main reason for being so hard on shoplifters. The shops simply cannot afford the loss. So many people out there think these merchandisers are making so much money they should just be able to lose stuff off their shelves and not even feel it. But it simply is not true. I cannot tell you how many ten- to fourteen-year-old girls have compromised their lives and their futures over about $4 in merchandise, because the stores would prosecute! The hope is that the more frequent the busts, the fewer dollars they will lose in merchandise. I don't know if 100 percent prosecution actually helps, but I know for sure that it can't hurt. It is just a shame that people think they are entitled to everyone else's stuff, just because the other guy has it and they want it.

Anyway, back to my happy guy. He was sitting there smiling, and he started talking to me all about his life, like I really cared or something. The fact was that I did not really care, and I found him rather strange and annoying. It was almost like he reveled in the attention. He liked the idea that he was being watched over by some guy with a uniform. The cops were on the way, and that did not seem to bother him either. I wondered if he was trying to build himself a career in crime and started out small to work his way up? That thought was an odd one, but it was all I could think of as his motive. The police officer arrived, a very unhappy-looking female in uniform. I knew this was not going to go very well. She thought it was a waste of time, and she was right, in a sense. These usually just ended up as a citation and a release. She got his ID and the story. She took my statement, which did not mean much because all I did was to watch the numbskull along with the store clerk until she arrived.

Soon after the ID her suspicions were confirmed—another rocket scientist shoplifter and first offender. No wants, no warrants, no priors. Another sticky-fingered juvenile starting out life in a very stupid way. She did not like the way he was conducting himself, with his oily smile and oh-so-willing-to-be-arrested attitude, so she hand-cuffed him. During the course of all this, as he was sitting there, he started telling me about how he had a set of handcuffs at home. He bragged about how he could get out of them if he really wanted to. I did not like the tone of the conversation. It was not normal, but the more he talked, the more I learned, and information is always critical when you are involved in a criminal case. When the officer came back after about twenty minutes of phone calls, she looked more irritated than ever.

"So...what did you have for lunch?" she asked him.

I was puzzled, and so was he, at that odd question. Then she said, "Because whatever it was, it was more than I had. I have not eaten my lunch, and now I am going to miss eating it because of you.

Since I could not find a responsible adult to take you off my hands, I have to drive you to jail. That is going to take up my lunch hour. Doesn't that sound like fun? Oh boy!"

Well, the sarcasm was dripping off her words, as one can imagine. He was still comfortably seated on the plastic chair at the front of the store. Then I started telling the police all about our strange little man, here, and how he knows the way to break out of handcuffs. When she heard that, she did what I would have done in the first place. She turned the locks away from his hands and then double-locked the cuffs so that he could not pick his way out of them, then she asked me to help bring him outside to her car. She was not taking any chances with this one. She thought he would get a little froggy with her alone, so I was glad to help her escort him out. She put him in the car without incident, and they drove off to jail. A hungry, grumpy cop and little miscreant who was all proud of himself and the criminal history he was starting to build. I marvel at how people sometimes think about life and how someone owes them something just because they have more. If criminals worked at doing the right thing instead of investing all their enthusiastic efforts into the wrong thing, they would make something of themselves. I don't recall what else happened that day, but it was not much. It was a quiet day, other than that one thing, but the happy shoplifter, I remember.

Now that I look back on it, I really think he was preparing for a life of crime. This was his first arrest, he was glad to engage it, he had been practicing with handcuffs—I mean it seems to make sense that he was going to work his way into other crimes. I hope that somewhere along the line, he was corrected by the Corrections Department. Hopefully, he got enough arrests to his name that he finally straightened out. I had a childhood friend whose older brother just loved getting into trouble. He had his tough-guy image, his tough-guy friends and he would run around half the night looking for trouble. He usually found it, too. Then one night he found a little too much trouble and ended up with his frazzled self in prison. I don't know how much time he did, but he sure did not want to go back for more. His whole attitude just changed, and never went back. I have the idea that people don't know when they have hit rock bottom, until they know that the only way they want to go is back up instead of sideways or back down. I guess my buddy's brother decided his time in the joint was his rock-bottom.

WILDLIFE: DEER, SKUNKS, MOMMA RACCOON

I have faced some dangers that people might not really expect. At some apartment complexes, there are problems with feral cats and rats. I actually was facing off with a wild cat in the basement of a hotel one night. I was on patrol, and the cat somehow made it into the building from the loading dock. I tried to chase it away by hissing and hollering, by making myself look "big and scary," and by doing whatever else I could think of, but it would not go away. It was a mean old black cat. Finally, it got sick of me and reared up in a menacing way, yowling and howling in that eerie caterwaul that sounds like a baby crying. As soon as it went back on its haunches, I knew that it was going to spring at me, so I swung my 4 D-cell flashlight at it and WHACK! I smashed it in the head. It ran off, back out the door. The stupid cat knew the whole time where the exit was; he was just mean and determined enough to not use it. He thought he was going to fight me, and he did. I just won faster than he could.

I hated to do that to the little critter, but I certainly was not going to let him attack me either. I was not going to let him damage me. I know what tomcats can do to a person. They lunge high and hard, right for your face if you get them angry enough, and this one was angry enough. I was the only thing standing between that cat and the hotel. I certainly was not going to let him get past me. Can you imagine me chasing that creature through the hotel lobby? What a scene that would have been! I certainly did not want any of that to happen on my watch, no siree! My job was to keep things like that as small as possible and to get rid of problems with the least ruckus I could. I solved a lot of stuff at that hotel without anyone in the upper echelon having to hear about it, other than in my daily report.

There was an apartment complex that had an especially bad feral cat issue. These cats were so numerous, they were competing for survival sources. They were having turf wars and were constantly yowling and fighting. It was a really, really loud, nasty noise when they fought, usually at night too, when the residents of the property were trying to sleep. One of the things that the management wanted us to do was to keep the noise down, so we would shut the cats up with pepper spray. You wouldn't think that would shut the cats up; you would think the opposite, but I guess the cats would go into shock or something. I sprayed a couple cats that were fighting under a car. One of the old tomcats, well, I actually felt sorry for him, he looked miserable. His tongue was halfway hanging out; he was wet with the spray and just limped around half sick. He probably could not see well either. And it occurred to me that the pepper spray was oil-based as oleoserum capsicum form…oil-based pepper was all through that cat's fur. "So what?" you may ask.

Well, consider for a minute, and you will realize that the cat has to bathe itself with its tongue! *OUCH!*

Another night, I had a raccoon digging in the garbage. Or at least I thought that it was digging in the garbage. That is something raccoons normally do, so it was perfectly reasonable for me to try to chase it away. The problem was that it would not run off, no matter what I did. Stubborn, stupid animal! *Get out of here!* But it would not run away. Then I started to wonder why. I knew the animal was afraid, but it would not run off. It wanted to, yes. I could tell by the way the vermin turned its head, looking away from me like the schoolyard victim who was cornered by the school bully. The ol' raccoon really did want to run away. But why—wait! What was that noise? I heard it again, a faint chittering warble of some kind. Then I turned around and found out why the ol' raccoon would not run away. I was standing direction between a Momma and her young! That is never a good idea, I knew, from being raised in the country. The only instinct in the animal kingdom that is stronger than defending one's life is a mother defending her babies. There was no way I was going to argue with nature. I knew that battle was already lost because the only thing that would stop Momma Coon from protecting her babies would be to kill her, and that is not the business I am in. So I apologized profusely with my hat in my hand, and I carefully bowed out of the situation, leaving the little raccoon family all to itself. Garbage or no… I was not staying there.

I was patrolling in the middle of downtown Anytown. I saw deer tracks in the snow, and I knew they were deer tracks…no doubt, but I could not go back to the office and tell the guys what I saw; they would think I was crazy. Deer just don't come that close into town. The next night, however, something happened that I had to tell them at the office:

I was on the same post where I had seen the fresh tracks the night before. I was coming around a blind corner, so out of habit I stepped wide of it, and *wow*! I was face-to-face with about four deer. One buck and three does. When I say face-to-face, I was about only two feet away, and he was a nice buck too, with a full rack. I was armed, but not in the least tempted to shoot him. I will admit I had my hand on my gun because I knew what a buck could do to a man at close range, but I was also backing away from the buck at the same time. Fortunately, he did not decide to defend his does, but they ran off, and he followed them. I was excited to see deer that close, but I was terrified at the same time because I could not predict what that ol' buck would do. That was why I was backing away and had my hand on my 9 mm. at the same moment. Fortunately, the old adage "That critter was more scared of you than you were of him" held true. That critter did run off with the three other critters.

Now *that* was a story that had to be told! So I told it at the office when we all came in from the cold. I expected disbelief, but they all knew I told the truth. What happens in that particular Anytown is that the mountains freeze up and the grass cannot be eaten, so the deer get hungry and wander into the lower elevations where the snow melts and there is food for them. Well, the lower elevations in this case happen to be downtown, so it made perfect sense…

PEOPLE DON'T WANT TO BE TOLD WHAT TO DO

It seems to be a common human trait all over the world for people to not want to be told what to do. From the cradle to the grave, free will is something that people cherish. We have established the greatest nation in the world, ever in the history of earth, based upon principles written by wise founders who understood the value of freedom. Freedom of will allow us to fulfill the greatest of our potential, or we will be permitted to sink to the lowest depths of misery and woe. It is all about choice. As the populations in prisons all over the world attest to, it does not matter why people are in prison, no matter if their reasons for being there are political or criminal, or if they are innocent or guilty, all prisoners have one thing in common: They crave freedom from their restrictions.

This precious freedom is something that people the world over are willing to die for. Countless revolutions and wars against tyranny have been fought over principles involving economic, political, and social freedom. The ability to carry out one's will, whether that will be virtuous or evil, ambitious or lazy, is the most precious thing every person has. It is something that is engrained into the very soul of man and is not unique to the religious or profane, the educated or ignorant, the rich or the poor. It does not matter who we are or what status we have in life; the one thing that all of mankind craves is the freedom to exercise that will; whatever it may be that they wish to do. Another interesting point in this discussion is that the "lower animals"—that is to say, the beasts of the field and the fishes in the sea—also entertain this craving, this irresistible drive to do as they wish, even at the peril of their very lives.

People freely run the risk of life and limb to exercise their freedom of will. Emergency rooms across the world are filled to capacity with people who are exercising their free will. Graveyards are full of folks who decided to take risks against the best and wisest advice. We all are subject to it, the best of our wisest and the most profound of our philosophers all know what free will does in our lives. Books upon books have been written about motivation and positive thinking, about morals and law, about religion, God, and freedom. All of them agree that mankind has free will, and it does not matter if we believe man to be mere brute animals that terminate completely upon death, or we believe mankind to be headed for more exalted shores of silver glass and gossamer wings upon death…all of us crave the freedom to do as we wish.

Unfortunately, what we decide to do is often not in our best interest or the interest of all those around us. A lot of the time, our free will is selfish. What parent has never heard their child say to a sibling "You're not the boss of me!" even as they were being strongly encouraged by their sibling to not light that fire in the living room carpet. World history is rife with outlaws and conmen, with sinners and saints, all wanting to do one thing: *Exercise free will no matter what the consequences are for themselves others.*

Because of this soul-deep demand that we exercise free will and not always for the best, we have imposed upon us rules and laws. And it is a good thing too, because when we do not have rules and laws to govern behavior, we have anarchy. I have studied a little bit about anarchists and their ideas about justice. I have found that there are peaceful anarchists who just simply wish to be left alone to live in the woods. They want to have no rules other than the ones they wish to abide by. These persons will have their social circle, yes, but they will live apart from rules. Then there are more vocal anarchists who believe that everyone should live by their philosophy of no rules or laws and who are willing to establish settlements across the land that live by this no rules principle.

The ironic thing about such people is that when they have over-thrown the law, as they have seen it, these people do end up under law, but that law is now imposed by the most forceful personality with the biggest and most efficient weaponry. The one who was the most vocal and fought the hardest to establish the lawless society, now ironically becomes the dictator of that same society, establishing his or her own law, all the while swearing that they don't believe in law. Well, what these dictators ultimately declare is a law that allows them to exercise their own freedom of choice exclusively and completely. They don't care about anyone else's freedom choice, and by force they will become the law and one who makes the rules…the very thing they said were fighting against in the first place. Why? All because they want to follow no one's will or rules but their own, yet at the same time are willing to impose that will upon others. Because of this natural tendency to only follow one's own rules and to force others to do the same, we have created a system of rules and laws that we all hope will even out the playing field. If one person is bigger than another and tries to take that smaller person's means of living away from them, then the law and rules will allow for that bigger person to be stopped. And to have such laws and rules means that someone has to be there to enforce the execution of the laws and rules.

Thus, we have now formed the need for courts and officers of the courts. We have need for governments and officers of those governments. We have need to enforce the laws and rules that people are just not willing to abide by under their own will. We see every day that someone is getting pulled over, someone is going to prison, someone is being executed because they did not want to follow the laws and rules. This is not to say that all laws, rules, and methods of governance are always true and just, and this is not the place to debate that. All I am saying here is that people don't want to do what they are told. They want to do what they feel compelled to do, regardless of the consequences to anyone else. Some people are so devoid of that inner drive to do good and to live selflessly, that inner drive we call a "conscience," that they must have laws to stop them because they will not stop themselves from taking what's yours, including your very life, if they happen to want it.

So now we see why we must have laws and people to enforce them. Enter the governments, the military, the police, the fire department, the departments of public safety, and so forth, all in place to protect us from each other, and even from ourselves. There are varying degrees of power of enforcement with each of these entities. There are checks and balances worked into the Constitution of the United States to prevent one branch of government from overpowering the others. We have laws that govern the enforcement of the laws and rules, all in the name of stopping people from hurting each other or themselves as they exercise their free will. I have gone the long way around to talk about the security profession's role and how they should approach people. I have done so because I deemed it necessary to establish the reasons for rules and laws and why people don't like being approached about rules and laws. It is very simple, really...they want to have their own way and they don't like that free will being threatened.

Understand that while security professionals act under law, they do not represent law enforcement. They cannot actually enforce the law. Security professionals, unless otherwise deputized under a law enforcement entity, cannot arrest people in the name of the law, but they can enforce rules on public property. The authority of the security officer does not come from The Constitution or governing bodies, other than the authority each of us has as a citizen of the United States. This gets us off onto the tangent of citizen's arrest, probably one of the most widely misunderstood and abused powers afforded to US citizens. We are not here to address that. We are here to address the best ways to approach people who are breaking the rules. We are here to understand where the security professionals' authority to act comes from, and why they need to approach people in ways that will not misrepresent their role.

First of all, a security uniform does *not* represent law enforcement. A security uniform represents the enforcement of rules and policies on private property only. It is very important to remember that, for all persons concerned. Equally important is that people remember that a police uniform does not represent security enforcement, either! People tend to forget that there are some things that security may enforce that police cannot. There is an important distinction here that the cops, security and the general public may easily forgot and it is an important are of law: Private security may not enforce the laws written by the local, state or federal government on their assigned property; police may not enforce policy or rules that are unique to the given private property until the policy or rule violation in question becomes a matter of laws being violated, which the police are duly authorized by the property owner to enforce while on that property.

Kind of a mess, huh? Yeah, I know. But these legal distinctions are important both from a constitutional standpoint and from a security enforcement standpoint. We must understand that cops acting as security are not on private property to enforce any laws outside of what the private property owner has asked them to enforce, serious crimes such as assault or murder excepted. We must also understand that while security can enforce rules and policies of the property owner, they cannot enforce the law even if asked to do so by the private property owner. But if the police do witness a serious crime such as a shooting or other felony, they may then enforce that law on that property with or without the property owner's consent. I am not even sure of all the legal technicalities and caveats involved in the situation because I am not a lawyer or judge. So *none* of this is to be considered legal advice; I am merely writing about what I believe to be in the law.

Let us consider a simple trespassing scenario: a young man wanders into a shopping mall wearing gangster-style apparel. He is dressed all in one solid color common to a gang that is locally well-known and operates in Anytown. Let's randomly call them Anygang. So this young man is dressed as an Anygang member and is stopped by the mall parent squad, a group of citizen volunteers who are present with the mall's permission to stop potential problems at the door. Upon arrival of the potential Anygang member, two of the parents stand up and ask the young man if he has seen the mall policies, listed on the large poster right in front of him. He stops, peruses the poster, and says "Yesh, I done 'em! Now what, li'l mama?"

"We can't let you into the mall dressed like that. You will need to change your Anygang-type attire before entering the mall."

"Well, li'l mama, who gonna stop me? You an' old pops standing there with his big gut?"

"I'm calling security."

"Well, I don't care li'l mama 'bout what you and yer ol' man do. I'm coming in."

The young man presses past the parent-volunteer table and enters the mall. The parent volunteers were instructed not to resist anyone, but to immediately report anyone who was entering the mall against the rules, so they call security and give them a description of the young man. The security dispatcher calls it out to the security team, and they also notify the police at the on-site mall substation. The young man in gang attire does not even cross the food court before security and police stop him. Security takes the lead, and police hang back to see how it goes, just as a backup to the security officer.

The young man is dressed in full Anygang attire and is clearly in violation of the mall policies. Security approached him, and he spoke first, "Yo, what up? I see homey dun brought the po-lice! A real PEE-DEE! Well, I ain't done nothin'!"

"Sir, you are in violation of mall policy. We have you on camera being stopped at the parent volunteer table, talking to them and then forcing your way past them."

"What? Li'l mama said I could come in. They let me in. And I gotta right to be here. You ain't forcing me out."

"You are dressed in gang-style attire, in violation of mall policy. We need you to leave the property immediately."

"I ain't no member of Anygang."

"I never said you were, but we don't allow anyone in here who is dressed in gang colors. If you did not see the rules coming in, you know them now because I have just explained them to you. You need to leave now."

Meanwhile, more security officers arrive, and a crowd starts to gather. The police are still standing by, watching closely and waiting to see how things unfold. One or two more police officers arrive. They are standing back, all of them, just watching the scene.

"Well, I ain't leaving. I came here to buy T-shirts, and I'm gonna do it." He started to walk away, but two security officers stepped into his path. He stopped and glared at them. They stood there with their hands at their sides, away from their duty belt. No need for pepper spray. That was a last—*last*—resort measure. No need to make this guy feel threatened either. Not yet anyway. Not unless he made a dangerous move.

"Oh, ho, so de five-o gonna make me go?" the young man asked. "You got no idea who I am." He throws up an Anygang sign. Only Anygang does that..."posers" are harshly beaten or even killed for throwing up those signs in public, so this young man is now identifying himself definitively as an Anygang member. The security officers don't budge or flinch. They are blocking his way and asking him to leave. Things are getting tense, but no laws have been violated other than, potentially, a trespass, but security has not called it yet. Police are still standing by, no assistance has been called for, but a crowd is forming now, and the security supervisor knows that this situation has to end, one way or the other. The crowd is getting bigger, Anygang thrives on any attention they can get in public, and more members of Anygang could show up any minute.

The security officer looks over at the supervisor who nods. *Trespass him now!* The first officer on scene, who typically runs the scene unless supervisory intervention is needed, tells the Anygang member who is now positively identified by his own use of gang signs that he is now to leave the property or face a trespassing charge. The Anygang member looks the security officer in the eye, steps forward, and lifts his T-shirt, showing "AF" tattooed on his belly in elegant script which on the street means "Anygang Forever."

"I ain't leaving til my business here is done. I ain't leaving for you, dem other fools over dere, or the PO-lees. You ain't got nothing on me, Mr. Paul Blart."

"I understand, sir. You are hereby trespassed and not able to return to this property ever again for violation of the dress code, refusing a direct request from authorized mall volunteers to leave the property, and causing a disruption inside the mall. Your refusal will result in your arrest by police."

"Ah said I ain't leaving—and I got business here!"

The police move in immediately, as the Anygangster reaches for the back of his belt and under his shirt. A gun is in his hand, security steps back and to the side, strikes the gun-hand downward as police rush in to knock the gangster down to the ground and arrest him. Security officers surround the immediate scene in a circle, facing outward. A couple of people start to object to the police action taking place, and they try to approach, but are immediately discouraged by the security officers pulling out their cans of pepper spray. They have used them before, as the crowd knows. The police officers not involved in the arrest now are working to disperse the crowd. The scene is cleared, no injuries, no shots fired. The Anygang member is taken to the police substation for processing and subsequent book-ing on several charges, including the concealed weapon without a license, aggravated assault, trespassing, etc.

Needless to say, he won't come back to the property for a long while. End of story. Now let's look at this picture-perfect scenario and how it unfolded by the book, with the understanding that this story is not factual but is actually based on several different events I experienced in my career. I handpicked several events I had witnessed or heard about and stitched them together into a fictional creation so that we could discuss for a moment the relationship between security, law enforcement, and the general public.

Notice that the parental volunteers were not security personnel in the strictest sent, but they did perform a security function. Their job was to act as a plain-clothes, friendly liaison to the public, with a friendly reminder about the rules. They were not in an enforcement function, and when they were challenged, they immediately retreated in the verbal exchange and told the person they were going to call security. Security in this case was quickly on the scene for a couple of reasons. First of all, they wanted to take care of the volunteers by having someone intentionally posted nearby. Secondly, security was not busy with any other calls at that time, so with security on the scene, the volunteers were taken completely out of the situation.

Now, security has the ball in this scenario, and they quickly are able to determine that this person is not going to acquiesce very easily if at all. But at all times, they remain cordial and professional. The police are on the scene, but security seems to have it under control, so it was appropriate to allow security to handle the situation. The security officers are the ones who understand the mall policies and procedures; they are the ones in control because the police are on private, not public property. Had this been a setting such as on a public sidewalk, or if this scene happened to move off the private property for some reason, then security would back off and police would be in control. In this case, on private property, police are there as peacekeepers, and they give a uniformed presence to the situation, which sometimes discourages things from getting out of hand. A security officer's uniform, by the way, can have the same effect. In some people's eyes, a badge is a badge, and that means trouble for the troublemaker.

In this case though, the troublemaker does not care about uniforms or badges. He cares about getting his way. He cares about being the one that's going to tell everyone else how it's going to go. He wants to be feared, and he's trying to intimidate first the civilian parental volunteers. Then he tried to intimidate the uniformed and trained civilian force of security officers. Security did not relent; they kept after him, no matter how much he cursed and yelled. They did not move out of his way; they did not get drawn into a shouting match with him, and they stayed cool and collected. They knew the cops were there and they knew that they could call on them as soon as they needed, so they did. The young man would not leave after several verbal requests, and he was escalating the situation by his behavior as he got louder and more belligerent with each passing moment. When he was warned a final time that he was going to leave, or be arrested, he was trespassing and committing a crime, security then turned the situation over the police.

When the cops started to get involved, the gun came out and a quick-thinking security officer stepped to the side and forced the gun hand down. The cops, already on their way, tackled the suspect and took him away to be processed into the American legal system. The story ends here, with all the parties acting within their role and having done so perfectly. We see here the complete picture, with all the defined roles and teamwork perfectly intact.

DISCLAIMER—I am going to clarify a couple of things right now. I do know a security professional who disarmed a young man with a gun. He was trained to do so. I don't believe that it is the role of security to disarm people, but if the moment calls for it, then sometimes it must be done. Disarming a gunman is better than standing there and letting him shoot you...but only slightly less dangerous. Now I also want the reader to understand that this gang member character is a collection of several different troublesome people I have met in my security career. The people I had in mind were White, Asian, Black, and Latino. I had about eight different young men and their traits in mind when I created Anygangster. The language that

I was using was a common gang slang that was used on the streets, no matter what the race. Nobody in particular was being picked on. And again…*understand that this entire situation is fictional and for illustrative purposes only!* In reality, it is very difficult to get people to coordinate so perfectly and to carry their respective roles so neatly. Trust me on this… I have never seen a call go this perfectly. This is certainly a work of fiction, but it is one created to just show the world how we wished it worked every time.

Things will always go wrong when there is a wild card in the mix, someone who is unpredictable, such as an angry young man who needs to prove something to his criminal gang friends. There is always a wild card, because we don't know every person we are dealing with at a shopping mall. I can't tell you how many times someone has popped out of the crowd to interfere with security business. It might be a pretty girl who happens to like the person being dealt with, or some macho stud trying to impress the damsel in distress. It can be a parent who appears out of nowhere and starts blasting you for "harassing" their child. They may even blame you for their kid acting up. Whatever the case, whether the person is a criminal who does not want to get caught or someone having a bad day who does not want to be told what parking space to use…they don't want to be told what to do. Most people do not; I know that I do not want anyone to tell me what to do.

When you have to tell someone what to do, it is best to be as friendly as possible. It is best to identify with them if possible. It is important to remember you don't know who are dealing with. Maybe the person you are approaching is the mayor's spouse, the brother-in-law of the CEO of your company, or maybe they are some savvy old guy who has a master's degree who is writing a book about security practices and who will mention what a doofus you made of yourself when you approached him. About the most annoying thing security can do, at least in my eyes, is to approach me with "Can I help you?"

First of all, when you are trying to interview someone or get even the tiniest piece of information from them, *you never ask a closed ended question.* In other words, never ask a "yes or no" question. All someone has to say to "Can I help you?" is "No," and it gives you nowhere else to go. It puts you on the defensive because now you have to think of another question. Asking someone if you can help them is appropriate in a venue where they are expecting it, such as if you are at a reception desk or in some other position you are expected to help someone, but that is the only type of venue.

Now when I am approached by security, in…say, a parking lot, parking garage, or some alley somewhere where I am not expecting to be approached by anyone, and they say, "Can I help you?" the first thing that comes to mind is "Why? Am I in danger of some kind?" Or even worse, "Who are you, and are you trying to distract me so I can be robbed or maybe slugged in the head in some stupid 'knockout game' situation?" I have been approached like that, twice, by the same security team. This particular team was working for a church, and I was there on business with that church. I was not there to be helped; I was just there on business and did not expect to be approached. I was on my way out; but I stopped in a sensitive area, one I had full rights of access to, to take care of some emails on my phone. I looked out of place. They were correct to approach me, but they were in suits, similar to the suit I wore, and they did not identify themselves.

This serious-looking man in a suit just appeared rather suddenly, and said, "Can I help you?" I started looking around because, one, I did know who he was. Two, I was not expecting anyone to approach me. Three, I picked up on his body language that he was somehow disturbed. Four, not knowing who he was put me on the defensive. Five, he was wearing an earpiece, and that was concerning. Six, he also responded to my very real, if subtle distress. Seven, he had other guys coming to join him, and I did not like that at all. Eight, his approach was not very kind, and I would have never thought that he was from a church, much less the one I was dealing with. Now, yes, we did work this out okay, and nobody got kicked in the groin or hustled to the ground; there was no public beatdown, no blood being shed.

And who knows what *they* could have done to *me* when I was finished with all that? *Ha!*

Now in all seriousness, yes, I was ready to fight because of their bad approach. I was not trying to be hostile, and I was not looking for trouble, but I seriously thought I was in trouble. These guys did not know who I was; they did not know about my education and training. They did not how I was raised to look for body language and the signs of being set up for something. They may not have necessarily had the look of attack about them, but they were out of place and distressed, and to me, that meant there was some kind of danger. They thought the danger was *me*, and I thought it was *them*, but fortunately, we all kept our cool and ironed it out quickly. They were mildly perturbed with me because I turned out to be okay, but I was not "looking" okay in their minds.

So yes, again, they were correct to approach me. They were right, absolutely right in trying to do their jobs. But in this case, it all could have been much smoother, and they could have avoided the misunderstanding and all the distress by not coming at me like they were trying to do something. They looked suspicious to me, and my looking suspicious to them did not help communication at all. It made me reluctant to communicate or cooperate with them when their approach was all wrong. The correct approach would have ended my reaction to them immediately.

The correct approach would have been, "Hello, my name is John Doe from church security." I would have been immediately relieved and ready to cooperate. There would have been no misunderstanding on my part, and I would have explained myself fully, and disarmed all their misunderstandings as well. One man could have done the job, and three more would not have been pulled off their post for no reason. It would have taken thirty seconds.

The idea of the correct approach does not apply to just the plainclothes security officer. It applies to everyone who is a security professional. It all goes back to the idea that people in general don't want to be told what to do. People don't like being pushed around. A little professional courtesy will go a long way. A little kindness can win you the world. I cannot possibly work my way through every possible scenario with you, but I can say that if you will approach people respectfully and kindly, you will get a lot further than if you come off authoritative. Of course, the authoritative approach is necessary in dangerous situations, but probably 96 percent of security situations are just not dangerous, and most people will want to cooperate and won't want to get into any kind of trouble.

I would actually suggest taking some courses or reading some books on how to influence people, how to get along and how to communicate with people. I have found that a willingness to communicate will diffuse a lot of misunderstandings and problems in this field. Naturally, there are those imbeciles who will want trouble, who will not respect you no matter what and who will escalate the situation into deterioration. You can't help that. But generally speaking, people will want to communicate, and if you show respect, they will respond. You will just have to learn by experience when a command presence is immediately needed, or when someone can be talked down. And read all the books you will, take all the classes you like…experience will *always be your best teacher*, though the classes and study will give you tools and ideas, which will make this whole communication upon approach thing much easier for you to learn.

CONCLUSION

These are some of the history and realities of the security profession. Personally, I wanted to really see some changes happen, and I thought I could help cause that, but the fact is that I cannot change the face of the industry. The things that I propose, the needed changes, are just too expensive for people's tastes. Security has been assigned a role by the people they serve, and that role will always be what it is. Companies will never do the right thing because it is too costly. They will not make the changes on their own because it affects their bottom line. The only times companies beef up security is when there is a financial incentive, a PR issue that has been broadcast across the land, or some kind of personal motivation such as a CEO being threatened. Other than that, it is a costly business, and they are not willing to pay the hard dollars needed.

To see security personnel trained and educated to the level of the job they are given would make them very expensive to hire. Security companies would have to pay them what they are worth to keep them. That cost would be passed on to the client. Most clients don't understand what it really takes to become the kind of person that should be trusted with their $30 million in real estate, bricks, mortar, and technology. It takes more than what nine bucks an hour will buy, I will tell you that much. And if you really think about it for a minute, people want to pack up their stuff, head home for the weekend and BBQ at the beach with not a thought for the high rise building they are leaving behind, yet they have just left it in the hands of people who barely finished high school.

Professionals with advanced college degrees conduct millions of dollars of business a year out of this building. People of high standards and professionalism are in and out of that building all day long,

345

for the whole five-day work week. High dollar trades are being made. Business is being transacted. Computers are actively recording everything. All week long, great things are happening. But then, at the end of the week, they want to turn this building over to poorly educated young people in uniform, making just over minimum wages, and the executives wonder what can go wrong. My gosh! There needs to be some changes in this field and fast.

But change won't come until state standards are changed for the security industry, and the states probably won't change their licensing standards much until the Feds make them do so. In the meantime, we have an underpaid, undertrained, underequipped, and largely uneducated population being hired to protect our public safety on private property. They will not spend the needed dollars on security until they must, until they are forced by law and circumstance. The warning I have attempted to present here will go largely unheeded, I know, but I hope the perception of security has changed to some small degree in the eye of the reader.

I know that it is tough to prove a negative, that you cannot prove what did *not* happen because security was present. You cannot prove that there was no theft of computers because security was present. You cannot prove that this or that act of vandalism or arson did not happen because someone saw that camera turning toward them or heard that security patrol whistling his way past what he thought were just kind strangers. This is a hard world, and it is getting harder all the time.

But the only thing that motivates people to take the correct measures to protect themselves are hard lessons. The rampaging shooter kind of lessons. It always seems like it will happen to the other guy's house, the other guy's business in the other guy's state. But I am here to tell you that as unpleasant as it is to hear, Columbine was somebody's school. The James Holmes shooting happened in somebody's theater, in somebody's neighborhood, to somebody's kids. Nobody ever thinks it could be them, including the people that those events affected the most closely. Whenever sudden death comes, it never has any respect for anyone's other plans they had that night.

The shooting at that theater in Colorado took place because a sick man made a sick decision. But there is one thing that would have made all the difference. People saw a man walk out of theater through a fire door down by the movie screen. They saw him block that door from closing with some kind of obstruction. But because they thought it was "none of their business if he snuck his friends in," they said nothing! The next thing they knew, theater goers who were enthralled with Bane doing his thing on the screen became a bunch of sitting duck targets. Then some became running targets. Then the gunman went out to the parking lot and quietly surrendered to the police.

Had I been there, I would have been the "ratfink," and I would have let him leave, yes, but I would have kicked the block out of the door, secured it, and then reported it to management. I am not saying that because I am a security dude, or a geek, or a tattletale, but because I was trained to do that by my old man. I have been trained to spot the unusual, to know when I am being followed, to know when someone is targeting my wife's purse. I would have done that thinking nothing more than someone trying to sneak his friends in. I am not saying that Holmes would have changed his mind, or that no one would have died that night. I think that he was determined to kill people. But I will say that he would have found that theater door locked, and he would have had people looking for him, and that would have very likely made a difference.

We don't need a bunch of wannabe cops; we don't need dudes with a bad attitude taking care of our property. We need people to be alert and to have enough concern about one another to actually take care of each other. If we watch out for each other, we will have a lot less crime because we will reduce the opportunity of the criminal to ply his trade. These are the kind of people we need in the security field. The kind who are willing to sit on that freezing loading dock, checking in trucks and keeping the parking lot clear of trespassers. We need the kind of people who want their friends and family visiting that mall to be safe. We need the kind of people who are sincere and kind, but who can get tough when the need arises. These are the people we need. We need them to be savvy, smart and educated. We need them to care. When we get such people in the security world, they always end up leaving for their good and that of their families, and I don't blame them.

God bless all our first responders, particularly those who get involved and hold things together before the police, fire, and medical crews arrive. These first responders, professionals or not, uniformed or not, armed or not, are the kinds of people societies across the world need to help us all stay safe.

Thank you, dear reader. Good night and sleep well, knowing that people are out there watching out for each other.

Oh, and by the way…at the time of this writing, Doc Whitey, my dad, who inspired me to enter this field by his example, is now resting in peace. And I am sure that even though the burdens of this mortal toil no longer exhaust him, even on the other side he is still watching over us…

ABOUT THE AUTHOR

George E. Kellogg was born in Ohio. He was the oldest of five children, and his father was a South Dakota native and a Vietnam veteran. His mother was born to a migrant steel worker's family in Pittsburgh, Pennsylvania. When George was fifteen, his family moved west to Arizona.

George started his college education late in life, graduating from Mesa Community College in Arizona as a member of Phi Theta Kappa. He holds an associate of the arts degree in general education, and finally earned a master's degree in the science of security management from Bellevue University in Nebraska.

George also spent some time in Colorado, and lived in Washington state, where he served a two-year-long mission for his church. Today, George and his wife, Valerie, who encouraged him to publish this book, along with his adult son Steven, reside in South Salt Lake City, UT.

CPSIA information can be obtained
at www.ICGtesting.com
Printed in the USA
FSHW011532170221
78656FS